D1388059

Gael García Bernal

and the Latin American New Wave

Also by Jethro Soutar

Ronaldinho: Football's Flamboyant Maestro

Gael García Bernal

and the Latin American New Wave

JETHRO SOUTAR

PORTICO

First published in the United Kingdom in 2008 by
Portico
10 Southcombe Street
London
W14 0RA

An imprint of Anova Books Company Ltd

ISBN 9781906032258

A CIP catalogue for this book is available from the British Library.

10 9 8 7 6 5 4 3 2 1

Typeset by SX Composing DTP, Rayleigh, Essex
Printed and bound by WS Bookwell, Finland

This book can be ordered direct from the publisher.
Contact the marketing department, but try your bookshop first.

www.anovabooks.com

Contents

Acknowledgements

Particular gratitude goes to everyone who gave up their time to be interviewed. To Meg Thomson; Federico Gónzalez Compeán; Iván Trujillo; Ludwicka Paleta; Carlos Hidalgo; Manu Hinojosa; Antonio Urrutia; Teresa Suárez; Diana Bracho; Tita Lombardo; Mariestela Fernandez; Dominic Santana; Matthew Parkhill; Kristine Landon-Smith; Peta Lily; Rufus Norris; the chain that was Sam Dubberly – Liz 'McGuire' Griffin – Alberto Muffelman – Bere Manjaraz and other fixers such as Sarah McWhinney and Guajo (*obrigado cara*). In Mexico, *muchísimas gracias* to Vic and Velia for their incredible hospitality; to Rosa for her fine cooking; to Pablo and Friné; to Eria and especially to my number one *güey*, Diego, for looking after me; *mucha suerte* to Hidalgo again, Charlie Gore, Hector and all who made me so welcome on the set of *SPAM*. Many thanks to my agent at Curtis Brown, Shaheeda Sabir and to Barbara Phelan, my editor at Anova. Special appreciation goes to my wonderful chief sub Maggie Lett – I'm very lucky to have you – and middleman Geoff 'El Gringo' Rowe; Ian Soutar for sub-subbing, access to a private library and general guidance – not to mention giving me the film bug in the first place; Kathy Loizou for films and other materials; similarly to Anwar Brett; and to Quentin Falk for occasional mentoring. Thanks to Josie for helping me start from scratch with *Bad Education*, Kriss for looking into DVD distribution, Dan for tracking down *Sin Noticias* . . . and Elisabeth for spicing up the prose; to Van for trying to supply the insider angle; to Sonny and Victor for creative encouragement; to Richard and Lucy, James and Paula, and Alex for keeping a roof over the stray writer's head. And no thanks to the *cabrón* who stole my bag at the *6 piso* fiesta in DF (great party though).

Prologue

A car hurtles down a street at breakneck speed, the driver swerving as best he can to avoid everything in his path. Blood is splattered all over the back seat and bullets are raining in on the vehicle, fired by those in hot pursuit. Danger is clear and present, disaster imminent.

So begins the Mexican film *Amores Perros*, pumping the audience with an immediate shot of adrenaline.

What they were seeing was fresh, exciting, compelling; boundaries were being pushed, rules being broken. Viewers were hooked straight away, perhaps conscious that they were witnessing something special, something significant.

That opening scene didn't just set the stage for a great movie; it also announced the arrival of a new cinema movement and a new star. Other Latin American pictures may have prepared the public for a new wave of cinema from the region but the sheer energy rush of *Amores Perros* ensured it would be best remembered as the leader of the continental pack. Similarly, the endeavours of many film-makers went into forcing Latin American cinema on to the global consciousness but it was the charisma, the screen presence and devilish good looks of the man behind the wheel, Gael García Bernal, in that seminal sequence that ensured the movement's star was born.

Bernal shouldn't have even been in *Amores Perros*. Although hardly an unknown in Mexico – he had been a child soap-opera star in his homeland – when the movie shot in 1999 he was but a humble drama student in London and accepted the call to make the movie against the wishes of his professors.

Today, Bernal is one of modern cinema's most thrilling talents. He has the sex appeal to draw fans to a movie simply to see him and swoon but he is also a superb actor, respected by industry professionals and critics alike.

He has been careful to avoid many of the usual trappings and pitfalls that typically dog movie stars. Not for him the glamorous Hollywood lifestyle: after several years as a Londoner, he returned to live in his native Mexico. He is proud of his roots and determined to make a positive contribution to the country of his birth by being both politically active – highlighting the plight of the poor – and by supporting the local film-making community.

It is his choice of films which best exemplifies Bernal's ideals. He enjoys declaring that the closest he has come to making a movie in Hollywood was with the *Babel* shoot in Tijuana, on the opposite side of the US–Mexican border to Tinseltown and California. He has made films in England, Spain and France and taken the lead only once in the US, and that was for an independent art-house flick, *The King*.

Most of his films have been made in Latin America. His portrayal of a young Che Guevara on the path to self-awareness in *The Motorcycle Diaries* represented something of an epiphany for the actor too: Bernal came to understand that despite their differences the various nations of Latin America have a great deal in common. He resolved to champion the continent's cause and has become something of a mascot for the Latin American film-making community.

The last decade has seen an absolute boom in Latin American cinema with films from the region proving box-office smashes both at home and abroad, and picking up all manner of prizes and plaudits across the globe. Bernal has worked with the top directors of Latin American New Wave cinema (including Alejandro González Iñárritu, Alfonso Cuarón, Walter Salles, Fernando Meirelles and Hector Babenco) and starred in most of the major success stories (*Amores Perros, Y Tu Mamá También, The Crime of Father Amaro, The Motorcycle Diaries, Babel*).

Bernal burst into the limelight at the same time as the movement and so recounting the tale of Gael García Bernal introduces and encourages the telling of the story of the Latin American New Wave.

This book portrays the rise of Bernal, from growing up on the streets of Mexico City to treading the red carpet at Cannes, filled with the background colour and details that shaped one of international cinema's hottest properties. It also charts the course of the 21st century's first major film movement and puts it in its historical and cultural context. Frequently the two strands are one and the same as Bernal's struggles as an actor form part of the bigger picture of the difficulties faced by the region's film-makers to simply get pictures made.

The triumphs in the face of adversity of both the Latin American New Wave and Bernal are shared. This is the wonderful tale of how circumstance and talent came together to propel the underdog into stealing the spotlight on the world stage.

On a Role

These days Gael García Bernal may be one of the most respected actors in the world, but if it hadn't been for a pair of roller skates he may never have answered his thespian calling.

Teresa Suárez directed him for his first serious acting role, in a play called *El Rapto de las Estrellas* (*The Kidnapping of the Stars*). Suárez remembers that Bernal was only drawn to the stage once he realised the potential rewards: 'I had selected Diego Luna for this work of theatre and he arrived at rehearsals accompanied by Gael, his best friend. Gael, who was only nine, at first said he wasn't interested in the play. But then he asked me if the actors were going to get paid. I said they would, and so he said, "Well, I want to act too then, because I need to buy new roller skates."'

Luna, who would of course go on to make *Y Tu Mamá También* (*And Your Mother Too*) with Bernal, had successfully auditioned for his role and in fact there were no more parts up for grabs when Bernal arrived on the scene. But such was his winning charm that Suárez ended up writing one in especially for him. 'He can be very angelic when he wants to be,' she says by way of explanation.

El Rapto de las Estrellas was the debut work as playwright of Alejandro Reyes. He approached Suárez with his script, she having had some theatre experience after helping Julio Castillo, an old college friend and a distinguished theatre director, stage *Dulces Compañías* (*Sweet Company*). Suárez helped Reyes rework the idea and managed to secure a run at the Poliforum theatre in central Mexico City. 'Between the two of us, we wrote it, produced it, acted in it, did everything,' recalls Suárez.

The story concerns two children who are left at home to watch their favourite television programme, *Nefasta*, about a wicked witch. In the episode in question, Nefasta (played by Suárez) kidnaps Scorpio and jumps out of the TV set, landing in the front room with the children. They follow her as they fly up to space and she uses Scorpio's venom to poison the other stars of the Zodiac in a bid for world domination. Pancho Mosquito (Reyes) tries to stop her with the aid of the children.

Bernal played the part of a beaver who confronts Nefasta, gets in a fight with Gemini, loses and is captured and put in a cage. Thus Bernal ends up spending most of the play in a cage.

1

Yet he had plenty of lines and Suárez describes it as a lovely role. Bernal was a natural. 'The truth is that he did it very well, was very confident and forceful. I really liked how he played it – it was very cool. This was his first real acting experience and it was very enriching to work with him.'

First experience it may have been but there were immediate signs of talent: 'It was very obvious. What you noted was that he really gave a lot to it and he had a natural spark.'

In order to promote the play, Suárez organised several commercials to be filmed, of which Bernal was the star turn, dancing like Elvis Presley in one, impersonating a *Quechitos* crisp in another.

'It was rewarding working with Gael,' continues Suárez. 'What's more, children take in a lot more. They used to fight with us – of course, they were kids – and I would have to convince or reassure them, but they all became great friends too.'

At such a young age, the balance between acting and playing can sometimes become confused but there was little doubting the youngsters' efforts and intentions here. 'They created, they acted. As the children of actors they were always going to take it seriously. Gael's father had done a lot of theatre; he was a very good actor. Likewise his mother.' As well as Bernal, Luna's parents both had theatrical backgrounds, as did Julián de Tavira, another cast member who would go on to be one of Bernal's lifelong friends.

'I knew Pati [Patricia Bernal, Gael's mother] and all their parents,' says Suárez, whose responsibilities as director often included providing childcare. 'Because the parents of Gael, Diego and Julián all worked in the theatre they were often away touring. So every weekend, we would finish the show and then they would all come back to my house to stay the night. We would play and do improvisations.'

Being the offspring of actors has natural advantages for a budding stage star but it comes with a particular form of pressure, a perceived level of critical expectation: 'Gael's parent's were thrilled that he got a part but on the day of the premiere he was very nervous; they all were. There was one boy whose parents weren't actors and he was much more relaxed.'

But Bernal didn't let the side down. 'Many children of actors go into acting but are not very good. But Gael really is, whether it's in his blood or not. I think he is the best actor in Mexico today.'

Casting and rehearsals began in early summer 1988. As the children were on their holidays, there was no clash with school during rehearsals and performances then took place only on Saturdays and Sundays. The play ran until late 1989, although Bernal didn't last the full course. 'Gael was in it for a year, then once he began the soaps and everything he got tired with it and we got new actors in.' Still, Suárez is quick to point out that one whole year required a lot of dedication and discipline, which set him in good stead for his future career.

Teresa has adapted *El Rapto de las Estrellas* for the screen as a part live-action, part animation feature film. The project is in the early stages of development but it may take slightly more than a pair of roller skates to tempt Bernal on board this time.

Nevertheless, Suárez is also rightly proud that *El Rapto de las Estrellas* first gave Bernal the acting bug: 'He did kind of fall into acting but once he started to do it his sense of curiosity was roused.'

On the back of the play, he was offered roles in a number of Mexican soap operas. One such part was that of Peluche in the 1989 television series *Teresa*, the vehicle which launched Salma Hayek to domestic stardom before she went on to conquer Hollywood too. Bernal's role in Teresa was more of the cameo kind than as a cast regular and he made a similar fleeting appearance in *Al Filo de la Muerte* (*The Blade of Death*), a soap starring and directed by his father, José Ángel García. Bernal's first real role came in *El Abuelo y Yo* (*The Grandfather and I*), a soap opera that turned him into a national star.

El Abuelo y Yo first hit the screens in March 1991, when Bernal was twelve. It concerned a bitter old man whose cynicism gradually melted away once he took two young children under his wing, namely Bernal in the role of Daniel (who keeps the skating theme going by travelling everywhere on a skateboard) and Ludwika Paleta as Alejandra.

'[Alejandra] was a rich girl whose parents were getting divorced and paid no attention to her, their only child,' explains Paleta. 'Daniel was an orphan who lived on a neighbourhood estate. His mother was dead and his father had just died too and he was alone, living on the estate and being cared for by neighbours. And amongst the neighbours there was an old man, always grumbling.'

The old man, or Grandfather of the title, was played by Jorge Martínez de Hoyos, a distinguished actor in Mexico until his death in 1997.

'Daniel used to go to his house to give him food and look after a dog that the old man always let him take out. And so those two characters, the old man and the boy, started to have an affectionate relationship and, although he wasn't his real grandfather, he sort of adopted him because, well, he started to love him,' continues Paleta.

'Lola, who was the cook in Alejandra's house, used to go to this estate to give food to the poor and Alejandra, my character, always wanted to accompany her. And that is where she met the boy and began to fall for him – well, at least, liked him and always wanted to see him. And they became friends and so began their relationship,' recalls Paleta fondly. 'And things became so bad at home that she decided to go off with them and fly in a hot-air balloon and to work in a circus. It was beautiful, a lovely story. A different sort of soap to the typical melodramas.'

What marked *El Abuelo y Yo* out as being so different at the time was its use of children as its focal point. The soap touched on meaty issues of class and race but all through the innocent eyes of youth. Paleta again: 'It was a story about children but which adults could watch. A strange thing happened in that adults started to get emotionally involved in the love story of these two children.'

This wasn't without its risks: a kissing scene involving the two young leads was a thorny issue at the time. 'There was a kiss between two children, which you don't usually get in a soap, so it was very controversial and on the day it was shown the ratings went mad,' continues Paleta. 'Some people said, "How dare this happen?" and others said, "Oh, how sweet," so it created a bit of a debate.'

For the young actors, it wasn't so much the risqué nature of the scene that worried them when filming it. 'I was terrified because I'd never kissed anyone in my life before – I was twelve – and I don't think he [Bernal] had either,' recalls Paleta. 'It was a scene in which the characters met on the estate and there was a dolly so the camera circled right around us and there were doves flying and everything: all very pretty, but not even in real life had such things happened; children just didn't really kiss at that age. And with all the crew watching – it was terrifying. I couldn't sleep the night before.'

The fact that Paleta and Bernal had become boyfriend and girlfriend off screen didn't exactly help. 'We spent a lot of time together and just grew close and became sweethearts. At that age you have no responsibilities so it was all very natural.'

By a remarkable coincidence, Paleta, who was born in Poland but relocated to Mexico aged three (when her concert violinist father moved over for work), is exactly one day older than Bernal, so they would celebrate birthdays together. 'I remember not long after we had met, so before we were together, it was my birthday and Gael gave me a gift which was, well, a very adult sort of gift: a pretty package with some lovely earrings. I was quite overcome and very impressed.'

During the making of the programme, Bernal and Paleta combined filming with a regular school life. 'We went to school as per normal and then after school we went to film. And in summer, the two months of summer holidays, we were filming the whole time in Puerto Peñasco, Sonora – a place in north Mexico with desert and a beach where we filmed the hot-air balloon and the circus.'

While Bernal had, via *Teresa* and *Al Filo de la Muerte*, enjoyed the briefest of tastes of the television world, Paleta had already made a name for herself in soaps before *El Abuelo y Yo* with a starring role in another popular series, *Carrusel*. These days she remains a soap-opera actress, contracted to Televisa, the station behind *El Abuelo y Yo*.

Paleta is adamant that, not only were they acting in *El Abuelo y Yo* but that they had their minds set on future careers. 'We all wanted to act. We all knew that we had been born for this and that it was what we wanted to do. It was acting, a commitment, although it was still quite instinctive, I mean we knew we were acting but it was quite natural too.'

Diego Luna also had a role in *El Abuelo y Yo*, smaller than Bernal's but permanent nonetheless, while Julián de Tavira made a guest appearance. Two other young regulars on the show, Osvaldo Benavides and Flor Edwarda Gurrola, went on to forge successful acting careers (Benavides also becoming a lifelong friend of Bernal). Paleta certainly saw it as a good base to launch a career from: 'I think so. It was a soap that was well written, well directed and well acted – it still influences a lot of soaps even today.' In fact, it was remodelled and remade in 2003 under the name of *De Pocas, Pocas Pulgas* (*The Good, Good Stuff*).

Pedro Damián was the brains behind *El Abuelo y Yo*, the creator of the series, its producer and director. On the eve of the show's ten-year anniversary, in January 2003, he told *El Universal* newspaper, 'I think I have a good eye for talent and creativity in future artists. I took the chance to find some good actors who are now big stars. Seeing them triumph gives me satisfaction because for most of them I was their first taste of TV or theatre.'

One of Damián's best memories is of the enthusiasm of the young Bernal: 'I remember that this soap was hard going, we had to work long hours every day and he was always willing and cheery. It is not easy to find a boy as noble as Gael to interpret an orphan who lives alone and finds his first love.'

In fact, Bernal's efforts were acknowledged when he was awarded the 1993 Bravo for Best Child Actor from the Asociación Nacional de Interpretes (ANDI – National Assocation of Performers). At the ceremony, he thanked Damián for having given him the opportunity.

Bernal was earning himself a reputation for combining his kind nature with a tough working streak. *El Abuelo y Yo* certainly required plenty of dedication, as Paleta explains: 'It showed on TV for a year but for us it ended up feeling like an eternity because before it aired there was a workshop, then we recorded it and then it was turned into a play and we toured the whole country with it. So in the end it was about three years.' Damián was also in charge of the play and most of the television cast, including Paleta, Bernal, Luna and Martínez de Hoyos, were involved too. The premise was the same although the theatre production was aimed at a younger audience than the television version with its crossover appeal.

Once the *El Abuelo y Yo* theatre run had come to an end, both Bernal and Paleta took a few years off from performing. Paleta looks back and explains why: 'Because it was very difficult to go through adolescence and be famous, be different from everyone else, from your classmates. Having started working aged eight, people would ask me for autographs, recognise me in the streets. For my school mates it was strange and for me even stranger. I wanted to be a normal person. I stopped acting until I was seventeen.'

In 1996, Paleta reappeared in *María la del Barrio*, a show that went on to be named soap of the year. Around the same time, Bernal made a brief appearance in *Roberto Zucco*, a play directed by Frenchwoman Catherine Murnas and starring Alejandro Reyes (who sadly died shortly after) and Luna. More significantly, Bernal made the short film *De Tripas, Corazón* (*Guts and Heart*) in 1994.

As for Bernal and Paleta the couple, the end of *El Abuelo y Yo* marked the end of an era and at the age of fifteen they went their separate ways, off to different schools. Their childhood romance had run its course but they kept in touch, remained good friends and would eventually travel to London together.

Child of the Theatre

Gael García Bernal was born on 30 November 1978 to Patricia Bernal and José Angel García, a pair of young actors. *El Rapto de las Estrellas* may have provided Bernal with his stage break but he was born into the theatre. His mother was 18, his father 22, and little Gael had not been planned. Unable to afford a nanny, his parents were forced to take their boy to work with them and so Gael spent his early years in the care of their theatre company. This initially meant going on tour, as Bernal would later recall: 'We lived like gypsies, from theatre to theatre, and that was what I thought the world was like.'

Soon, the stages and rehearsal spaces of the cultural centre of the University of Guadalajara, where his parents both worked, became Bernal's playground, as well as his second home. Certainly, some of Bernal's earliest memories are from there. In a platform conversation with Juliette Binoche at the Toronto Film Festival, the French actress asked him about his infancy. 'I remember the smell of the theatre they worked in – it was wood combined with the smell of people. In Mexico it generally rains at night, so it also had that smell of wet dirt,' he recalled. 'I remember walking beside the centre's walls and thinking how long they were. The spaces seemed infinite.'

At the university, seven theatres, auditoriums and studios backed on to one another, fighting for space. 'I remember going from one theatre to another without going outside – just going backstage to see other shows, like twenty minutes to see a bit of some other play because there was a really funny part in it, and then going and having an ice cream.' He said he would take the plays a bit too seriously and didn't like it when his parents were performing in a tragedy and came to harm, hoping each night that the play would have been changed for a comedy; he loved watching his folks playing funny.

Then still an only child, Bernal's best friends were the children of other cast and crew members, one of them being Diego Luna. Bernal's and Luna's mothers were great friends; baby Gael, then one year old, was even taken to meet the newborn Diego in hospital in Mexico City. Tragically, Luna's mum, Fiona Alexander, a painter and set designer, would die in a car crash before Diego was three, leaving the boy in the exclusive care of his father, Alejandro Luna, also a set designer.

The theatre inevitably marked the march of the years in Bernal's early life: aged three he took to the stage for the first time in the role of Jesus Christ to his mother's Mary (as an acting debut it was fairly straightforward: sit on donkey with bottle of milk); by the age of four he had learned to read, a skill perfected by studying his parents' scripts; aged five, he learned his father's whole part in a play.

In such an environment, Bernal had little time for children's customary stuffed toys, preferring games of make-believe, although he did treasure a little blue bike. Aged four, he fell flat on his face, leaving him with a faint scar that endures even today. 'It didn't mess up the bone that much but it definitely looks punched on one side,' he has admitted.

Bernal enjoyed his unconventional upbringing. 'It was fun to see your parents play like children when the parents of friends never did any such thing and were much more solemn. That reality opens up beautiful possibilities for learning. I am thankful for having received such an open education in that environment.'

Nevertheless, he did sometimes feel too unusual. 'I often wanted my parents to have a job like the ones of my classmates. But at the same time what happened to me and made me different to the others was to feel that my parents could choose with freedom what they wanted because they were part of this world of the spectacle.' He says that being associated with the theatre allowed for certain caprices: the family could dress however they cared to, arrive late everywhere, generally get away with anything.

Something else that made him feel different from his contemporaries was his name: Gael is as unusual in Mexico as it is anywhere else. His mother has spoken of Gael calling himself Carlos Alberto because he was ashamed of his rare moniker: pretending to be someone else seemed like the obvious solution to growing pains for this son of the theatre.

'Being an actor is the only thing I didn't choose,' Bernal has said. 'Since a child, I've always been an actor. I even thought that my parents were actors because I had chosen them to be so. My parents didn't promote my vocation but to be close to them I had to be in that theatre environment.' A few years after his stage appearance as Baby Jesus, he joined in with a play at the Festival Cervantino in Guanajuato, aged eleven. This wasn't quite a matter of being an acting prodigy either: he would have to travel with his parents anyway and as a performer, the theatre company were obliged to pay his expenses.

Bernal was born and spent his childhood in Guadalajara, a city he has described as 'six million people living on one great big ranch'. Guadalajara is indeed cowboy country, a city that invented the ten-gallon hat and whose male citizens still go about town wearing them today, while *charreadas* (rodeos) remain a popular pastime. Located in the state of Jalisco on the central plains to the west of Mexico City, Guadalajara, with four million inhabitants, is Mexico's second largest city (after Mexico City with a population of some eighteen million). There is a degree of rivalry with the capital as well as a healthy sense of local pride.

Guadalajara is said by some to be the most Mexican place in Mexico. Such a claim is hard to argue against given that mariachi music is a product of the city and that the small town of Tequila, which gave its name to the amber spirit, is located just up the road. Guadalajara itself has a pretty centre with several beautiful colonial buildings clustered around a series of squares. Many of the buildings' interiors are decorated with fantastic frescoes by José Orozco, a more accomplished muralist than Diego Rivera, or so the *tapatios* (as the people of Jalisco are known) will tell you. One of the squares is decorated with busts of Guadalajara's most famous citizens throughout the ages. Orozco is thus honoured and perhaps he will be joined one day by Bernal, and even film director Guillermo del Toro, also a native.

Bernal moved with his parents to Mexico City to spend his teenage years and it was in the capital that he started to act in earnest and his life began to develop. But he retains a strong sense of pride in his home city. When people ask his origins, he always says he is from Guadalajara and frequently refers to it in interviews. He has even spoken of his dismay at never having seen a film set in Guadalajara, declaring himself determined to put that oversight right. He still has extended family in the city, including several cousins.

Nevertheless, Bernal did most of his growing up in the capital, the metropolis of Mexico City, DF to the locals (after Distrito Federal – Federal District). Bernal initially lived with his mother and father on Avenida Nebraska in the Colonia del Valle district, a middle-class neighbourhood just southwest of the main hub of the city and based around Insurgentes Sur, one of the main thoroughfares. In what can be a chaotic, out-of-control city, Colonia del Valle is one of the more pleasant districts with parks close by and a number of cultural institutions. That said, few cities in the world can compete with Mexico City in terms of traffic congestion and Insurgentes Sur sees its fair share of circulation and jams.

His parents being fringe theatre actors, Bernal's was a family of fairly modest means during his infancy, but once in Mexico City his parents were appearing in television soap operas and circumstances grew to be more comfortable. That said, all was not well at home and Bernal's parents would split up shortly before he made his own acting debut proper in *El Rapto de las Estrellas*. Bernal moved in with his mother, who relocated to the outlying Cuajimalpa *colonia* (in Mexico, districts are labelled *colonias*, or colonies), on the southwest city outskirts.

Patricia Bernal is a well-respected actress, veteran of various successful stints in several hit Mexican soap operas, not least *Yesenia, El Pecado de Oyuki* (*Oyuki's Sin*), *Angeles Sin Paraíso* (*Angels But No Paradise*) and *Gente Bien* (*Good People*). In all, she has appeared in over fifteen soap operas, thirty-plus theatre productions and several films. Her dream is to one day star alongside Gael.

Mother and son resemble one another. Indeed, Bernal has talked of the horror of seeing himself in drag for the first time in *Bad Education*: he was the spitting image of his mum. Their bond is strong, their relationship open and amicable. 'When we see or call each other we chat like the good friends we are,' she says.

Patricia Bernal has shared in several of her son's major triumphs, accompanying him to the Oscars ceremony in 2001 (when *Amores Perros* was nominated) and to Cannes in 2004, for the presentation of both *The Motorcycle Diaries* and *Bad Education*. 'I am very proud. He is a marvellous son and he has marched forward himself,' she declares. 'Gael is a very free and independent person and he has known how best to care [for] and nurture that freedom. He is very disciplined and has always focused on what he wanted. I feel that your children are lent to you and you have to do your best to make them happy.'

After splitting from Bernal's father, Patricia got together with Sergio Yasbek, a television and film producer. Bernal got on well with his mother's new partner. So much so that Bernal prefers the term father to stepfather, as Yasbek has always been a paternal figure to him. With regard to the initial split and its impact on her eldest, Gael, Patricia Bernal says, 'A separation always leaves its tracks but he knew how to cope.'

Bernal is closer to his mother than his paternal father, with whom his relationship is said sometimes to be strained. Yet all rub along well enough for both Patricia and José Ángel to usually accompany Gael to the Mexican premieres of his films.

José Ángel García is a successful actor in his own right, star of soap operas such as *Tu y Yo* (*You and I*) and *El Premio Mayor* (*The Biggest Prize*), although lately he has specialised more in direction, on shows such as *Las Vías del Amo* (*The Tracks of Love*).

García is proud of his son's success and appreciative of the hard work that has gone into achieving it. As he told *El Universal*, 'I am the first to recognise the application and seriousness with which he has made his choices, the quality of his work and the diligence with which he opts to commit to certain scripts, because he receives proposals from all over the world. I think he always makes the right choice because he is not motivated by anything other than commitment to his career.'

Spanish magazine *Fotogramas* asked Bernal what he had inherited from his parents: 'A sense of play and self-evaluation, because theatre serves this function. Without self-evaluation you would not evolve, you would have no sense of humour; everything would become frighteningly solemn or would produce a false belief that you know everything. Theatre encourages self-evaluation, for you to look at yourself.'

He then added: 'And not to want to be like your parents, obviously. I mean to strive to be better parents than even they were with you. My childhood was beautiful but I want to be a better father than my father. Well, that's what we all aim for.'

Throughout his time in DF, Bernal was enrolled at the Edron Academy, an Anglo-Mexican institute located in the city suburbs, halfway out towards Cuajimalpa, the area he and his mother moved to. At Edron, Bernal learned to speak English, which would set him in good stead for his future studies and work. He kept regular school hours, fitting in rehearsals and performances in the evenings and at weekends. In fact, the school was arts-focused and used to such pressures, having something of a reputation for churning out stars of stage and screen.

That is not to say Bernal didn't stand out: as the lead in one of the country's favourite soap operas, he was inevitably quite the celebrity. Such attention at school is often not welcome or even well intentioned, as his *El Abuelo y Yo* co-star, Ludwika Paleta, explains: 'Well, yes, it was difficult. After the show, when I started at a new school, they bothered me a lot. At that age, adolescence, classmates are like that – but that's also where I made my best friends.'

Bernal was the victim of similar teasing, often picked on and called the Televisa Kid by his contemporaries. When asked about being considered a heart-throb by the *Observer* newspaper several years later, Bernal recalled those difficult days: 'Very honestly, it is hard for me to see an outside perspective on myself. It is hard – and I don't share it. I wake up every day, look at myself in the mirror and I am the same person who looked into the mirror every morning when I was scared shitless of going to school.'

The hormonal Bernal perhaps didn't help himself. 'I had a phase of hating everyone. Well, they thought it was a phase, but it lasted from fourteen to eighteen. I was a little pretentious.' As a perfect example, he recalls how he would often confront other kids he caught wearing a Che Guevara T-shirt. 'I would see people wearing it and give them shit about it. Say: "Why are you wearing that? You don't know anything about him. Who was he?"'

Despite all this, he was popular and had a wide circle of friends. Besides an interest in art-house cinema that might see him skip school in order to go and watch a François Truffaut movie, his main pastimes were typical of any adolescent boy: rock music and football. He played in a band and for several football teams as well as avidly following the Pumas, a top-flight side from Mexico City. Bernal also told *Rolling Stone* magazine that as a teenager he and a dozen friends would juggle in front of cars stopped at traffic lights in order to earn spending money for a night out on the town.

The young Bernal liked to travel and spent months one summer trekking through the Mexican sierra. By then, he had already visited Cuba several times too. A grandfather had been born in Cuba but fled Fulgencio Batista's dictatorship and ended up in Mexico. By the time of the revolution, he had fallen in love and so made Mexico his home, but Bernal would go on family holidays to see relatives on the island. Aged sixteen he set off to Cuba on his own and spent a summer at the San Antonio de los Baños film school, a college established by Gabriel García Márquez, studying scriptwriting and photography. 'For a man, to go to Cuba at sixteen on his own was very, very nice,' he has since said teasingly.

By this time, Bernal had appeared in the short film *De Tripas, Corazón*, sparking an interest in cinema that would also lead to him taking a course in New York, at Robert De Niro's prestigious Tribeca film-making school.

With his *preparatoria* (the three-year pre-college course) at Edron complete, Bernal enrolled at UNAM (Universidad Autónoma de México – Autonomous University of Mexico), the leading academic institution in Mexico City and considered to be Latin America's very finest. Just three months after commencing his Philosophy degree, a strike broke out, one of many that would blight the university for the next few years. Bernal eventually grew tired of waiting and explored other options, but the missed opportunity still rankles: 'I ended up not studying. This pissed me off in truth. There are many things I have not experienced, not read.'

With the strike showing every sign of becoming an ongoing affair (a student strike led to a teachers' action that paralysed the university for a year and a half), Bernal decided to broaden his horizons and flew to Europe in search of adventure, and so began his London years.

Boy in Shorts

Over the years, Bernal would become a regular at the Oscars, both presenting awards or as part of the entourage on nominated feature films. His first brush with the Academy Awards, however, came via a short film made when he was just fifteen, *De Tripas, Corazón* (*Guts and Heart*).

The film is set in a small, traditional Mexican village and Bernal plays Martín, a milk delivery boy who develops a crush on Meifer, an older woman, the most beautiful of the working ladies in the hamlet's brothel. In an early scene, his contemporaries boast of their sexual encounters and tease Martín about his inexperience. They set about initiating Martín into the adult world by providing him with a chicken to do the deed on for the first time; as his chums hold the fowl steady, Martín pulls his trousers down before thinking better of it and running away.

He is then not invited along with the other boys when they make their first foray into the brothel itself. Bernal's character watches through a hole in the wall, resigned as he sees Jesús, the butcher's son and Bernal's chief tormentor, go upstairs with Meifer. Then, unbeknown to the others, the bragging Jesús gets stage fright.

The next morning when Martín is doing his milk round as usual, Meifer calls him over and they begin to kiss. The film ends as Meifer pushes the boy into her home and closes the door behind them.

The short's director was Antonio Urrutia, who explains how it came about: 'The producer Bertha Navarro had worked on *Cronos* with Guillermo del Toro and he and the Universidad de Guadalajara invited Bertha to come and do a workshop with people in the city.' (Urrutia, like Del Toro and Bernal, is a Guadalajara native.)

'The workshop brought people from Sundance to help script-writers from Latin America and I worked as a translator at the workshop, then in the evenings I worked on my own script with a few of the participants,' says Urrutia. 'Bertha got interested in a few of the scripts, one of which was *De Tripas, Corazón*. We managed to get a little money from IMCINE (the state film fund) and some from the Universidad de Guadalajara and with twenty thousand dollars we produced this short.'

What appealed to Navarro was that *De Tripas, Corazón* was both different and traditional. 'All the shorts that were being made in Mexico City were trying to be

13

very vanguard and here we weren't. It was a very provincial story and Gael is very provincial too, very *tapatio*.'

So it helped that Bernal was a local, a *tapatio*, but he got the part via the traditional route. 'Bertha knew Claudia Becker, the most important casting director in the country, and she said to me, "I have the perfect actor for your film," and presented me to Gael,' continues Urrutia. 'I met him and Martín Altomaro and the other two boys and there was great chemistry between everyone. And so we went to work.' Martín Altomaro was Jesús. The role of Meifer went to Elpidia Carrillo, an established Mexican actress who was then best known for appearing in *Predator* and who has since appeared in Ken Loach's *Bread and Roses*.

The cast was nearly bolstered by another illustrious name. 'There was a role for Diego Luna but he ended up being on holiday – we were shooting in summer – so he didn't appear in the end.'

The shoot went ahead in 1994, lasted just over a week and took place in Concepción de Buenos Aires, a small village in the south of Jalisco state. 'We were only a small crew, about twenty people, but it was a big deal for the village: they were very impressed; we might as well have been making *Gone with the Wind*,' recalls Urrutia.

Nevertheless, the locals didn't recognise Bernal from his *El Abuelo y Yo* days straight away. 'Gael had very straight well-kept hair in the soap, all very neat and pretty, and afterwards he didn't like it and thought he looked like a Mormon. So he cut it all short. At first people didn't realise who he was because he looked very different but soon people recognised him: "Oh, it's him from *Abuelo y Yo*."'

Bernal and the other young male cast members proved quite a hit with the local talent. 'They sent the village girls crazy, and they were good-looking girls too,' laughs Urrutia. 'It was a small production so there wasn't much money and so Pastora, my wife, was there to make us food for lunch and in the evenings, burgers or sandwiches or something.

'At night Gael and Martín and everyone would go and play spin-the-bottle with the girls of the village. The girls were crazy for them. So at night if they weren't filming they'd head off and Pastora would then have to round them up and say, "Bedtime" because they would have to be up at seven to film.

'They were like a little family, a right gang of terrors. There was a bar in the village with loads of porno posters on the wall – the bar we used for the film was a set – but in the real bar there was *Penthouse*, *Playboy* and *Hustler* all over the walls, in this tiny little village.

'And they [Bernal and his chums] would turn up all excited and as the owner of the bar was helping us a lot with things to put in the bar on the set – bottles and stuff – we would always go to his bar to get drunk after filming. And the boys were allowed to come in: they were only fifteen but it was fine; I remember they used to drink grenadine punch. So, anyway, they became very good friends.'

His new best buddies were very jealous of Bernal's final scene. 'Oh, his mates were all like, "Wow, you are going to get to kiss her and everything." But he of course was very nervous, mixed with desire. And Elpidia was a real beauty, a right handful too, and I said to her to grab Gael's hands and put them on her bosom,' recalls Urrutia, laughing. 'So when we were filming that last scene, the door shuts and I could hear in the microphone Gael on the other side panting, "Huhuhuhu, oh man, oh *cabrón*," because he was just a boy after all.'

Bernal too remembers the movie fondly, having since said in an interview, 'That's basically the best film you can do about a young kid, no? I mean, the discovery of sexuality coming amongst the whole discovery of oneself. *The 400 Blows* really gave a lot to cinema when it came out, because it started the trend of these films about young kids searching for something.'

In referencing François Truffaut's Nouvelle Vague debut, Bernal highlights the short film's universal appeal. Urrutia jokingly uses the chicken scene to make the same point, saying that people around the world would come up to him after seeing the film to say they had that same ritual in their country too: 'So things like the myth of the chicken is even universal. I wrote it because I had heard about it. Nobody ever told me for real, "I fucked a chicken," but you hear about it. And this now becomes another element of the film: twelve, fifteen years ago, Gael is there, trousers down, all worried in front of a chicken.'

Urrutia believes that Bernal's physical looks were also an important universal factor. 'The short is very Mexican, the whole environment, donkey, horse, the old motorcycle. And then the presence of Gael: very Mexican but a very universal type, very familiar-looking too. So in all these shots you have a very rural Mexico of the rockies and then this very Mexican guy but who is also very handsome. So a nice mix and at all the festivals people said, "Oh, Mexicans can be different to the squat, dark stereotype."'

The short was Bernal's first experience working on a movie set and he said that from that moment on he knew what he wanted to do with his life. According to Urrutia, it was pretty clear he had a future in film. 'It was obvious, the difference he had in his emotional work compared to the others. It was very evident. Gael was on a different level.'

Urrutia would be the first film-maker, though certainly not the last, to appreciate the Bernal gaze. 'I like actors who work with their eyes. As a child I loved Steve McQueen, who can be on screen for thirty minutes without speaking: it's all in the eyes. And Gael has this; he can be on screen for four minutes and respond, "Yes, no, maybe", and the rest of the time respond with the eyes, listen with the eyes, move with the eyes. That's what I admired most about Gael and I told him, I said, "Wow, man, it's great that you can do this."

'Gael's work was very serious: even though he was young, he was very committed, very focused, and this really struck me. And don't forget that it was my first film too: the first time I had operated a 35mm camera. When I said "action" for the first time, Gael came along riding the bike. Something that will stay with me forever.'

De Tripas, Corazón went on to win 27 international prizes. As for the Oscars, it was nominated in the Best Short Film category but had the misfortune to come up against *Dear Diary*, the first ever project to emerge from the Dreamworks stable. 'What's more, they had made it with ABC, the company that had shown the Oscars for the last nine years,' recalls Urrutia. 'Winning the Oscar is a matter of lobbying and one of the directors told me, "For every vote you manage to get, they'll get a hundred." I think I got two.'

Bernal's involvement in *De Tripas, Corazón* came as a result of his connection to casting director Claudia Becker. She may just have had some input into his next short film too: it was made by her son, Andrés León Becker. *Cerebro (Brain)* told the tale of a young boy mixed up with drug dealers. He meets a girl at a cocaine refinery and becomes entranced by her, to the point that she appears to him in visions of various shapes and forms. The 23-minute film was written and directed by Andrés León Becker, who would go on to photograph Bernal in *The Crime of Father Amaro* as part of the second-unit crew. *Cerebro* itself gained only limited exposure, screening at a handful of festivals after premiering at the 2001 Guadalajara Film Festival.

Another short starring Bernal debuted in Guadalajara the year before, although this one proved slightly more successful: *El Ojo en la Nuca (The Eye of the Nape)* was made in conjunction with the CCC (Centro de Capacitación Cinematográfica – one of Mexico City's main film schools) and went on to win Best Foreign Short at the student Oscars.

El Ojo en la Nuca was another writer-director piece, this time from Rodrigo Plá. Born in Montevideo, Plá's family fled to Mexico City when he was a boy following persecution at the hands of the dictatorship that ruled Uruguay from 1973 to 1985. The short tackles this very theme, telling the story of Pablo (Bernal), a teenage boy who returns from exile to hunt down the military figure who killed his father.

Military goings-on in the region are also at the heart of *The Last Post*, a BAFTA-nominated British short concerned with the Falklands War, in which Bernal plays an Argentine soldier.

The Last Post begins in Buenos Aires as a woman opens a letter and screams in horror. We are then transported to the battlefield where Mark, a young British soldier (played by Kevin Knapman), is being overwhelmed by events going on around him. He inadvertently shoots a comrade and, in shock, decides to desert his unit.

Wandering lost and aimless, he comes across what appears to be an abandoned Argentine post. As he explores, he wakens José Francisco (Bernal), who manages to free his rifle and train it on the British soldier to gain the upper hand. José Francisco asks his hostage several questions in Spanish, which are not comprehended, although the pair soon reach some kind of truce, some kind of understanding. Bernal shows the Briton a photo of his girlfriend and they share a cigarette.

Soon, four British paratroopers approach the position. Before they arrive, José Francisco hands his rifle to Mark, allowing the Briton to make it look like he had captured his opposite number. The newcomers survey the scene and frisk José Francisco, finding the photo and a letter from his girlfriend. They order the soldier to kill the Argentine prisoner, presenting Mark with an awful dilemma. In the end, José Francisco is clumsily shot in the back and, as Mark contemplates the horrors of war, the others line up for a photo with the dead Argentine. The final sequence cuts back to the opening scene and the content of the letter is revealed: it is the photo of the soldiers posing over the body of the woman's dead boyfriend.

The film was made by Brighton natives, the Santana brothers: Lee did the writing and producing, Dominic the directing. Neither has a military background but they do have friends who served. 'A medic in the marines told us the story, amongst others, and it was just an amazing story about the letter, so awful. People ask us, "Is that true?" – and it is,' recounts Dominic. He says that he has a pretty good idea which regiment it was, adding that it was not necessarily the one used in the film and that the Argentine Ministry of Defence investigated and corroborated the story; there was even talk of tracking the girl down to make a documentary.

Ultimately though, it was the human element that interested the brothers. 'I didn't want to be dragged into the rights and wrongs of the Falklands War or for the film to be anti-British. I think it is about what happens to individuals in conflict,' Dominic explains. 'I didn't want to make a political film. I don't think it is even a war film: I think it is about humanity.'

Dominic had been working in television but wanted to break into film and was trying to get a screenplay developed. He was told to make a short first, although advised to make it funny: 'Common wisdom at the time meant that, if you were to do a short, you were told to do comedy. But we didn't want to do one of those extended gags.'

The brothers had heard another Falklands War story, that of a soldier shooting a colleague in friendly fire, having to come to terms with it and deserting, and so combined the two stories. 'We wrote *The Last Post* and it was all done really quickly. The script was written in about three days and we didn't go to anyone for any backing because it would take too long,' continues Dominic. 'I think from the concept we were shooting it three weeks later.'

Having been impressed by Kevin Knapman in a Granada television production, they cast him as the British soldier. He was represented by Gordon & French, who also had the then London-based Bernal on their books. 'We were looking for an Argentinian actor and we auditioned a dozen Spanish actors but none of them fit,' says Dominic. 'Then Donna, Gael's agent, said, "You know this guy's really up and coming," and so she showed me a head shot [of Gael] and I thought he had really fantastic eyes and a sensitivity that I thought we needed for that part.' That both boys look so fresh-faced in the film does indeed add weight to the piece.

'We came in, had a meeting – he didn't even read – and I said, "Yeah, OK – we'll do it." She said, "Trust me, he's going to be really big." I actually hadn't even seen *Amores Perros* by then.' This was late summer 2000 and, although Bernal had by then made the film, *Amores Perros* was not released in the UK until May 2001.

Getting Bernal on board did come with certain minor conditions. The actor was already signed up for a television film about Fidel Castro, to be filmed after *The Last Post*, as Dominic recalls. 'He had really long hair with a headband thing and he said he couldn't cut it because he was doing Che.'

Bernal was happy to fit the film in to help build his body of work. 'I guess at that time he was looking to do a profile. We approached Gordon and French and it was pure luck. We didn't really dream that Bernal was going to be such a big name. But he is Argentinian, or half-Argentinian, which was fantastic. His mother is Argentinian, or so he told us, and he took this Argentina badge with him. So I like to think it had some resonance for him to do it.'

In fact, Bernal's mother is Mexican through and through. Either there was some kind of breakdown in communication or Bernal was prepared to lie to ensure he got the part. Certainly, given Bernal's political convictions – he is both an anti-war campaigner and a champion of the Latin American cause – it seems the sort of film that would have appealed to him, or one that his agent at least knew he would go for. 'I don't think Donna would have put him forward if she didn't like the script and where we were coming from,' concludes Dominic.

The main shoot took place over a week, although Bernal was only required for three days; the brothers then headed over to Buenos Aires to film the beginning and end. The Brecon Beacons represented the Falkland Islands, appropriate enough given that the Special Forces trained there. 'We stayed in Cardiff at some hotel and then every morning we drove out to the set, which we built in a quarry,' says Dominic. With time a factor, it was evidently a relatively intense shoot. 'We didn't go out at all. On set we got on very well but we didn't socialise much, just did our own thing. Because it was summer we were shooting until eight o'clock. I remember when it was finished I dropped off the Land Rover we had hired and had a pint in some Welsh village and thought, "Thank fuck for that".'

Be that as it may, Bernal was a pleasure to direct. 'He was very easy to work with, very giving. He was very natural and quite technically accomplished also. Even just things like smoking his fag and stuff, and repeating that action but at the same time with a great range of emotions – and fantastic eyes.'

It was Bernal's responsibility to capture the Argentine accent. 'I don't really speak Spanish, even though I'm half-Spanish myself. I knew that it [the Argentine accent] is more Italian, more sing-songy, and he sounded like that. I talked to him about it and we left him in charge of it and trusted him.'

As for improvisation: 'We didn't have a huge amount of time for that so we pretty much stuck to the script but we would try different lines. He would say, "I don't want to say that." I'd go: "OK, fair enough, what do you want to say? OK, let's give it a go." As long as it didn't change the meaning, and nobody does things in the same way anyway, I'm happy.'

The combination of a lack of Spanish speakers on set and room for dialogue manoeuvre did lead to one amusing incident. 'There is a moment when he takes out a photo of his girlfriend, and it's actually the girl I was going out with at the time, and she was Brazilian,' laughs Dominic, noting the irony given the rivalry between Argentina and Brazil. 'When we were shooting we actually had no idea what he was saying. We then went to Spain and it was shown in Valencia at the festival there and it [the photo scene] got this roar of laughter from the audience and I had no idea why. He was actually saying, "She has a fantastic arse."

London Calling

With his university studies in limbo, in September 1997 Bernal took off to Europe for a bit of adventure. There were no firm plans but London seemed as good a place as any to start. After all, Bernal's father had headed to the English capital on a similar trip in the early 1970s and regaled his son with the tales of his experiences.

Bernal's European travels were not supposed to end in England – given his love of the country's literature, there were dreams of Russia – but as anyone who has visited London can easily imagine, his savings were eaten up pretty quickly there. Thus he was forced to look for work rather sooner into his trip than he had perhaps envisaged.

He did a spot of modelling for a boutique in Hoxton and found a cash-in-hand job on a building site at the weekends, surprised by the decent wage a builder could earn in England compared to Mexico. He then settled into what would become a longer, more stable term of employment mixing cocktails and waiting tables at Cuba Libre, a bar and restaurant on Upper Street in Islington, north London.

The prospect of a prolonged stay in London started to take shape. The university strike back in Mexico City rumbled on and so Bernal began to consider his options, one of which was to study drama right where he was. His father had taken drama classes in the city on his visit twenty years earlier so there would be a nice symmetry to Gael doing the same. With nothing to lose, he put himself forward for an audition at the Central School of Speech and Drama.

'I decided I wanted to study acting and looked at a few drama schools but it was very late in the year,' he has said. He settled on Central because it was the only one still open to applicants and he could 'remember reading in an interview somewhere that Laurence Olivier had gone there so I applied and luckily got in'. Olivier did indeed learn to tread the boards at Central. Other ex-alumni of the prestigious school include Vanessa Redgrave and Judi Dench.

Luck no doubt played its part but given that some 3,000 hopefuls apply to the school every year and only 30 are taken on, no little skill on Bernal's part must also have come into play. His audition piece, a soliloquy from *Macbeth*, was sufficiently impressive to make Bernal the first-ever Latin American to be admitted to Central. His English was still fairly rusty in those early days and he struggled to grasp the message when he was first told his application had been successful, but he would later call it 'one of the happiest days of my life'.

'Originally I thought I would take lessons in the evening for six months or maybe a year,' he said. 'Then to my surprise they offered me the chance of doing the whole course, and I was lucky enough to get a bursary which meant I would be there for three years.' Yet Bernal claimed he still didn't consider acting to be a career choice at this stage, viewing it more as a means to see the world than a serious profession. 'My dream, my objective, was to work in a theatre company and travel all over the world with the theatre company, be it in England or Mexico,' he said, adding that he still imagined himself returning to finish his degree at UNAM.

Others see it differently. Diana Bracho, one of Mexico's most distinguished actresses, has known Bernal for a long time. 'The fact that he went to the London drama school in the first place, then stuck it out through what I know were very hard times, proved his dedication to the craft,' she says. Juliette Binoche suggested to Bernal that acting must have meant a lot to him then. 'I didn't think of it being a lot when I was there, but in retrospect, yeah, I think it was quite heavy. I could have done with going somewhere that wasn't as hard as London, especially with no money.'

Times were tough. His place at Central came with a modest grant but he would still have to fit his studies around the evening job. He told the *Telegraph* of the speciality cocktail he nurtured at the Cuban bar, a tipple designed not for customers but to perk up the other barmen at closing time. Having deposited shot glasses in the freezer at the start of his shift, he would whip out the frosted glasses and fill them from his 'secret stash' of vodka; the *coup de grâce* was then applied with a few drops of Tabasco, which would rise up through the vodka 'like a lava lamp'. Bernal christened his concoction *Vete al infierno* (Go to hell).

Work could be hard and inevitably monotonous but there were good times too. Bernal is remembered fondly by the few members of staff left over from his era and the actor makes a point of dropping by Cuba Libre most times he's in London.

Besides the struggle to make ends meet, there was the basic issue of being a long way from home in a city that can be pretty cold, confusing and impersonal. 'The food and the weather were big adjustments for me,' Bernal said. 'Finally, I relaxed into it. I decided you never totally adjust to a new place. You just find a way to make it work for you.'

Particular aspects of life in the capital certainly surprised him. On arrival, he had the rather romantic expectation of coming across a vibrant city abuzz with vanguard musical, political and cultural activity. He was ill-prepared for the apathy he encountered, especially on the politics front. He has spoken of his shock on discovering that students would rather spend their time in the pub or submit themselves to pharmaceutical testing than seek out a political rally.

'I think my attitude also has something to do with my family. They work in the theatre, underground theatre, so maybe I was pretentious, or snobbish perhaps,' Bernal has since concluded. Perhaps, but more likely it was a simple matter of culture shock. Britain may have its fair share of problems but, relatively speaking, they are nothing to get too excited about when compared to the politics of Mexico, where barefaced injustice and corruption frequently occur and protest matters.

'I found it difficult coming from Mexico,' Bernal has said in this regard. 'In Mexico, there's this feeling that everything you do has a political complexity. Which it does. Whatever you do, whoever you say hello to, whichever part of the neighbourhood you go to ... Everything has this huge political complexity, as well as social, emotional and sexual.'

He has also surmised that whereas in Mexico City he could be 'twenty different people leading twenty social lives', in London, when he called up friends with the suggestion of something to do, they would usually excuse themselves saying, 'No, I am just chilling out ... ' Another of his London observations was that 'people go home every night to think, sleep and clean. London leads to introspection.'

That said, Bernal did make some very good friends in London. Indeed it was in London that Bernal met Pablo Cruz, along with whom he and Diego Luna now run Canana Productions. Cruz tells a nice story of being asked to act as a reference when Bernal was trying to rent somewhere to live. In preparation, Cruz had concocted a letter that claimed Bernal to be the main character in some fictitious television series. Before he had a chance to present it to the landlady, he realised that Bernal had stolen a march in the poetic-licence stakes when she asked him, 'Is it true that he [Bernal] is the brother of Andy García?'

Of course, Bernal had indeed starred in a television series, *El Abuelo y Yo*. Ludwika Paleta, his opposite number on the soap, had remained a friend and even travelled to Europe with him. 'I went to England with Gael but I went to live in Oxford with a girl I knew there, to learn English.' Paleta's stay was relatively short-lived. 'Two months before I left I met the man who would be my future husband, so after three months I decided not to stay and enter drama school like I had thought of doing.' She returned to Mexico, although keeps fond memories of her time in England: 'I would go to London every weekend and stay with Gael.

Then when he started to study, I used to meet him from college and we would go out with his course mates.'

Bernal had arrived in London knowing nobody, with nothing more firm on the contact front than the address of a friend of a friend. He spent his first weeks sleeping on people's floors then roaming around, moving from one place to the next, always looking for the cheapest option with minimum commitment. Entering Central meant that he was able to hook up with other students and he soon moved into a shared flat in Finsbury Park. He also counts Kilburn, Golders Green, Stoke Newington and Muswell Hill among the London neighbourhoods he has called home.

Paleta remembers that Bernal 'lived in a two-storey house that his parents rented for him, which was quite far out – a bus and a tube ride I think'. The underground brings out mixed emotions for Bernal: 'The different mnemonics like smell or atmosphere – the swampiness of being in the Tube in the summer – bring back for me feelings of a place where I spent perhaps most of my post-inflicted adolescence.'

Whatever a post-inflicted adolescence might be, life in the Big Smoke forced Bernal into growing up pretty fast. 'Of course, millions of people live like that – with no money and no family close by. Without that support, it was hard to kick things off. But for me, London sends you down a route of introspection in a way that no other city does. It was an introspection compounded by loneliness.'

Yet in professional terms, all this introspection perhaps proved to be no bad thing. 'London is a great place that throws you, like if there was a bunch of lances pointing at your inner self, so that you deal with your introspection, your inner demons, thoughts and experiences,' he told *Time Out*. 'I think that's the reason why they [the British] are such great actors and actresses.' And just maybe a contributing factor as to why he has become one too.

When asked about how the general approach to acting differed in Britain from anywhere else, he cites spontaneity as a defining factor. 'In Mexico it's much more in the Eastern European tradition of acting that requires, like, "let's make it clear", then wait, "then let's think about it", then wait. In England people just stand up and do it.'

Bernal found advantages to this get-up-and-go attitude. 'For me it was great to be able to experience and to be put through that stage of just going and doing it, because sometimes thinking about it is a refuge that can make you feel that you're doing something terribly interesting, but when you stand up and do it, it's terrible.'

He also suggested that actors in Britain not only trust in themselves more but in the part and the audience's ability to interpret what they are seeing too. Of his British contemporaries he noted, 'They are incredibly specific and they let their complexity come from within. And they trust their complexity, that what's going on is alive and it's going to be complex, you don't have to colour it in so much.'

This last point is interesting in that Bernal credits his drama training in London for a quality that so many directors have come to appreciate in him over the years; his not overstating things but rather supplying his characters with an element of mystery.

Those comments take on extra resonance given the conviction with which Bernal advocates going to drama school. In a *Guardian*-sponsored talk Bernal gave at the National Film Theatre (NFT), he was asked how important he thought studying was for a prospective actor. Here is what he had to say:

> Very important. For me, I'm a strong believer in academia in this sense. I really feel that whoever wants to act really should go to drama school. You should really try it because it's the best place where you can fuck it up real bad and it's the safest place to do that. It's the place to throw yourself out there and give yourself to it: you'll cry and you'll have a very bad time but you'll also have a huge awakening of something. There are good drama schools and bad drama schools, good teachers and bad ones, depending on the day sometimes, and how you receive things. But I think if you're completely open to someone's subjective interpretation of your work, it's incredibly important. Because when you come out of drama school, that's all you have – people's perception of you and your work. You might have an idea of what you're doing, but when you're on stage, you get lost. And that moment of losing yourself, of not knowing what the hell you're doing and thinking that you're going deep into a whirlwind and hoping that someone will catch you at the end, that is called a performance. That's when a director catches you, and that's when the audience acknowledges your leap of faith into something that's so incredibly unknown. This is why drama school is important.

The course at Central was broken down into various disciplines, including acting, movement, voice work and clowning. Students also participate in college theatre productions, for which they are then assessed. One of Bernal's first was *The Three Sisters*, directed by Alan Dunnet. Dunnet was Bernal's acting tutor throughout his time at Central and fondly remembers his young Mexican charge as a good student and modest individual.

Bernal also took part in a production of *Mother Courage and her Children*, under the directorship of Peta Lily, now with Youth Music Theatre but then his clowning tutor. This is the Bertolt Brecht play from 1939 and concerns the eponymous Mother Courage as a woman determined to profit financially from the war (in this case, the Thirty Years' War) but who ends up losing both her sons to the conflict. Bernal played the younger son, Swiss Cheese.

Given the lack of budget and the material's need for props, Lily conceived of a clever ruse of making it a play within a play: the overall piece would be about the homeless of north London putting on a performance of *Mother Courage and her Children* on the street. Thus a shopping trolley could substitute for a cart, a broom could become a cannon and all the required props could be easily improvised.

This required the students to not only prepare their characters from *Mother Courage and her Children* but also to adopt a homeless alter ego. One of the students decided upon a figure prone to preaching from a soapbox, another settled upon a rent boy. 'Gael came over and asked, "Can I play it as someone who is stoned all the time?" I said yes, of course,' remembers Lily.

'He was wonderful and seemed to stay in the role all the time,' she adds. A matter of living the part, perhaps? 'Yes, there did seem like there might be some method acting involved.'

As there were so many students to accommodate in the play, several roles were shared – there were four Mother Courages for example – but Bernal had Swiss Cheese all to himself. 'One or two of the others didn't seem to get what he was doing with Swiss Cheese,' remembers Lily. 'The whole way I had chosen to do the play was a bit left-field but he was fully committed to it and his role. Some of the others would be worried about demonstrating this or that to the tutors but he didn't care what others thought and believed in what he was doing.'

Bernal is said to have been a less-than-punctual student but *Mother Courage and her Children* was performed in his second year and Lily recalls, 'He was always on cue, highly professional.' He is also known to have been very popular with the other students, although for this show 'he didn't seem to mix loads but then I think that might have been because of how he played his character – everything being so internalised'.

'It was a one-night performance and was long with no interval – but the audience stuck with us,' says Lily. 'He was very watchable. There is a scene where the preacher sings while Swiss Cheese is being killed. In the play you don't see it but I did it with little vignettes of torture so he was flanked by two army people and moved around on a chair as the lights came in and out until he dies. I remember it was a very poignant scene.'

Bernal brought the same commitment displayed on the stage to class. 'He was very focused. I also taught him for clowning and it was the same thing – he threw himself into that too. By then he was already cast in *Amores Perros*, I remember he told me, but he was still totally committed.'

The final play Bernal performed at Central was *The Lights*, overseen by Kristine Landon-Smith, co-founder of the Tamasha theatre company and an experienced stage director. Bernal made quite an impression. 'He was extraordinary to work with, way ahead of the other students,' says Landon-Smith. 'He had this very fresh way with movement and it was evident in every single performance and rehearsal. It meant that there was excitement whenever he was on the stage because it made it live and real. He really was extraordinary.'

The Lights is a play by Howard Korder about life on the underbelly of New York. Bernal's group at Central gave four performances with him in one of the lead roles.

'He has an amazing improvisational quality. I remember with text work, it would sound like he was improvising and you would have to look at the script and you would be surprised to find he was still on text,' continues Landon-Smith.

'He had a wonderful sense of timing, which meant he could be very funny as well. Plus he liked to leave characters unformed. Often kids like to finish things off but he liked to leave them unformed, to add an edge,' says Landon-Smith, confirming that Bernal was endeavouring to put into practice the observation that had impressed him about drama in Britain.

For her part Landon-Smith notes that, 'His whole approach was of a slightly different discipline. Whether that was because he was Mexican, I don't know, but it could have been.'

The different approach extended offstage: 'It was funny because he was always the last to arrive and you looked at him and sort of thought, "I wonder what he was up to last night?" But then you would start and he would lead the way, totally immersed. He could never do things sort of half-mast – he was always totally immersed.

'One thing with him was that he found it impossible to do something the same way twice. Other students often try to do things the same way, to repeat them, but he really couldn't and not because he was trying to always change it but because he was just so instinctive.

'I've not seen that quality from anyone else, and I've worked with many talented young actors who went on to form good careers,' she concludes.

Bernal himself was just about to embark on his good career. 'It was very funny because I remember he would say, "I'm doing this low-budget film in Mexico and need time to prepare – can I have Friday off?" And of course I said yes,' recalls Landon-Smith. 'That film turned out to be *Amores Perros*.'

In fact, his studies at Central almost prevented him from participating in *Amores Perros*. Bernal was invited on board halfway through the second year of his three-year course, but the school has quite strict rules which stipulate that students should not take working roles during the first two years of their studies. Alejandro González Iñárritu, the film's director, had to come over and speak to the school in person, explaining that he had the consent of the boy's parents. Finally a compromise was reached: Bernal was free to film but only during the four weeks of his Easter holidays; he was not to miss classes.

The shoot got under way in Mexico City as planned in April 1999, but a delay to the schedule meant Bernal would not be back for the start of the summer term. He was worried he might be thrown off the course. As Bernal explained to the audience at the NFT:

> So I told Alejandro, and he came up with a very good Latin American solution to this problem – he said that a relative was a director of a hospital and he would be able to get me a medical certificate to say that I had contracted some big tropical disease on my last visit to Mexico. That was perfect because I had no hair when I got back from *Amores Perros* and people believed me completely. I only missed one week of drama school, so it wasn't that bad. But my movement teacher told me to take it easy and my classmates sent get-well cards to me in Mexico, so it was embarrassing.

The following year Bernal had more explaining to do when he got back from filming *Y Tu Mamá También* to continue his third and final year at Central as news broke that *Amores Perros* had been selected to play the Cannes Film Festival. These acting outings were obviously more than a bit of holiday work experience.

Yet by then, Bernal's acting future seemed secure, diploma or not, and so he decided to leave Central having completed seven of the course's nine terms. This is now a cause of mild regret. 'Perhaps with hindsight it would have been better to have returned to my acting classes,' said Bernal. 'I was very young and I preferred the idea of finding out about life rather than returning to school.'

Although he was no longer attending Central, Bernal kept London as his base for several years to come. At first this was down to sheer convenience: 'I had taken over so many things [from Mexico] that just the thought of moving them somewhere else made me feel lazy.' There were also certain advantages to a Mexican matinee idol not living in Mexico. 'In London I live very isolated and I like that. I have friends, I have a life and I like being out of my natural environment,' he would say.

But London also proved a good hub for a jobbing actor. From London, Bernal was approached to star in *The Last Post*. He also headed to Almería, Spain, for a guest appearance in an episode of the US television series *Queen of Swords*, a sort of *Zorro* meets *Red Sonja*. Bernal played one of two men captured by the evil governor Montoya until the Queen of Swords risks her life to free them. Perhaps not a career highlight for Bernal, it did help pay the bills.

In the summer of 2001, Bernal was invited on board the London-located movie *Lily and the Secret Planting*. With rehearsals and preparations out of the way, filming began in August but was abandoned after just two weeks when Bernal's co-star, Winona Ryder, fell ill. When it became clear that Ryder would be unable to return, attempts were made to kick-start the project with Kate Winslet taking over, but such efforts came to nothing and the whole production fell by the wayside.

But he would get to shoot a movie set in the capital the following year: filming on *Dot the i* got under way in spring 2002 with Bernal still a Londoner. *The Motorcycle Diaries* followed and this film seems to have made Bernal realise that his destiny lay elsewhere, namely back home in Latin America.

Spanish magazine *Fotogramas* asked Bernal in December 2001 what changes had taken place in his life, to which he replied: 'A lot. For example, I have my own house in London, something which makes me very happy.' But by April 2004, the same publication was asking him why he had let go of his London home: 'Because I live in Mexico and can't afford it.' The interviewer didn't seem to accept this explanation and so Bernal had to justify himself. 'Look, I'm making Latin American films. I haven't done a single one in Hollywood, which is when you start to earn the big bucks. Latin American cinema doesn't leave you with anything. I have made five films and I am still running about because I haven't paid the rent on my flat.'

On his decision to leave he told the *Sunday Herald*: 'London is gone, that's a bit sad, but it's like a rite of passage, leaving the place [where] you studied. This is hard to explain, but I remember being in Mexico and wanting to live somewhere else, and now I can remember the same feeling about London. I was hungry and now I've eaten.'

The opportunity to return to London for a short spell presented itself in 2005 when Bernal was approached about performing in *Blood Wedding*, thus returning to the London stage for the first time since his drama-school days. The lure of London was too great and he accepted, spending the whole summer back in the capital, holed up in Shoreditch while performing at the Almeida Theatre, curiously enough just around the corner from Cuba Libre.

Whenever in London on professional engagements, promoting films, attending award ceremonies or festivals, he always seems pleased to be back and amazed at the course his life has taken since he first arrived in the city. London has had a major influence in shaping his destiny and the English he speaks, honed at an Anglo-Mexican school and then perfected on the streets of London, will retain its British twang as evidence.

Amores Perros

Bernal was in a London pub enjoying a beer with friends when he got the initial call from Alejandro González Iñárritu about *Amores Perros*. That was in early 1999 but the *Amores Perros* project had already been a long time in the works.

Alejandro González Iñárritu and Guillermo Arriaga first met in 1997. Iñárritu, a successful director of commercials, was looking to make his debut feature film and was scouting about for a scriptwriter. A screenplay by Arriaga caught his eye and the two arranged a meeting. Arriaga started to script a story that Iñárritu had pitched him, a comedy, but he got bogged down: he found it hard to develop other people's creations. He told Iñárritu about another idea he had been toying with, a scenario involving three intertwining stories. That idea became *Amores Perros*.

The resulting film turned out to be a phenomenon, a smash-hit success both in Mexico and all around the world, enjoyed by moviegoers and critics alike. It was a victory of talent and dynamism in the face of the adversity that was making movies in Mexico, but also a story of an unusual set of circumstances that came together perfectly to provide the right platform.

One happy coincidence was that, while Iñárritu and Arriaga were exploring their concept for a film, another ambitious group was busily putting together AltaVista, a company to make Mexican films. Film production in Mexico had traditionally been a state-supported affair, but private investors had begun to look at the sector. Compañía Interamericana de Entretenimiento (Inter-American Entertainment Company – CIE) was a successful events-management firm dedicated to the entertainment industry. They believed that, although cinema attendance was down generally and was no longer the popular pursuit of its heyday, educated urban youth as a demographic group were regularly going to the pictures. The stage seemed set for a domestic film to target an intelligent young audience.

AltaVista had money to pour into films but no bottomless pit, and film-making was an expensive industry. Money was too tight for star names or special effects so they needed projects that would be director-orientated and story-driven. Scripts started to flood in, with Federico González Compeán and Martha Sosa in charge of uncovering the ones with best potential.

Iñárritu's and Arriaga's script stood out and in spring 1998 Sosa managed to agree the right to first refusal with them. By November that year, AltaVista's parent companies, CIE and Sinca Inbursa, gave the *Amores Perros* project the thumbs up and a budget was set: US$2.4 million, of which 86 per cent would come from AltaVista and 14 per cent via Alejandro González Iñárritu's own Zeta Film.

'It was an enormous risk, irresponsible even,' says Compeán. 'At that time, without a doubt, it was the most expensive film ever made in Mexico but, reading the script, knowing Iñárritu's talent, that he had worked well with actors for a long time in commercials, knowing his enthusiasm, his tenacious foolishness, the conviction of (Alejandro) Soberón (chief executive of CIE), of Martha Sosa, of the whole team . . . we just said, "Let's do it".'

They had known Iñárritu since his days as a radio disc jockey when CIE would donate tickets to the concerts they were organising for him to give away in competitions. It would be Iñárritu's first film but he was far from unknown. In the late 1980s, at the age of 23, he had become Mexico City's favourite radio presenter and went on to become producer and director at the station, WFM. By the 1990s, he had left radio to move into television, taking over the production of commercials on Televisa, one of Mexico's biggest networks. From there, he founded Zeta Films, a cross between an advertising agency and film production company, which quickly became a dominant player in the commercials market.

There was no doubting that he was the master of the publicity spot but an early foray into longer works had ended in failure: he directed the pilot for a television series called *Detras del Dinero* (*Behind the Money*) which never made the grade. 'Many people thought we were crazy,' admits Compeán. '"Making a bloody film with a director of commercials, how disgraceful, fancy investing so much money in this young upstart, a novice, who makes commercials and commercial radio." But we had the last laugh.'

Arriaga was hardly new to the game either. A successfully published author, he had already had one novel adapted for the big screen, *Un Dulce Olor a Muerte* (*Sweet Smell of Death*), although Arriaga admits that his input on the movie was minimal.

AltaVista, Iñárritu and Arriaga agreed on five fundamentals for their film: there would be three stories worked around one car crash; camera work would be documentary-style and the print tinted; the dog fights would be handled with extreme care; the cast would be made up of unknowns; the soundtrack would be pumping.

Iñárritu and Arriaga were sent away to trim down the 170-page first draft. Thirty-six versions later, they were happy.

That the process took so long was in part because writer and director were quite contrasting characters and had different views about many things. Others helped them blend their ideas together, not least Antonio Urrutia, director of *De Tripas, Corazón*, who invited Iñárritu and Arriaga for a long weekend of script development at his wife's house in the country. Ultimately they made a fine working partnership, whatever friction there was positively aiding the creative process.

The basic premise was to weave together the stories of three different characters and their dogs via a car crash. In the first story, a boy discovers that the family pet is top-dog in the barrio and enters it into fights for money; in the middle chapter, a pampered pooch gets lost under the floorboards in its owner's newly acquired flat; in the third, a vagabond wanders the streets with his canine companions, reflecting on the sacrifices he made in life by becoming a guerilla freedom fighter.

Each tale carried an element of truth: Arriaga's own dog killed the local prize-fighter in the writer's youth; somebody had told Iñárritu about a missing dog whose eventual whereabouts became known only via a horrible smell from below; and Arriaga had heard of a teacher who disappeared to join the guerillas and was never seen again.

The lives of dogs and owners collide, quite literally, in a terrible car crash. The first car is driven by Octavio (played by Bernal). He is fleeing the heavies of a gangster he has just stabbed as a dog fight got out of hand: Octavio's mutt was about to win the bout when his rival's owner put a bullet in him. That Octavio has entered the world of dog fighting is partly as a consequence of his love for Susana, his sister-in-law, with whom he is having an affair. He is trying to raise funds in order to realise his dream of whisking her away from the cramped house they all share, away from his brute of a brother.

The second car has the beautiful young model Valeria at the wheel. Her lover, Daniel, a man several years her senior, has just left his wife and kids to move into a new flat with her. She has gone out to buy champagne to celebrate. Soon she will be wheelchair-bound, career over, confined to the apartment with nothing more to do than feel sorry for herself and try to tempt her lapdog out of the hole it has fallen into.

At the side of the road is El Chivo, a bedraggled old man who in his younger days gave up a happy home to follow his beliefs and join the revolutionaries. These days, back in the big city, he observes from afar the daughter he abandoned and who knows nothing of him. Embittered by his experiences, he earns a living as a hit man. Accompanied by the pack of strays which have become his only companions, the old man rescues Octavio's dying dog from the crash scene and nurses it back to health, only for the hound to follow its fighting instincts and kill all the other dogs when their master's back is turned.

As well as following three individual stories, the narrative offers an overall continuity. Arriaga has said that he used the first to recount his own childhood spent growing up in the tough Mexico City barrio of Unidad Modelo. The second is not so much about the woman but about her lover, the middle-aged man tempted into giving up everything for the charms of a young beauty. The third is of an older man looking back on his life with regret.

Arriaga explains the logic: 'We had said that it was important that all the social classes were in there. We wanted to make a story in which the first part narrates the past, the second the present and the third the future, bearing in mind that the last one ends with a spark of hope, that after reaching the lowest hell he has the capacity to redeem himself through love.'

Each tale is about loves (*Amores*) and dogs (*Perros*) and the film also has fun with the concept of dogs being like their owners: an innocent boy and an innocent dog become killers; a pretty woman and a pretty dog suddenly find themselves in a living hell; a hit man comes across his canine counterpart.

The hit man is played by Emilio Echevarría, the most experienced actor in the film, with a successful theatre career behind him. He and Bernal were the only two actors in the movie not to go through casting: Iñárritu was adamant that they would both be involved right from the start.

One of Iñárritu's many commercial assignments had been to make a series of clips for MTV, which ended up winning several industry prizes. In one, a boy sits in a bedroom and cries. Bernal was that boy and the depth and dedication that he brought to such a small, simple and fairly insignificant role impressed Iñárritu. (Bernal jokes that he thought long and hard about Dumbo to bring the tears on.)

Urrutia, long a good buddy of Iñárritu after they worked together on commercials, recommended Bernal too, although he warned Iñárritu that the actor wasn't as impressive with dialogue as with emotions (in *De Tripas, Corazón* he speaks very few lines). Iñárritu called up Bernal in London and told him to film himself reading something and to send it over. Having never before done a casting, Bernal was understandably bemused by the request but did exactly as asked. Perhaps his theatre training had been paying dividends: Iñárritu was satisfied with his delivery and called Bernal back to tell him he had got the job and that a script was on its way.

'When I first got the script I read it so quickly,' says Bernal in *The Faber Book of Mexican Cinema.* 'The intensity that you see in the film right from the very beginning was also there in the writing. I was totally mesmerised by it and shocked by the pace of it. And it was well written and extremely moving and I just savoured each page.'

Next came the challenge of persuading Central to let Bernal participate. Making the dates of the Easter break fit in with the shoot schedule back in Mexico City was no easy task. In the end, the shoot had to be rejigged and the start delayed by two weeks to accommodate Bernal.

Assembling the crew proved an easier task, given Iñárritu's vast contact base from his commercial days. Iñárritu and director of photography Rodrigo Prieto had worked on numerous commercials together, as was the case with Brigitte Broch, the production designer. His assistant director, Carlos Hidalgo, and production manager, Tita Lombardo, were also old colleagues.

'It was very good fun,' recalls Hidalgo. 'There was lots of pressure because Alejandro is the sort of director who, from the chauffeur to the director of photography, pushes for the limits. This makes it challenging but it is also good fun because Alejandro has a good sense of humour, so on set there is always laughing and joking and he makes it enjoyable.'

Despite their shared experiences, this was still Iñárritu's first feature film and Lombardo says that at first it showed. 'Alejandro was very nervous on his first day arriving on set. We had all worked together on commercials for years so it was quite striking to see him like this, but as soon as he said "action" for the first time the nerves evaporated and he commanded the cast and crew like he'd been doing it all his life.'

The ten-week shoot ran from April to June 1999, Bernal being involved for the first three weeks only. However, most of the crew had been on the job for months already.

'Alejandro is very demanding,' reiterates Hidalgo. 'We prepared this film for fourteen weeks and for the last six or seven we worked seventeen, eighteen-hour days. In the preparation. By the time we started filming we were knackered.'

Part of the preparation work included scouting for locations. This led the crew to some insalubrious parts of town and into some tense situations. 'All the dog-fight scenes were filmed in a very poor *colonia* called Tacubaya, a very rough area. But we chose the setting and Alejandro loved it and we went back a few weeks later because Brigitte Broch, the art director, had another project to go to, so she had to have everything ready and built before filming started so that she could go to join the other picture,' says Hidalgo. 'We went back to review what had been built and it was brilliant.

'But while doing further scouting, with the van and cameras and everything, along came an armed gang. What was amazing was that they were kids of ten to twelve years old but with guns and everything.

'Even more amazingly, Alejandro didn't realise what was happening: he was on the phone and there was a kid scruffing him by the shirt and holding a gun to him and Alejandro thought it was all a game. It took him a few minutes to realise this was serious and that we had to give them everything – and then off they went.'

This inevitably forced a change of plan. 'We were stunned by this and had to send the film's security team to talk to the authorities; the authorities said that quite simply the police don't enter that particular neighbourhood and that we would have to negotiate directly with the capo of the area. So our security went to check things out, found the important capos and negotiated with them the safe passage of the film.'

Once filming was under way, harmony broke out. 'We used a few extras from the barrio: they liked the idea of appearing in a film and they became our friends. Obviously, these people were just people off the streets: the capos themselves had no wish whatsoever to appear on screen.

'But after a few weeks of filming there was a very nice gesture from them. Of all the things they had taken from Alejandro, the thing he most valued had been a chain that commemorated the first communion of his daughter. After a few weeks of filming, the capo mayor came along and said, "I believe this is yours," and gave it back to him. It was an emotional moment, something we just never expected.'

The dog fights themselves then made for more ventures into the underworld and further danger. 'We did lots of interesting research, including going to dog fights, which were horrible. I love dogs and it was just horrible. It was incredible to see: the thrill that human beings have for suffering, for watching these animals suffer, is frightening. There were drunkards, people drugged up – an atmosphere that was absolutely illegal in every way.'

Disgusting it may have been but the trips served their purpose. 'It helped us to understand how we had to film the fights without hurting the animals. Alejandro chose a dog for each of the fights with the main dog, so ten dogs. And from those ten dogs they made ten dummies, with the same colour hair, and ten sleeves, because the trainers of aggressive dogs have special sleeves. We filmed the close-ups of the bites with the sleeves and the dummies and for the wider shots the dogs wore wax gum shields painted in their same colour and so they knocked each other over but didn't bite.'

Dummies and gum shields or not, these were still very dangerous dogs. To *Fotogramas* magazine, Bernal compared the experience to being in a bullring: 'From that shoot I most remember my panic when faced with those animals that we had to learn how to control. We had three weeks of daily training with fighting dogs in order to know how to dominate them, because we had killers in our hands which would bite you if you didn't control them. I felt like a bullfighter in front of a beast of pure animal instinct.'

Hidalgo was scared too: 'Very and all the time. It is like having the presence of death there with you all the time. If the dog got free, it would kill the other dog or bite someone; they were very aggressive dogs.'

This comes across vividly in the movie's dog-fighting sequences, which are ferocious, violent affairs. Given the film's overall themes, of humans as animals and the callous way in which they inflict suffering on one another, this is necessarily so. There is also a neat parallel towards the end of the film when two humans, who had been trying to trick and kill one another, are chained up just out of touching distance of one another, a gun placed between them.

Despite all the precautions that ensured the dogs were in no way harmed in the making of the film, the RSPCA in the UK couldn't resist condemning the film's fighting scenes and urged the British Board of Film Classification to act. These scenes had caused no such outcry in Mexico. Iñárritu said that dog fights are a cruel reality and found it curious that, in a film which highlighted the miserable plight of Mexico's downtrodden, this was the issue that most concerned people. 'This is nothing other than First World fascism whereby they worry that an animal may be getting hurt but don't offer the slightest assistance to the people who suffer the same violence,' said Iñárritu. 'Nobody has asked me if I killed anybody in the car accident.'

The answer to that last question is, luckily, no. 'It was a very difficult scene to rehearse. We practised for eight hours while Alejandro filmed other things,' says Hidalgo of the car crash. 'And there was time pressure because Rodrigo wanted to film at four fifty-three, which was the precise moment when the sun reflected perfectly off the whatever . . . it had to be between four-thirty and five. So we practised and practised: at half speed; at full speed; with extras; with doubles; with doubles, extras and cars; with doubles, extras, cars and wagons. And so we went, assembling the scene.

'Then at four, it suddenly started raining. So el Gordo [Compeán] was sweating and sweating because it was a very expensive scene and he didn't want to have to do it all again.

'And then at four-thirty, magically, it stopped raining. But then the stunt driver said, "Hey, I need another practice because the wet road changes everything." So we agreed to do one more practice. By now there were lots of people watching: we had an area where they were safe but could watch and wouldn't be in shot. Then a taxi driver came along and decided to park his car in the street. We said, "You have to move it, you are in the middle of the shot." And he said something like, "I couldn't care less, the road belongs to everyone," and he left his car there.

'So we did the other practice and the rain did indeed change everything: the driver braked but hadn't calculated right and smashed the front of the car. So we had to repair the front.

'It is now five-thirty and so we had to do the take. The taxi was still there and the impact of the crash was so strong that the main car went straight into the taxi, direct hit. So, quite apart from having to pay the taxi driver for the smash, the taxi was now part of the continuity matching. To close these roads you only get permission on Sundays, so we filmed the crash itself on the first Sunday and on the second we had to match the crash and film all the post-crash scenes. So the bloke couldn't work all week with his smashed-up car and then had to bring it along the following Sunday for us to film before we sent him off to get it mended.'

Given that the main car went skidding off at its own free will, it could just as easily have ploughed into the watching hordes or into Echeverria, who was standing foolishly close to the action in order to appear in shot. As for Bernal, says Hidalgo: 'We had to use a double for some of the driving but Gael is generally the sort of actor who likes a bit of action.'

Bernal arrived with just two weeks of rehearsals to go so he had some considerable catching up to do. In Faber, Iñárritu tells of being concerned that Bernal just didn't get who Octavio was. 'He asked me if I thought that his character would play tennis in the afternoons and I remember saying: "What are you thinking? This guy is lower class."'

Hidalgo suggests that Bernal's late arrival might have been a factor. 'Maybe from arriving late he had a slight disadvantage as compared to the other actors but I think Gael understood straight away that he was a few steps behind and that he would have to exert himself and get up to speed.'

Bernal himself said that the dog-training helped him, that the animal instincts of the dogs could be compared to the way Octavio is forced into making split-second decisions that decide his future, indeed whether he lives or dies.

Amores Perros may have been Bernal's first film but he wasn't afraid to use his instinct and improvise. Prieto cites the scene when Susana confesses to Octavio that she is pregnant again. When Octavio then stands up, Bernal marched his character way beyond the floor marker where he was supposed to go. He got so close to the camera that it lost focus just a touch and as Prieto panned around to follow him some film equipment crept into shot. But Bernal's ad-libbing gave the scene such extra emotional charge that the take made the final cut.

That he was so close to the camera in the first place was partly a consequence of the claustrophobic house Octavio shares with his mother (played by Adriana Barazza, who would reappear with Bernal in *Babel*), brother, sister-in-law and their baby. There was also a conscious decision to provide the different segments of the film with different styles. While the first would feature tight shots and close-ups, emphasising the intensity, the second would prefer wider, open shots to highlight the void Valeria's life had become.

There was another reason for this technique: by always shooting Octavio in close-up, he appears bigger on the screen, making the character greater in stature. This effect was achieved either by placing the camera near to Bernal and using a wide lens or, in the example of his going back and forth to the car at the final dog fight, by following with a steadicam at his back. Given that Bernal, at five foot seven inches, is no giant, it was a significant approach.

'It was mostly to do with the story, with how Alejandro decided to narrate the first story, because it was a very intimate story,' says Hidalgo. 'But he thought that he needed to make Gael grow. Gael in real life is small, skinny and short, and it seemed to Alejandro that he needed to give the character lots of strength via the camera and that Gael's story should be told from a much closer camera angle. It was an intentional thing.' Then he adds, 'But Gael just has incredible screen presence anyway.'

Iñárritu himself has said that Bernal has a supernatural relationship with the camera. Many commentators made reference to Bernal's eyes in *Amores Perros*, to the intensity of his glare. Making wonderful use of his eyes would become a Bernal trademark over the years but in *Amores Perros* there was a little cinema magic at play.

Once a film has been shot, the negative is usually bleached to clean off excess silver before being fixed, but Prieto and Iñárritu decided to miss out the bleach process. This emphasises the contrasts between colours, brightening the likes of the white of an eye.

It is said that Rodrigo Prieto and Alejandro González Iñárritu had made an advert for a bank in which they used a hand-held camera and bleach-bypass process. 'The world of commercials is a huge field of experimentation because, as there is almost always money, you can experiment with new technologies, new materials, new looks,' says Hidalgo. 'This means that when you get on a Mexican film and there are many more economic restrictions, you have already done your experiments elsewhere. I think Rodrigo had worked a lot on silver retention before *Amores Perros*.'

Missing out the bleach process still carried some risk – the negative can ruin without it – but helped give the movie its distinctive look, making everything seem more vibrant, somehow more real.

The shaky, in-your-face camerawork of the first story was married with fast editing and an ad-man's flair for grabbing the viewer's attention. Combined with the monochrome effect, this made for a breathtaking start to the film, announcing the film's arrival with a bang, that here was something different.

The edit process itself proved a rather tortured time for Iñárritu. In the same way that Arriaga's script went through 36 reincarnations, Iñárritu had chopped and changed for 7 solid months but still had a 160-minute movie on his hands. Antonio Urrutia saw a rough cut and knew it was too long. Urrutia got hold of Guillermo del Toro to see if he could help. Del Toro watched a copy and called Iñárritu to tell him that he had made a masterpiece but that it was twenty minutes too long. Soon, del Toro showed up at Iñárritu's door to help him cut it down, sleeping on the floor for three nights until they got it done.

Fellow director Alfonso Cuarón, then preparing *Y Tu Mamá También*, had also been in touch with del Toro. Cuarón had seen the first cut of *Amores Perros*, which came in around the three-and-a-half-hour mark, and told del Toro he should see it. More than anything, Cuarón had been blown away by Bernal, to whom a script of *Y Tu Mamá También* was promptly put in the post.

The *Amores Perros* end product came in at just over two and a half hours long. It never drags and in part this is because the audience is kept on its toes piecing together the various strands of the narrative. As well as being between three different stories, several flashbacks have the film jump around in time too. This means that the film grows in depth as it progresses, scenes relating back to earlier ones and enriching them with greater context. Thus the viewer's interpretation of events slowly builds as the blanks are filled in and parallels drawn.

Cinephiles were quick to make comparisons with Quentin Tarantino's *Pulp Fiction*. While there are certainly similarities, Iñárritu and Arriaga themselves have dismissed the connection. It seems to be more a question of the novelist's range of scope being applied to cinema and Guillermo Arriaga was after all a novelist. If anything, Mexico's soap-opera addiction is a better audio-visual reference. Indeed, familiarity with the methodology of soap-opera storytelling, whereby different scenarios involving different characters are intercut, is credited as to why *Amores Perros'* unusual structure barely raised an eyebrow on home turf.

The real genius of the screenplay's mosaic structure is in highlighting how these people's lives were not destined to coincide: it takes the dramatic shock of a car crash for them all to come into contact. In one of the world's largest cities (at 18 million, Mexico City then trailed only Tokyo and New York), it is an indictment of the lack of interaction between different social classes. Octavio represents the proletariat, Valeria is bourgeois and Chivo lives on the margins, outside the class structure.

The contrast between Octavio's overcrowded and clammy home with Valeria's spacious and airy flat is clear enough and the effect could have been much the greater: the social divide in Mexico is enormous and *Amores Perros* doesn't venture to the real extremes of society, the shack-living very poor or the mansioned mega-rich.

The film does, however, show how the city's disparate lives are sometimes forced to overlap and in *Amores Perros* they do overlap rather more than they intertwine in the manner of, say, *Pulp Fiction* or Robert Altman's *Short Cuts*.

Although the movie is very much a portrait of Mexico City, notable landmarks are conspicuous by their absence. The Latin America Tower can be picked out on the horizon but there are no other recognisable buildings or other telltale signs of places such as Metro stations, local taxis (distinctive green-and-white Beetles in DF) or buses. In this way Mexico City becomes generic, representing all modern conurbations.

Yet Mexico City is alive in every shot: the camerawork is almost documentary in its vividness. There are no street-colour cutaways as such but the screen overflows with the sights and sounds of the *chilango* capital. In a city this size, anything can happen and everything probably is taking place in some corner or other. It is chaotic and out of control but above all fascinating in its resistance to being deciphered.

Iñárritu calls Mexico City an anthropological experiment, explaining that no civilisation of the past has ever lived through a city so enormous, so polluted, violent, corrupt and, in spite of itself, full of beauty. 'Many Mexican directors are scared to shoot in Mexico City, which is why there are many stories in Mexican cinema about little rural towns or set a hundred years ago. It's difficult to shoot there, not just technically but because it's such a complex mix.' According to Lombardo: 'If you can make a film in Mexico City you can make one anywhere.'

Mexico City is practically another character in *Amores Perros*: in many ways it is the villain of the piece, a corrosive influence that has corrupted every one of the film's characters through its extremity. In the final scene, El Chivo turns his back on the metropolis the locals call the monster, offering a message of hope that he may thus escape its violence.

The treatment of El Chivo is particularly curious. He seems to be being punished for his past links to the revolutionary left while on the other hand the film shows up the neglect which the city – and by wider association the country – has suffered at the hands of its right-wing rulers. At the time of the film, the Partido Revolucionario Institucional (Institutional Revolutionary Party) was coming to the end of a seventy-year by-hook-or-by-crook grip on power.

In fact, El Chivo's revolutionary past is not explored and the movie actually downplays its characters' social circumstances. This would become a common theme in the Latin American New Wave movies: personal stories where the context appears to be incidental but in which, on closer inspection, every choice each character makes is necessarily a product of their environment. Octavio enters the dangerous underworld of dog-fighting because it is the only prospect open to him to earn the cash he so desperately needs to elope with Susana; Daniel treats his young lover to a new apartment because, as a white upper-middle-class media type, he can; a police chief plays agent to El Chivo's assassin because he is so poorly paid by the force.

Having long given up hope in the authorities, individuals take matters into their own hands or simply resign themselves to their fates. 'How do you make God laugh? Tell him your plans,' quips Susana. An ineffectual state not only led to the film-maker's having to broker a deal with barrio hoodlums but also permeates the entire film.

Frequently the absence of state is represented by the absence or incompetence of a father figure: Octavio's mother is single, his brother dreadfully ignorant about childcare; Daniel has chosen Valeria over providing a nuclear-family home for his two daughters to grow up in; El Chivo's daughter doesn't even know her father is alive.

As well as specifically targeting father figures, the film shows masculinity in general to be in crisis. Arriaga has spoken of it being a three-part tale of an everyman's life. The young Octavio gets confused between his own sensitive reaction to his brother's thuggishness and the machismo solution to the family's problems he thinks he finds in dog-fighting. Daniel, meanwhile, might do the cooking but he is making a mess of everything else. El Chivo has tried and failed to change the world through force; redemption seems to be coming to him through a discovery of his compassionate side and, at the end, Octavio and El Chivo are ready to abandon the city, having hopefully learned from their mistakes.

The women of the film are blessed with more pragmatism. Octavio's mother, Susana and the wives and daughters of both Daniel and El Chivo are seen as passive victims of male ponderousness. Valeria is somewhat different, representing as she does the superficiality of her professional world and class, but she too becomes a victim of silly-boys' games – being hit by the speeding Octavio – and like Susana is trapped in an adulterous relationship.

All three actresses – Vanessa Bauche as Susana, Goya Toledo as Valeria and Barraza as Octavio's mother – are excellent. The males put in star turns too. Emilio Echevarría as El Chivo brings a magnetic menace to all his scenes. Álvaro Guerrero as Daniel provokes both pity and loathing for the situation he has got himself into.

But it is Bernal who commands most attention. As well as his gaze, commentators praised his handling of a character as complex as Octavio, bold and conniving, sensitive and vulnerable. In part because he is on screen for the dramatic, exhilarating opening sequence, at the wheel of the car and the film so to speak, much of the *Amores Perros* magic washed off on to Bernal. A star was born.

His performance earned him the Best Actor Award at the Ariels, Mexico's most prestigious annual industry accolades. By then, however, it was just one of many prizes that the film had picked up, the first coming at Cannes.

'Alejandro wanted to enter the film in the official competition but I managed to persuade him there was no need with his first film. It would be easier to win Critics' Week,' explains Compeán. His theory was that, if a Mexican movie came back from the French Riviera victorious, it would allow them to plaster 'Cannes Film Festival Winner' all over the publicity and it was unlikely anyone would much care what it had won. Critical credibility would also be required in promoting such a long movie.

It proved to be a smart move: *Amores Perros* duly triumphed and the achievement was greeted back in Mexico as a national victory almost of the magnitude of winning the World Cup.

However, there had been marketing strategy at play here too. 'We paid for ten Mexican journalists to go over to Cannes, which was a new initiative. It made a big, big difference,' says Compeán. '*Cronos* won the same competition (in 1993) but it had no impact at all – Guillermo del Toro and Bertha Navarro (director and producer respectively) had to put posters up themselves.'

The *Amores Perros* brigade had arrived in Cannes like gatecrashers and left as its hottest properties. Even their hotel booking was a last-minute job. 'The hotel was just one we managed to find that wasn't booked up,' says Compeán. 'Gael was in Europe and so we paid for his flight and two nights in a hotel. He asked for more nights but we had to say no, so before and after he had to stay with friends.'

The buzz generated by Cannes persuaded the film's distributors NuVision, AltaVista's partner company, to move its release date forward from August (Cannes being in May). The publicity machine kicked into overdrive.

Typically, a Mexican film might then have spent US$70,000 on advertising: on *Amores Perros* they splashed US$1.1 million, more than the production cost of most domestic films. Posters and stickers appeared everywhere, merchandise was given away, a song from the soundtrack ('*Lucha de los Gigantes*' [Fight of the Giant] by Nacho Pop) dominated the airwaves, a huge glitzy premiere ensured extra press coverage and Iñárritu worked a mention from all his contacts in television and radio: *Amores Perros* was everywhere. Mexico had never seen a domestic film pushed in this way before.

To match the scale of their ambitions, NuVision managed to persuade cinemas to take on more prints: from a provisional 40-odd, *Amores Perros* opened on 220 screens. The move proved worthwhile: some 270,000 went to see *Amores Perros* in its first weekend. It would go on to be the biggest box-office draw of the year and finished up grossing US$8.8 million in Mexico, making it then the second-most successful domestic film ever (after *Sexo, Pudor y Lágrimas* – *Sex, Shame and Tears*).

The picture proved just as popular overseas. Victory in Cannes was followed by the award of prizes at festivals as dispersed as Porto, Chicago, Los Angeles, São Paulo, Tokyo and Havana. Iñárritu was named Best New Director at the Edinburgh Festival, paving the way for UK distribution, notoriously a tough market to penetrate. In US terms, a Golden Globe nomination was followed by an Oscar nod for Best Foreign Language Film. Not only did this augur well for the movie's March 2001 US release, it triggered a re-release back in Mexico.

It was the first Mexican film to compete in the category since 1976 and *Actas de Marusia* (*Letters from Marusia*) by Chilean director Miguel Littin. The last time Mexico had figured at the ceremony in any capacity had been in 1997 with *De Tripas, Corazón.*

In the event, *Amores Perros* lost out to *Crouching Tiger Hidden Dragon*, so no disgrace there, but afterwards, Bernal and the gang convened at Salma Hayek's Hollywood home for a party regardless. In any case, the film would go on to win the equivalent BAFTA award and become the most internationally decorated Mexican film ever.

The degree of success surprised those who had made the film as much as anyone else. 'We knew the sort of person Alejandro was,' says Hidalgo. 'If you analyse his career, when he decided to do radio he transformed radio; when he decided to do adverts he transformed adverts. So there was an expectation that he might transform cinema too. But when we were making it we didn't realise that it was going to get as far as it did. We knew we were making something big, of impact, but not of the magnitude it did have.'

Arguably, Alejandro González Iñárritu did transform cinema. Says Hidalgo, 'I think that one of his great virtues, as with all good leaders, is that he is the type of guy who listens and who enriches his projects with other people's ideas and always trusts those around him as being as capable, if not more capable, than himself. This makes the project, the idea, the scene grow. There was a good atmosphere off-set, lots of friendships were made. Alejandro is one of those people with a sense of recognition. It doesn't matter if you are the chauffeur or the tea boy, at the start of the day he wishes you "good morning" and he thanks you at the end of the day. Gael is like that too: he was a boy whom all the staff liked a lot.'

Amores Perros changed Bernal's life, as he told an audience at the National Film Theatre:

> I saw it for the first time in Cannes and it was the first time I'd seen myself on such a big screen. And it had a huge impact on me – it was the strangest feeling. I was completely taken in and moved by the way the film transcended our experience of making it, the way it captured it. Suddenly the penny dropped; I understood the nature of cinema.

When it's good, cinema can be one of the most important things in a person's life. A film can be a catalyst for change. You witness this and it is an incredibly spiritual experience that I'd never lived before, well, maybe only in a football match. But that's when everything started for me in film. I never thought I would do a film, that all seemed so far away.

Bernal was credited simply as Gael García on *Amores Perros*, which was of course his debut feature, a fact that hadn't escaped the crew's attention, as Hidalgo explains: 'In Mexico, when you make your first film you have to be baptised: it brings you luck so that you will make many more films. I was fortunate enough to be given the honour of christening Gael on his last day of filming.

'He was due to go back to England the next day or day after and Gael hated us because we tipped a whole bucket of green paint from the green screen all over him – I think he had green paint in his ears for the next two weeks or so. So that was his baptism and it served him well because he has made a lot of cinema since *Amores Perros*.'

Latin American New Wave
Part I: Mexico

Although a blitz of a marketing campaign was a major factor in the domestic success of *Amores Perros*, the film was also the beneficiary of a happy coincidence of timing. The euphoria in the Mexican press that greeted the movie's triumph in Cannes helped persuade the picture's distributor to move the release date forward. Not only did this ensure that the Cannes-generated buzz was maximised but it also meant that the launch of *Amores Perros* coincided with the Mexican general election. And this was not just any general election, but one in which the Partido Revolucionario Institucional (Institutional Revolutionary Party – PRI) would be deposed after seventy-plus years of power.

That the PRI had ruled for so long was the consequence of decades of authoritarianism, electoral fraud and corruption. Suddenly, open democracy was winning out in an explosion of national political consciousness. Vicente Fox of the Partido Acción Nacional (National Action Party – PAN) campaigned on a call for change and, although conservative, he won the backing of left and right as voters across the country clamoured for political legitimacy and accountability.

Amores Perros burst on to the scene amidst this tidal wave of revolutionary fervour. That the film tackled contemporary issues in such a bold and unflinching manner captured the mood on the streets perfectly. Portraying the country's problems on screen was seen as further evidence of the emergence of a more mature Mexico, one prepared to recognise the elements of which it was ashamed. Just as the long-awaited victory for democracy was a source for national pride, so too was this new determination to face up to the country's faults as a first step towards solving them.

'Oh yeah – politics helped,' producer Francisco González Compeán is happy to admit. 'Basically, it was a great film, full of talent, but we were helped by the luck factor too.'

But that the cinematic success of *Amores Perros* had much to do with the peculiar political climate of the moment was nothing new: the highs and lows of Mexican cinema have been indelibly linked to politics throughout history.

In the late nineteenth century, Mexico was politically stable and economically prosperous, at least on the surface. (In reality the regime of President Porfirio Díaz (1876–1911) was harsh on civil liberties and noteworthy for concentrating the spoils of industrialisation into the hands of the few.) Thus Europe's latest craze, the *cinématographe*, which the Lumière brothers showcased in Paris in December 1895, soon arrived on Mexican soil. After first being demonstrated in Rio and Buenos Aires, the new image-projector was shown off in Mexico City in August 1896.

The first Lumière offering had been footage of the arrival of a train into a station and the brothers would continue to document the everyday. Meanwhile, fellow Frenchman Georges Méliès went off at a different tangent and pioneered more imaginative fare with *Le Voyage Dans Le Lune* (*Journey to the Moon*) in 1902. Film-makers everywhere planted a foot in one of the two camps. Early Mexican film productions followed the former example, with newsreel documenting events of national importance providing the staple.

By the time of the Mexican Revolution, a violent Civil War spanning the years 1910 to 1920, factual film-making as a practice was so established that General Pancho Villa accepted payment from the Mutual Film Corporation to allow his battles to be recorded and to conduct executions during daylight hours to better capture the key moments on camera.

With peace came Mexico's attempts at restoring order and recovering its economy. Cinema developed as an industry with a studio system and domestic stars, but the US had already stolen a march and established itself as the dominant global player. Hollywood was founded in 1911 on the Los Angeles periphery, making the most of cheap land and labour, low taxes and a wide range of film locations: within the immediate vicinity were deserts, mountains, forests and the sea. Prior to World War One, the French and Italians had dominated the cinema scene and most movies screened in Latin America were European. The war scuppered production in the Old World and Hollywood stepped in to fill the void.

Hollywood refined a popular formula, which included happy endings, clearly defined goodies and baddies, and a cinematic style of seamless editing, the better to not distract from the storytelling. Such movies were typically character-driven and so movie-star culture inevitably emerged.

Establishing a cinema industry was an expensive business, given the investment in technology the whole film-making process required. Financial constraints in Latin America hampered production, with local efforts obviously less technically accomplished than US or European versions.

Unfavourable economics also affected distribution. The movies became big business in the US, where thousands of cinemas opened; in Latin America, the only places with movie theatres right through the 1920s remained major conurbations – Mexico City, Buenos Aires, Rio and São Paulo. Therefore, while the US domestic market was big enough for a film to turn a profit on the home front and thus be offered cheaply abroad, Latin American countries were still trying to establish cinemas away from the major cities.

A substantial distribution network was essential if a domestic film was going to reach its audience and cover costs. Latin American entrepreneurs interested in cinema concentrated their energies on trying to set up such a web rather than on film production itself. In order to fill cinemas and establish their infrastructure, the businessmen distributing films were bound to favour the polished products from Hollywood rather than a local picture, which risked paling in comparison.

For anyone anywhere wanting to make movies, the safest bet was to copy Hollywood's winning formula, and Mexico did this with musical melodramas. The advent of sound in the 1930s then gave Mexico a kick-start as it forged a niche in the Spanish-language market, churning out movies based around a star and some form of show. *Comedias rancheras* became the genre of choice: a *ranchera* was a popular ditty nostalgically recalling life back on the ranch. These cowboy musicals made stars of the likes of Pedro Infante and Jorge Negrete.

A boom in cinematic production was linked to wider economic growth in the country: disruption to general industry elsewhere during World War Two allowed Mexican exports to prosper. Thus Mexico began to dominate Latin American cinema: by the 1940s, the Mexican cinema industry was one of the largest in the world and the period would come to be known as *L'Época de Oro* (The Golden Age). Classics of the period include *Allá en el Rancho Grande* (Out on the Big Ranch), the quintessential comedia ranchera; *María Candelaria* starring Dolores del Río, back in Mexico after being a Hollywood star of the silent era; and *Ahi esta el Detalle* (*Here is the Point*), which helped Cantinflas become a comic star in the Charlie Chaplin mould.

Successful in terms of output, the Golden Age is not so well regarded critically these days. Although there are some real gems in the canon, given state involvement (a special tax law protected the industry), films from the period tended to depict an idealised, harmonious version of Mexico, the country the government wished to portray. In many ways the Golden Age movies were the precursor for the escapist television soaps that would come to dominate a few decades later.

The *comedias rancheras* in particular were overloaded with Mexican colour. The likes of Octavio Paz, a Nobel Prize-winning author and essayist, praised this idea of *mexicanidad* as a demonstration of national character and identity. Opinions change: these days Golden Age films are more frequently dismissed for being elitist, sexist, racist and class-bound; in other words, old-fashioned.

The Golden Age ended as soon as Hollywood reasserted itself after the war but Mexican cinema continued to ape Tinseltown. By the 1950s, the trashier elements of US culture began to filter south. New B-movie genres emerged: Lucha Libre films showcasing masked wrestlers such as El Santo (The Saint) and El Demonio Azul (The Blue Demon) and bordello melodramas known as *cabareteras*.

Both before and during the Golden Age, stories celebrating the leaders of the Mexican Revolution, chiefly Pancho Villa and Emiliano Zapata, regularly appeared. Russian maestro Sergei Eisenstein started, though sadly never finished, an epic called *¡Que viva México!* (*Long Live Mexico!*).

If Mexican films of quality were few and far between in the 1950s and 1960s, some of the finest movies ever shot on Mexican soil were produced, courtesy of another European guest: Luis Buñuel. The master of surrealism had fled Francoism in his native Spain and wound up in Mexico in 1946. His 1950 flick *Los Olvidados* (The Forgotten Ones), depicting a gang of youths who live by their wits on the streets of Mexico City, remains a masterpiece. Brutal in its realism, this merciless portrait of inequality and desperation packs the same punch today as it did on its release. Buñuel would make some twenty films in Mexico, *Nazarín* in 1958 and *El Ángel Exterminador* (*The Exterminating Angel*) in 1962 being perhaps the best known.

While the 1960s produced few Mexican movies of note, one major, tragic and shameful event would have an impact on future film-making. In keeping with the spirit of the times, students took to the streets of Mexico City in 1968 to denounce the authoritarian government. With Mexico City due to host the Olympic Games later that year, President Gustavo Díaz Ordaz was anxious to project a sense of order to the wider world and sought to quash the protests violently at their inception. This naturally led to further unrest and, on 2 October 1968, the students were joined by sympathisers for a rally at the Plaza de las Tres Culturas, just north of the capital's centre. Government troops opened fire on the crowd, killing some four hundred protesters. (*Y Tu Mamá También* director Alfonso Cuarón is presently planning a film to chronicle the tragedy, with Bernal pencilled in for a leading role.)

Such shocking brutality would stun and scar a generation and, in the 1970s, those who lived through the events of 1968 emerged on to the cultural scene with much anger to vent. Waving the flag for cinema was a whole band of new talent: Felipe Cazals, Arturo Ripstein, Jorge Fons, Paul Leduc and Alfredo Joskowicz. *Canoa*, made by Cazals in 1975, was perhaps the highlight of their body of work.

Economic factors also came into play: the 1970s had heralded a boom in business thanks to rising oil prices, so the sudden crash in the cost of crude hit Mexico hard. With its considerable oil reserves as guarantor, Mexico had been able to borrow billions of dollars on the international markets, money it suddenly owed with the value of its assets severely reduced. The 1980s brought major recession and the cinema industry suffered from the general tightening of the purse strings, a state of affairs that would prevail into the 1990s. Cinemagoing fell significantly as punters chose the cheaper option of a night in front of the TV, while the arrival on the scene of the VCR complicated matters further.

The government went through the motions and fulfilled its cultural obligations of financing a certain number of films each year, but there was little concern for whether these productions were actually seen by anyone.

As if the situation weren't desperate enough, President Carlos Salinas de Gortari then pushed through the North America Free Trade Agreement (NAFTA – agreed in 1992 to begin in 1994). Quota laws, which had forced Mexican cinemas to dedicate around a third of their screen space to domestic product, were now seen as unfair protectionism and were slashed.

Unable to compete with the special-effects-laden fare flooding in from their neighbours, a dedicated few kept Mexican film production ticking over with low-key works of quality which targeted the festival circuit rather than a mainstream audience. Arturo Ripstein triumphed at the Venice festival with *Profundo Carmesí* (*Deep Crimson*); Carlos Carrera came up with *La Mujer de Benjamín (Benjamin's Woman)*. Both were financed through the Instituto Mexicano de Cinematografía (Mexican Film Institute – IMCINE), which had been established in 1983.

Bucking the trend somewhat were two directors with bright futures ahead of them making their feature debuts: Alfonso Cuarón went over the heads of the dominant film-making unions to make *Sólo Con Tu Pareja* (*Love in the Time of Hysteria*); Guillermo del Toro went private to fund *Cronos*. Both films were successful, the former domestically, the latter more so abroad.

However, if one production has come to encapsulate Mexican cinema in the 1990s it is Alfonso Arau's *Como Agua Para Chocolate* (*Like Water for Chocolate*). The government's approach to film-making at the time was to encourage a small number of well-made features by reducing funding and promoting private investment. This led mostly to a swathe of sex-and-violence trash but *Como Agua Para Chocolate* proved different and was a dream come true for the regime.

Based on Laura Esquivel's successful novel, *Como Agua Para Chocolate* was a large slice of magical realism, ignoring Mexico's very real social problems and discontent in favour of a romanticised version of a happy-go-lucky country respectful of conservative values. This was the sort of Mexico the government liked to believe existed and liked even more to show to outsiders. Perhaps it was no coincidence that among the film's private backers were the Mexican Ministry for Tourism and the State of Coahuila, where the movie was set. (Domestic airline Aviasco and IMCINE made up the rest of the funding.)

The film shoot itself was disastrous and some locals were none too taken by the resulting film, a picture as idyllic as the book, but many were and the film played for six straight months in Mexico and went on to become the most successful Mexican film of the decade. Overseas, it ended up being the highest grossing foreign-language picture of 1993 in the US. Furthermore, the very fact that it veered towards escapism and played to stereotype showed that in *Como Agua Para Chocolate*, the Mexican film industry was beginning to work to market principles, to target its audience.

Despite the success, Mexican cinema slumped into an ever deeper crisis: no more than twelve movies were made annually in 1995, 1996 and 1997; the number of cinema tickets sold countrywide had dipped from 400 million in 1980 to 60 million by 1995.

The government (which, as we know, had been the PRI in one guise or other since 1929) then used up what credibility it still had in cinema circles when it pushed IMCINE to try to prevent the distribution of Luis Estrada's political satire, *La Ley de Herodes* (*Herod's Law*). Chronicling the underhand practices of a village mayor in 1940s Mexico, *La Ley de Herodes* not only suggested that the corrupt politicos in the film might belong to the regime but boldly cited the PRI in name, a first for a domestic production. That IMCINE had backed such a subversive picture in the first place was a mystery in itself and the state-backed institution was forced into selling its 60 per cent share in the movie. The government's clumsy attempts at censure made the film something of a cause célèbre and the scandal enabled Estrada to have the film released on some 250 prints, comfortably more than any previous Mexican film, and defiant cinemagoers turned out in droves. Nevertheless, the whole saga served as a timely reminder of whom IMCINE was answerable to and producers began to appreciate the ideological freedom that private financing brought.

What's more, by now IMCINE was providing at best only a third of a film's budget, at worst just one fifth. Private investment became a major factor and under such circumstances commercial concerns had to match artistic ones. The whole dynamic changed, with directors having to actually appeal to their audience.

Compeán takes up the story. 'Before then directors didn't care if their film even got distributed because their business, or what fed them, was getting the film made. Some very interesting people emerged from this, like Arturo Ripstein, who is very well known in Cannes. But in Cannes only; in Mexico, very few people – the cultural elite – know of Arturo Ripstein. And this changed. Directors stopped making personal projects and opened their minds a bit and said: "I would like people to see my films".'

Another repercussion of NAFTA had been the removal of government controls on ticket prices. 'Cinema prices were part of what is known in Mexico as the *canasta básica* [basics basket]. Cinema had controlled prices, the same as tortillas, maize, frijoles and other such things. But they [NAFTA] freed up the cinema prices and there followed the important investment of Cinemex in multiplexes,' explains Compeán.

Cinemas could now charge what they liked and so a wave of US-style money-making multiplexes came to be built. With them came a new make-up of cinemagoers. Having long been put off by shabby facilities (Compeán recalls seeing rats) the new state-of-the-art screens and theatres attracted the affluent middle classes.

Of course, multiplexes also meant more screens and, domestic production all but having ground to a halt, these filled up with Hollywood fare.

Into this void came *Sexo, Pudor y Lágrimas*, a Mexican comedy drama revolving around the bedroom shenanigans of two middle-class couples and their circle of friends. Unusually, the film was released by a foreign distributor, Fox, on several prints. It opened unspectacularly but went from strength to strength and snowballed into becoming the highest-grossing domestic film ever at the Mexican box office.

Whilst a polished and well-acted film, its formula was nothing new internationally and European audiences proved immune to its charms, yet in Mexico it had offered something novel and the industry woke up to the realisation that there was a market for local produce when it reflected the lives of cinemagoers themselves.

Sexo, Pudor y Lágrimas had also been a successful play prior to being adapted for the screen and so cinema now pulling in the theatregoers was also a factor.

Compeán worked for CIS, an events-management company specialising in pop concerts. Its president was Alejandro Soberón and he had made films back in the early 1980s. 'He remembered the days when four hundred million tickets were being sold and was convinced we could win some of them back,' says Compeán. 'We had done concerts and theatre and so cinema was the logical next step. We formed Estudio Mexico Films with AltaVista as a production wing, NuVision as a distributor. The intention was to make bigger films with bigger budgets, because we came from doing big shows and we knew there was a market there.'

They understood that the market had changed, that it now was the same as the big concert and theatre crowd. 'When they used to sell four hundred million tickets, it was the poor who went to the cinema and the rich who watched TV. In 1995 [the year of the relaxing of ticket-price restrictions] the rich started to go to the cinema and the poor to watch TV.'

The almost complete absence of a film industry for most of the 1990s had left a generation of film-school graduates with no product on which to apply their skills. Almost all of them ended up working for companies making television advertisements, the one area of audiovisual production where the cameras were always rolling. This meant that Alejandro González Iñárritu and his ilk were well versed in commercial practices and in targeting an audience.

As well as understanding which consumers they were driving for, they also knew the sort of product they wanted to provide, as Compeán explains: 'The theory was that the Mexican public wanted to see themselves up there, to say, "There is my *colonia*, that's my city, my character, the taxi I know," to see themselves reflected up there. There were so many stories to tell in Mexico and we hadn't told them yet. From the US we know all about the rednecks, New York, San Francisco, Las Vegas, everywhere else; we know all about the crazies who kill people, those who go to the canyon, whatever. But we have not told our stories and when a foreigner comes to tell the story for us he always puts a Mexican in a sombrero and a mariachi suit. One thing we all agreed on with *Amores Perros* was for it to be a matter of, "This is my country, this is Mexico – it's ugly too but we have good stories to tell."'

Amores Perros followed the *Sexo, Pudor y Lágrimas* blueprint but was at the same time more original and daring (helping it appeal abroad where its precursor had not). Here was a Mexican film which depicted people who looked, lived and talked like real Mexicans and that showed the country's underbelly, giving it added credibility. The dominant demographic of the cinemagoing public was now the young and the educated, and the social issues raised by the film gave them the extra resonance they were looking for given the changing political climate.

The cinema landscape appeared to be changing too: *Amores Perros* was so fresh – and so successful – that it seemed to herald a new dawn in Mexican film-making: audiences eagerly awaited what might come next. They were not disappointed: *Y Tu Mamá También* lit up screens with its depiction of the lost generation of Mexico's youth while providing social commentary on the country to boot. As Bernal himself would say: 'I think the film hit a chord with many young Mexicans as no other film had done before.'

Y Tu Mamá También

Bernal frequently cites Julio, his character in *Y Tu Mamá También*, as the one dearest to him, the movie's shoot as among the happiest experiences of his life and the picture itself (along with *Amores Perros*) as the one that makes him most proud. The film's international success, coming hot on the heels of *Amores Perros*, certainly confirmed him a star.

At first glance, it is a classic road movie: two oversexed adolescents embark on a journey of self-awareness. What makes *Y Tu Mamá También* special is that, while this is indeed the basic premise, there subtly emerges a great deal more for the viewer to chew over.

Julio is one of the movie's three chief protagonists. At the film's outset, he and best friend Tenoch (Diego Luna) are seen squeezing in a last quick screw with their respective girlfriends, who are both bound for Italy for the summer. The boys are not overly upset to see them go; rather they look forward to a few months of freedom to get high and chase skirt before going off to university.

At a party held by Tenoch's wealthy father, a politician, the young bucks discover Luisa (Maribel Verdú), an older Spanish woman, whom they invite to join them on a trip to the beach, the so-called unspoiled paradise beach of *La Boca del Cielo* (Heaven's Mouth) no less, which they invent on the spot. Luisa is married to one of Tenoch's cousins but when she learns of her husband's infidelity she decides to take up Julio's and Tenoch's offer: the boys have to get hold of a car quickly and throw together a plan.

Once on the road, the film begins to expand. There are two parallel journeys: the physical one sees the trio travel out of urban Mexico City into the rural and downtrodden Mexico of the south; the other sees the immature and macho attitudes of the teenagers gradually transformed by the older woman, who herself is experiencing something of a liberating epiphany.

Although the boys compete for her attention by bragging of past sexual exploits, it is Luisa who seduces them one by one: first Tenoch, then, to redress the balance, Julio. But her first conquest triggers a confession: Julio, feeling slighted by and jealous of his friend, admits to having had sex with Tenoch's girlfriend. When Julio then has his fun with Luisa, Tenoch reciprocates the confession: he too has slept with his best buddy's girl.

The boys begin to fight; Luisa loses her patience with the young men and threatens to abandon the trip unless they start acting by her rules. The journey continues with Luisa in charge.

With the issues of infidelity yet to be properly resolved, the trippers miraculously reach a beach, which lives up to the one they had imagined. An idyllic afternoon is spent out on a fishing boat and it really does seem like they have reached their paradise.

But there will be a sting in the tale. That evening, the three of them get drunk and all manner of confessions surface. The boys laugh at both their own and each other's unfaithfulness before Luisa expertly steers them into the bedroom and a *ménage à trois*. They awake horrified by their taste of homosexuality from which, we learn, their friendship will never recover.

As a sad postscript, albeit one that gives the whole story an added dimension and pathos, it transpires that Luisa had been dying of cancer all along.

The premise of a road-movie love triangle is not new but the film's rebellious spirit and social conscience, the camera frequently becoming distracted by everyday snapshots of daily injustice, keep it fresh. Meanwhile, the charm and poise of both Bernal and Luna ensure that their characters, horny, spoiled, impetuous and insolent though they are, retain our allegiance and even our sympathy; after all, they are only teenagers anxious to reach maturity.

The idea for *Y Tu Mamá También* first surfaced some fourteen years before the film hit cinemas across the world. Cuarón, then a fresh-faced film graduate, was trying to come up with a suitable scenario to make his first film. The main priority was for it to be low budget. Emanuelle Lubezki, ultimately *Y Tu Mamá También*'s cinematographer but a long-time friend and collaborator of Cuarón, the pair having met at film school, suggested a road movie to the beach. In fact, Cuarón remembers his exact words: '*Imagínate un road movie de unos güeyes que van a la playa, güey.*' ('Imagine a road movie about some dudes who go to the beach, dude.') The project may have taken over a decade to reach fruition but the spirit of that original suggestion certainly made it through.

Cuarón thought the idea as good as any and, along with his screenwriter brother, Carlos, set about pulling a script together. They made progress but never got finished and in the meantime the screenplay for the comedy *Sólo Con Tu Pareja* took shape and would become Cuarón's debut work, released in 1991. Written by Carlos, *Sólo Con Tu Pareja* tells the tale of a yuppie womaniser on the verge of suicide having been tricked into thinking he has Aids. The film proved a triumph on release and Cuarón was soon fielding offers from Hollywood. (There he made *A Little Princess*, another success story.)

The brothers kept returning to the idea of *unos güeyes que van a la playa, güey* and would periodically develop the script further but could never quite get the right balance. They were wary of it ending up a typical Hollywood-style teen movie and Cuarón, having had to sit through a string of such films with his teenage son, was adamant: 'I wanted to steer clear of the *American Pie* style comedies that treat adolescents as if they are idiots.'

In the end, something dramatic had to occur for *Y Tu Mamá También* to really start to take shape: no flash of inspiration, rather professional disaster.

Despite starring Gwyneth Paltrow and Ethan Hawke, Alfonso Cuarón's big-budget *Great Expectations* flopped. It was a very tough experience to deal with and made Cuarón question his film-making credentials, but things would get worse before they got better. Another project Cuarón had been dedicated to fell through: it was based on a script he had written about an out-of-work father and his son on a journey from Michigan to Detroit. Cuarón determined to learn from the setbacks and asserts that he said to himself: 'Why not try to regain my enthusiasm? I needed to make something closer to my roots, something creative which reflected my culture, my language, my upbringing.'

Heading for Hollywood had not so much been the fulfilment of a lifetime goal as much as a logical career progression but Cuarón realised that what he needed now was to return home and make a specifically Mexican film. So he called his brother over to his house in New York and they sat in the garden and started to rework the road-movie story.

The big decision they reached, which ultimately reignited their passion for the earlier project as well as, by extension, the film-making process, was that context would be as important to the movie as the characters; that is to say, the circumstances which surrounded the main protagonists would have to command a focus all of their own.

From here spawned the idea of putting erotic tension at the core of the movie. The film was supposed to be a coming-of-age piece and so, to get to the heart of the matter, sex would be the motivational force that drove the narrative along.

But all this contextualising wasn't limited to spicing matters up with a few sex scenes. The film would be about identity – of two adolescent Mexican boys looking for theirs as adults and of an older Spanish woman trying to come to terms with hers in later life: in the bigger scheme of things, the underlying theme would be of a nation with its own identity crisis. Mexico was thus put at the heart of the piece, as an adolescent country struggling to make the transition into adulthood.

The two Cuarón brothers themselves had been on a road trip in Mexico as youngsters many years previously and, although driving north (in the film they head south), began to appreciate the contrasting lives of the people who shared their great land. They looked at a boy walking along the roadside and marvelled that, though they were all Mexicans, there was very little they had in common with the stranger in terms of their circumstances or perceptions of the world, never mind of the country they shared.

Drawing on their memories, other autobiographical elements found their way into the story too: the siblings once attended a wedding at a bullring graced by the presence of the President of the Republic, just as Julio and Tenoch do, and the woman who had once been their maid played the maid in the film. Meanwhile, a scene in which pigs ransack their camp on the beach was taken from the real-life experience of Lubezki, the cinematographer.

Unusually for a Mexican film, the project was financed entirely privately. In New York, Cuarón had long been speaking to Ted Hope, co-founder of production house Good Machine, about working together. Back in Mexico, Cuarón was approached by the businessman Jorge Vergara, owner of the Omnilife healthcare company and the president of Guadalajara football club, about making a commercial of some sort. Cuarón said that he was busy with a screenplay and showed it to Vergara, who liked what he saw and told them to start the production right away. Together, Vergara and Cuarón formed Producciones Anhelo and the project was up and running. Vergara eventually ended up with a cameo as 'el presidente' in the movie.

After five treatments of the script, the Cuaróns were happy with what they had, although further amendments were made during the shoot. For one thing, opportunities and ideas inevitably presented themselves once on the road, but the actors themselves also left their mark and in some fundamental ways, as Bernal explained: 'Diego and I had to update the script for the present day since Alfonso and Carlos wrote much of it so long ago. The slang was old-fashioned.'

Manuel Hinojosa was the Assistant Director: 'For example, in the 1980s in Mexico we called video clips "video rollers" and this was in the script and Diego and Gael were like: "What?" So the pair of them, as well as Alfonso's son [Jonas], helped a lot in preparing the script.'

The importance of the language should not be underestimated: for one thing, by providing Julio and Tenoch with cutting-edge dialect, the film would gain credibility among Mexican youth and, more importantly, it would serve as a very perceptible barrier between the generations in the film and introduce the adult cinemagoing public to a world with which they were not familiar.

In fact, the youth-speak is so vital that it even made its way into the title of the film itself and stubbornly remained there even when the film was launched in non-Spanish-speaking countries. A rarity indeed.

Y Tu Mamá También – And your mother too. Clearly, as a title it is ambiguous and can be perfectly innocent depending upon context. It is also perfectly representative of the banter between the two boys, even of their attitude towards sex and the lack of respect felt for their parents. It is Bernal who finally gets to say the immortal words towards the end of the picture as Julio and Tenoch compete for bragging rights with regard to whom each of them has slept with: 'Your girlfriend, your sister and your mother too.'

'Cuarón spoke to me one day, we knew each other well,' recalls Diana Bracho, one of Mexico's most celebrated actresses and Tenoch's mother in the film. 'He said: "I'm making this film, it's my brother's story, and there is a very small role, but it is the Mama of the film's title and I would really like you to play it." So I'm the one who was "with" Gael, although you don't get to see it.'

The director also speaks of a broader resonance: that for one thing they are all only there in the first place because of their mothers but also that a mother has already done all this before; that she was once young and had to grow up and find her identity, got into adventures and probably lied and deceived along the way also. That Verdú's character is older and takes charge of them – to a degree mothers them – adds a further dimension.

They have further fun with language in naming the three lead characters: Tenoch Iturbide; Julio Zapata; Luisa Cortes.

Tenoch, as explained in the film, is an Aztec name cynically chosen by the boy's father in a bid to charge his own political persona with a dose of ethnic credibility. Tenoch's surname is equally intriguing: Agustín Iturbide was something of a tragi-hero of Mexico's war of independence with Spain; not only did he fight on both sides but after Mexico's victory, he kept the old caste system in place with himself in the role of emperor.

Emiliano Zapata was one of the main figures of the Mexican Revolution. Says Cuarón: 'We gave the revolutionary name to the lower-middle-class guy.'

As for Verdú's character, Hernán Cortés was the Spanish conquistador who first conquered the Mexico of the Aztecs in the sixteenth century.

A notable feature of the script is the significance of a narrator. 'In all of my earlier films, the point of view was subjective, seen through the main character,' Cuarón explains. 'I wanted to do something objective, seen from the outside. You learn about the characters through context. So in the new script a voiceover comments first on the parents of the two teenagers. Later it makes observations – present, past or future – about people like construction workers and fishermen, whom they encounter on the road.'

Thus we learn that the road accident which is delaying the boys' progress through town is the result of a construction worker having been fatally run down by a car because there was no pedestrian crossing anywhere near the building site where he worked; that the fisherman who has taken them out on an idyllic boat trip will soon have his livelihood destroyed by the erection of a beachfront hotel. The voiceover doesn't so much narrate the film as fill in the gaps: his additions don't add to the plot but enrich it through the circumstances which surround it.

While the characters spend much of the time inside the car, the voiceover usually comments on what is going on outside: these can be actual (evidence of death or displacement linked to the unsatisfactory state of politics and democracy in Mexico) or abstract (that which is confined to the heads of the protagonists, remaining secret and not shared); all is resonant and adds to the audience's understanding of the characters and their context, especially given the boys' apparent blindness to the social injustices surrounding them.

The voice itself is extremely dry – 'clinical' is how Cuarón describes it – as well as distant and cut off. In fact, all other sounds are faded out a few seconds before the voice has something to say. The effect is that it doesn't appeal to the spectator's emotions but encourages calm and considered reflection on what has been said and seen. The device is fundamental to the tone and shape of the film.

Interestingly enough, the voiceover in *Y Tu Mamá También* was provided by Daniel Giménez Cacho, who would later star opposite Bernal in *Bad Education* as the corrupt priest.

With the script complete, Cuarón began assembling his cast and had already fruitlessly auditioned hundreds for the role of the two boys when he got a call from a friend: Alejandro González Iñárritu had just finished the first edit of *Amores Perros* and wanted Cuarón to come over and offer his opinion. In the first scene, a boy is being chased by killers. Cuarón asked who the actor was; Iñárittu replied that it was Gael García Bernal. In fact, Iñárittu had been banging on to Cuarón for months about how great Bernal was in the film but the latter had taken it all with a pinch of salt; no more than Iñárritu's typical excitability. Now Cuarón realised he was indeed looking at his man.

Iñárritu told him that Bernal lived in London and so Cuarón duly dispatched a script. Bernal liked what he saw, later commenting, 'I think it is the best script I've ever read. I was laughing from the first paragraph.'

Meanwhile Cuarón had also sent the screenplay to Fernando Trueba, director of Spanish Oscar-winner *Belle Epoque*, to get his verdict. Trueba not only replied with positive feedback but also recommened Verdú, who had starred in *Belle Epoque*, for the role of Lucia. Cuarón organised a meeting with her in Madrid and arranged to meet Bernal there too. Bernal was keen to commit and also suggested his good friend Luna for the other role. Cuarón knew Luna well, had done since he was a child, and everything suddenly became obvious and clear: not only were the two boys perfect for the parts but their being friends already brought a whole new dynamic, one which could never be created artificially.

Luna hadn't seen Bernal since his friend had headed to London two years earlier but remembers receiving a letter from Bernal giving him the good news that the pair were going to make a film together. Luna assumed it to be a joke of some kind, especially when he then got a second letter from Bernal saying that Cuarón was going to direct them; he himself had still not been contacted by anyone else. But a phone call from the director soon followed and all became excitingly clear.

Filming began in February 2000 in Mexico City. Curiously, the very first scene they shot was the picture's last: Julio and Tenoch meet in a café for the final time. 'The first scene was in a Vips cafe on Reforma,' remembers Hinojosa. 'This was really for continuity so we could cut their hair and things afterwards. We then went to Tenoch's house that night, in San Geronimo, to a house that we had rented. We were to film there for three days and on the second day the council arrived to repossess the house – some issue with the owners. In the end, they sealed the doors but let us carry on flming inside.'

One of the scenes at Tenoch's house sees his mother arrive home and disturb the boys who are getting stoned on the terrace. 'For me it was only a two-day shoot,' recalls Bracho. 'The second day was a bit tortured, they were behind schedule when I arrived and the sun was setting.'

Given her distinguished career, Bracho is rather amused that it is her cameo on

Y Tu Mamá También that has brought international recognition. 'We filmed it very quickly and there wasn't really time to express yourself but it is curious because it is such a small role but as everyone has seen the film, many friends abroad, Italian, English, German, all called me: "What a surprise – we went to see a Mexican film and there you were."

'It was good fun. But I only had three scenes: one when I'm on the path and they're smoking pot and I'm getting back from my yoga class; one at the wedding, with a hypocritical show of admiration towards my husband, the horrendous politician and me, the classic Mexican wife of the important Señor; and one at the wedding when I was with the boys and the girl.'

The girl was played by Spanish actress Maribel Verdú. She had never even been to Mexico before and so the fact that the movie was shot in chronological order (after that first day) added an extra dimension of realism: as Verdú the actress gradually got to know and grow comfortable with her surroundings and opposite male leads, so too her character gets to know the boys and discover the country.

To maximise this potential, Cuarón was careful to keep the three main players apart before the shoot began. Bernal, Luna and Verdú did one rehearsal together in Spain (to make sure there were no obvious chemistry problems) but, once in Mexico, the already bosom buddies Bernal and Luna practised together and Verdú alone. 'Also it was to do with Maribel arriving later. Gael was the first one to arrive on set while Maribel arrived in Mexico at the end of the first week of filming. So really there wasn't any rehearsal time,' explains Hinojosa.

Thus the process of familiarisation between the actress and actors is played out directly on screen. Familiarity between the two young men was of course long established, Bernal said: 'It almost seemed as if we had spent twenty years in rehearsal for the film.'

The journey from capital to coast began, thematically and in practice, in Mexico City, located in the centre of the country. Heading south, the bandwagon progressed through Puebla state and then into Oaxaca, one of Mexico's poorest provinces. Here the shoot ended on the beautiful Huatuclo coast. So, as well as shooting chronologically, the crew all physically made the same journey as Julio, Tenoch and Luisa, although they did cut the odd corner. 'We had already done the journey for scouting and in reality, on the shoot, we missed out a chunk,' reveals Hinojosa. 'It has been relaid now but then the road from Oaxaca to Puerto Escondido was terrible. It took six hours to drive two hundred kilometres. Cuarón doesn't travel well and anyway, it would have been impossible to film with all the bumps. So we flew.'

They encountered many problems en route, not least with filming the route itself. Closing a road in Mexico is no easy business and in clips from the '*Making of Y Tu Mamá También*' angry drivers can be seen in tailbacks, outraged on discovering the cause of their delay. One woman is shown remonstrating with officials guarding the blockade: 'I can't believe you – the Highway Patrol – block the road for a movie. How dare you.' Cuarón says getting permission required a certain improvisation: 'You have to get it the Mexican way: giving money to a cop, to the government. And stopping people coming through is hard, especially in areas where people carry machetes.'

The most testing times for Bernal on the shoot were much more personal: as someone in the body of a 21-year-old pretending to be a teenager, 'I had to shave really closely every day to look sixteen'. He also initially refused to wear the Rinbros Y-fronts in which Julio emerges from bed.

'Rinbros are very tacky and uncomfortable and Gael hated to wear them,' says Hinojosa. 'We also made a sort of scrapbook of the shoot with stills photos and one day after filming everyone had gone to look at some parade but I had to take the photos first. Gael said: "You can photo me from the waist up but that is it." Knowing that Cuarón can be very particular, I said, "Come on – am I going to have to call the boss?" And I did have to call him and Cuarón arrived: "Stop acting like a little kid who won't do as he's told unless the headteacher is called. This is a photo of Julio not Gael. You can't look cool all the time so stop being so bloody vain."'

There were other inconveniences too, not least the heat. For the beach scenes it was typically 27 degrees in the shade, never mind in the sun with cinema lights beamed at you. In such temperatures, a car is the last place you want to be but cast and crew spent three weeks sweltering inside Betsabe, as the car was known. Or rather two cars: a pair of 1983 LeBaron estates were interchanged for the shoot.

'We spent a lot of time in that car,' said Bernal. 'In fact that was the hardest part of the whole process, much more difficult than taking my clothes off or doing the sex scenes. With those I think "you have nothing to lose" and just dive in but filming in the car for three weeks in the heat was the worst part.' Nevertheless, apart from the sequences of Julio and Tenoch fighting, Bernal's favourite scenes are the ones in which they are talking in the car and familiarity eventually breeds fondness: 'When we went to the premiere of the movie, we all went in Betsabe.'

One reason they spent so much time in the car was Cuarón's method of working. 'During the preparation, Cuarón is open to new ideas, scenes that present themselves while scouting for locations. But once the preparation is over, he sticks very much to the script, controls everything,' says Hinojosa. 'There is not much room for improvisation. Cuarón was very careful in sticking to the rhythm of the film. We always had two cars, one was always set up to film and often in the other one Alfonso would sit with the three actors, the script and a stopwatch. They would practise a scene and Cuarón would say, "That took three minutes whatever, let's try for two minutes." They'd get it down to two minutes, already tripping over one another, and he'd say, "now for one minute forty-five." Maybe it would end up being two minutes thirty in the film itself, but this process got them used to a pacey rhythm.'

Bernal found it hard to keep up with the pace. 'Gael as an actor is much more pausey and Diego was more comfortable doing things quickly. Gael is more technical and reasoning. Usually in his films he pauses, he reacts, he speaks.'

Cuarón could be a demanding director too. 'If it was a simple scene, it would be five or six takes, but on average it was a film of fourteen, fifteen takes per scene,' tells Hinojosa.

Bernal's approach to the sex scenes may have been to 'just dive in' but the nude sequences did require extra care and sensitivity. 'It's not that I don't have a problem taking my kit off, it's just that I can't imagine the film without it,' said Bernal, adding that he would have been more concerned had a perfectly tanned or hairy body been required.

Luna offered a similarly philosophical reflection: 'The only way is to lose your timidity. If I have to strip off I think that my body is making art and, for good or bad, I should be proud.' But Luna also had props to hide behind. 'My character had to be circumcised but I am not. With a prosthetic penis, I felt I was dressed: it wasn't my dick.'

When it came to the final sex scene, the climactic *ménage à trois*, the fact that the actors knew one another so well did finally come back to haunt them: performing a boy-on-boy love scene would perhaps be awkward enough without the opposite number being your oldest buddy. Bernal has admitted: 'It would have been much easier if the guy I had to kiss weren't my best friend in real life. It was like jumping into cold water. You just have to go for it.'

What's more, the crew had relentesly ribbed them about the scene, upping the ante. Hinojosa looks back with a smile. 'You couldn't avoid it because the relationship the two of them had with all the crew was so friendly. There had already been jokes for two weeks about the kiss.'

Joking aside, it was a very nerve-racking scene for Bernal and Luna. 'There was tequila and mezcal, that was what the boys needed. As with all the sex scenes, it was a closed set, very few people. We did it in a big warehouse where we built the set. Very hot and very uncomfortable,' recalls Hinojosa. 'The camera stays on the kiss and Maribel leaves the shot, ducking down. At the end of take sixteen I saw Cuarón take Maribel to one side and whisper something in her ear. On the next take the scene started to work,' laughs Hinojosa. Use your imagination.

According to Bernal, there was a sense of art imitating life with the more experienced Verdú guiding the way for her young co-stars: 'Thanks to Maribel, really she was the one that grabbed our hands and put them on top of the boiling pots and in the oven, you know? She was the one that dared.'

The scene is evidently important to Bernal: he has spoken of it being liberating in terms of his career; having tackled something so challenging and risqué, future hurdles would doubtless pale in comparison while, as an actor, he had broken the mould.

As for *Y Tu Mamá También*, for Bernal the sequence which built up to the kiss, a long shot which sees the trio get steadily more drunk and start dirty dancing before the action cuts to the bedroom, captured the essence of the whole shoot: 'I would reduce it all to the seven-minute take at the end of the film – everything was really precise and synchronised, all the crew having at least six tasks to perform and yet through teamwork and spirit it all came through perfectly.'

'It wasn't as hard as we thought it would be, partly because the actors were marvellous,' says Hinojosa. 'The idea was for as little movement of light and camera as possible. We had two days to do it: one day for rehearsing, the other for filming. On the first day, everyone went to prepare and then everyone said they were ready, so we thought let's do it and then we don't have to work tomorrow. And it came off about take eight or nine.'

Luna emphasised the on-set camaraderie: 'It was like a big family. Alfonso, his brother Carlos and the cinematographer were always there. Alfonso was always watching the actors – not through a monitor in another room but right up at the camera.'

'Actors usually like some special treatment, especially when you have someone of Maribel's standing. But there couldn't be seen to be any difference between the three actors so wherever Maribel was put up, so too Gael and Diego,' recounts Hinojosa. 'At first, Diego said he wanted to be with his mates so he came and stayed with the crew, but he soon went running back to Maribel. Not that the crew is particularly bad but there is always a party in one room . . . smoking, drinking, music. Gael had already smelled the danger.'

Not that Bernal and Luna were especially straight-laced. 'Both Gael and Diego were relative newcomers to film but both had spent their whole lives on sets. They were great fun, twenty-one years old and up for anything – and there was a lot of space for freedom on the shoot. We played football most Saturdays. There is a Saturday tradition in Mexican film whereby it is a day off, so you gather for a lunch and bit of a party. If you are filming in DF, you go home, but if you are on location, well you carry on. And Diego and Gael knew how to party – oh, yes. Very professional – they were never late on set or anything – but they bought a load of bottles of mezcal in Oaxaca and they loved to party.'

Lunch on the shoot would often be fresh fish. 'To get to the beach where we were filming we had to go by boat, so there were six boats maybe. One day someone had the idea of putting a fishing line out and caught a great dourado. So soon everyone was doing it and we caught loads of fish for our meals. One day, Gael came on the walkie-talkie and told us all to stop fishing, that we had taken enough from these waters. Cuarón then came on the walkie-talkie and told Gael where to stick his Greenpeace ideals and to shut up: we would fish for our food and whatever was left over we would give to the local fisherman. So then later when everyone was eating the fish Gael was sitting there trying to keep his dignity but sulking. In the end he succummed and ate the fish.'

The shoot ended at the beach but Bernal and Luna stayed on behind after filming their last scenes. Most of the crew had left but there were still a few library shots to take care of. Short of numbers, Hinojosa says the solution was obvious: 'Gael and Diego were enjoying themselves and didn't want to go so we contracted them as assistants.'

'They were both interested in the film-making process, Gael more on the technical side. When he wasn't in the scene he was always with the crew, the sound, asking El Chivo questions,' reveals Hinojosa, El Chivo being the nickname of Lubezki. All this interest would actually lead to Bernal filming a scene – the one in which Tenoch bursts out of the hut where he had just woken up beside Julio and is sick. 'Gael was hovering over the camera and was given it to hold and Cuarón said. "OK, then," and El Chivo said, "Sure, go for it." Diego didn't know and came bursting out of the door with a mouthful of sick, did what he had to do and paused before saying: "What the fuck, dude?"'

Bernal has described the project as having been made through the union of intelligent people and with affection right from the start, and he is full of praise for Cuarón the director: 'He would arrive at the location and talk through with the actors and block the scene and then think about where to put the camera. It is the good directors who do this. They work around the story, the actors and the life of the film.'

Cuarón manages to coax incredibly natural performances from Bernal and Luna. The director originally intended to use a cast of amateurs with the aim of better capturing the sense of realness but he realised that the parts required considerable depth too. That Bernal and Luna are able to provide such seemingly spontaneous performances while also allowing a sense of their character's insecurities to come to the fore is a major achievement for all concerned. It no doubt helped that, as Bernal has said on many occasions, of all the characters he has portrayed, Julio is the most like himself.

Julio's character is somewhat ambiguous. Although the poorer of the two boys, he is the one who blames the traffic jam on some kind of protest and often seems almost more ignorant to his surroundings than Tenoch. If both boys are spoiled, it is Julio who comes across as the more brattish.

It is thus even more curious that Bernal so empathises with Julio: 'I grew up in a very similar situation as Julio. I support Pumas, I made a journey with friends to the beach many times. It is the role that I have much more in common with.' (Julio wears a UNAM Pumas shirt in the film.)

As well as his affinity with Julio, starring opposite Luna helped complete the personal identification process. 'I've always known him. We went through a lot of the same experiences the boys shared in the film – well, not everything, of course, but stuff like going on road trips and smoking our first joint together.'

He has also cited *Amores Perros* and *Y Tu Mamá También* as the films he is most proud of, the latter because it showed the reality of life for his own generation and finally provided a film with which young Mexicans could identify. At a talk he gave at the National Film Theatre in London, when *Y Tu Mamá También* was reshown in 2006 as part of a festival of Mexican cinema, Bernal elaborated upon this theme: 'There is a big difference between the youth of developed countries and the underdeveloped ones. In Mexico, you get an excellent education and you know what is going on in the rest of the world but you don't have the opportunities to do anything. So, you try to make your life as unboring as you can.'

When asked about his character's obliviousness, even blasé attitude, towards the inequality around him, Bernal replied: 'In a country like Mexico you are not conscious of the importance of these violent situations or of unequal societies. You are so used to it from when you are small that it doesn't cause you the least amazement. You don't even question if it is right or wrong. What does suffocate you is being poor, being unable to get out of your problems and not being able to do what you want with your life.'

Julio as a character was no doubt immense fun to play: he and Tenoch swear like troopers, are completely irreverent and make fun of just about everything. At different times, they reveal themselves to be not only immature but also macho, egotistical, prejudiced and even racist. Nevertheless, they are lovable in their ways and the viewer is sympathetic to their cause. Making a character crude and brash while at the same time vulnerable and charming is quite some acting feat, but we also give Julio and Tenoch the benefit of the doubt because their faults are the product of confusion and naivety as much as anything else. All of us have to make that tricky transitional step towards adulthood, if not necessarily in the testing and imbalanced environs of Mexican society. The lack of communication between the generations is a constant theme in the film, as is adult failure in setting the right example. Julio, Tenoch and their contemporaries merely ask to be understood and for someone to show them the right path forward, as Luisa tries to do.

Verdú is excellent as Luisa. Her role is complex and required a deft performance in order to represent all the different factors pulling at the character's emotions. On the road, she is waking up to her own liberation as a woman while teaching the boys a few facts about life. As the older woman who has sex with both of the young men, hers is the mother-whore role as the film tackles machismo's notorious Oedipus complex. Yet she does so having taken control of the party, giving the film a feminist agenda, and is not shy in bringing up the latent homoeroticism of machismo culture, which leads us, as she will lead the boys, towards the picture's grand finale. As such, Verdú shows her character growing in confidence as the movie and journey progress. She is bold and sexy, wise but not too weary: hers is the mature voice the audience can best connect to, somewhere in between the adolescent hyperactivity of the boys and the cold-heartedness of the narrator.

There are some emotional scenes for Verdú when, through tears, she bears up to bad news received or given over the phone. These sequences sit slightly awkwardly within the film and even when their true cause is revealed (that Luisa was dying) don't entirely feel right. Verdú gives her all to these scenes but she, like the film, seems more comfortable when in the company of the two boys.

Her illness makes for a somewhat overly sentimental end to the film, a somewhat Hollywood-type conclusion to what is in the most part an original and fresh picture. In fact, the film ends with a double dose of sadness: less dramatic than Luisa's death, though just as regretful in its way, we are informed that the two boys never see each other again. Their friendship which, although not perfect seemed so strong and eternal, would never recover from the issues raised by the trip.

In relationships as intimate as theirs, when friends are entirely comfortable in the other's presence even when naked, it is often suggested that there is some form of latent homosexuality at play. And yet we never know for sure what exactly killed off their relationship. Was it the discovery of betrayal or was it their forbidden kiss?

And if we are to take the adolescents as representatives of Mexico, just how does this ambiguity impact upon the film's overall message? Perhaps that the country will set higher standards for itself in future and not stand for such treachery or, more worryingly, that the teenage nation will examine itself but be scared by what it sees, withdraw and shy away from home truths.

By extension, does the love triangle have a greater significance? Luisa is a woman being forced to deal with the very serious problems that have come to afflict her life, while the boys grapple with torments of their own making. The best of friends cannot be trusted to act honourably when desire comes into play: similarly greed has nurtured a culture of corruption whereby Mexico's elite continually betray their fellow countrymen. But if Luisa represents Old Europe, what should we make of the fact that she takes the boys to paradise and then so swiftly straight to hell? Luisa doesn't simply complete the triangle but rather shapes it to her tastes. In games of treachery, there are older, more experienced players than Mexico and its New World cousins, often competing for higher stakes.

Another painful reading of the message of the final chapter relates to class. From their names, through their parents' professions and the houses in which they live, through to the universities they will attend – Tenoch to the Instituto Tecnológico Autónomo de México (The Autonomous Mexican Technology Institute – ITAM), one of the most prestigious and expensive in Mexico, Julio to the public Universidad Autónom de México – (Autonomous University of Mexico – UAM) – we are frequently reminded that, although great friends, neither of whom are poor, there is a class distinction at play. This rears its ugly head once the boys start to insult one another: 'You dirty peasant,' cries Tenoch when Julio spits at him: 'You stuck up snob,' replies Julio. If two friends as close as these cannot shake the shackles of a class system, what chance has anyone else? By extension, if Mexico is to progress as a country, it needs to become a more equal, less class-based society. Unfortunately, *Y Tu Mamá También* never tells us how Julio's and Tenoch's unlikely friendship came about in the first place.

What we are told is how the mess that is modern Mexico came about: the closing scene refers to the end of the PRI's hegemony (in the election that followed the release of *Amores Perros*). This reference is in fact the only directly political moment of the film, although politics are at the heart of almost every shot.

The casual, seemingly accidental cinematography – traffic accidents, people being arrested, rural folk simply going about their impoverished lives – along with the voiceover cannot help but filter home. Sometimes the camera leaves our heroes and simply follows the bit-part, background players to show what they, the bit-part, background players of real life, are doing – slaving over a hot stove in the kitchen or taking food out to the chauffeurs in the car park.

Cutaways to contrasting images perform a similar purpose with their juxtaposition: a downtown student protest march plays against the boys larking about in that temple to consumerism, the hypermarket. The concept of contrast is perhaps most keenly felt with the road trip itself: the urban excess of Mexico City dissolves into the rural backwardness of the south. Once on the road, our heroes encounter the weird and the wonderful: a festival queen waves to the passing cars as her fellow villagers collect donations; an old lady does a jig in the kitchen. Mexico is thus incorporated into the narrative like another character in the plot.

The film was photographed by Emanuelle Lubezki, who had first drawn acclaim with his work on *Como Agua Para Chocolate* and was then nominated for an Oscar with *Sleepy Hollow*. He had worked with Cuarón on all his previous films – *Sólo Con Tu Pareja*, *A Little Princess* and *Great Expectations*. Despite the latter's lack of success, it was nevertheless praised for its beauty. It is said that for *Y Tu Mamá También*, Lubezki and Cuarón took care not to film when the light or landscape was too perfect or spectacular to better install the scenery with a natural, rugged beauty.

Yet sometimes there was no avoiding the beauty of the landscape, as Hinojosa explains. 'Things surprise you en route. Where we were filming the cows [a scene when the car comes around a corner to find a herd blocking the road], there were jacarandas, bright purple flowers, very pretty, and a tunnel of trees. Cuarón wanted the place to look very miserable and when we went [scouting] the trees were bare, there was rubbish, it was very ugly. But when we went again, it was March and beautiful. We were going to change location but decided beautiful could work.

'The idea was not to film when the light was too perfect, until we got to the beach. This was the concept. But the photographer is only ever going to make it look ugly to a certain point and *Y Tu Mamá También* is beautifully photographed.'

Some of those beautiful shots even have Hinojosa at the wheel. 'In the mornings we went out driving, me dressed as Gael, or dressed as Diego, because we didn't have the money for body doubles or anything, and drove around with the light reflecting off the car. Once the light got ugly, about ten o'clock, we stopped. Meanwhile, Cuarón rehearsed the actors. Then we would film in the car and try to make sure the light didn't reflect too much. In the afternoons we would film outside the car with the light nice. All natural light for the exteriors, except the beach.'

In the end, the marriage of realism and visual poetry is well managed: the audience understands that it may look wonderful, but scratch below the surface and all is not well.

To the film's credit, there is no preaching: we see what we see – the good and the bad – as observers and are free to draw our own conclusions. For this Cuarón faced criticism from various quarters. Conservative Mexicans objected to his providing an unflattering portrait of the country to foreigners, worried it may scare investors and tourists. He also managed to upset liberal circles by affording the upper classes a degree of sympathy.

The main charge levelled against *Y Tu Mamá También*, however, was that it addressed social issues superficially; that by offering so little by way of analysis, the social elements were used for mere decoration. One particularly vocal critic of the movie was Mexican film scholar Leonardo García Tsao. He attacked devices such as the sardonic narrator as mere ploys to dress the film up with false depth.

This does seem a little unfair given the film's dedication to context. The voiceover often comments on those moments when the camera has been distracted from our focal trio by realities elsewhere. These steadicam sequences are frequent and a fundamental part of the film, giving it a documentary edge and allowing the viewer an all-seeing-eye perspective.

Cuarón might argue that the way in which social ills are portrayed is a deliberate means of engaging with the film's target teenage audience, perhaps even shaming them into responding. Furthermore, that by raising issues without judgement, the film forces younger viewers to consider for themselves the questions raised.

Another criticism of Cuarón within Mexico is that he too readily embraces US culture and methods. But Cuarón is not ashamed about aiming to be successful, and indeed almost invited the anti-gringo cries by making a road movie (bastion genre of Hollywood) with a flashy soundtrack.

Although *Y Tu Mamá También* was subversive in its way, it was made primarily to entertain. Equally, while it does tackle and comment upon Mexican issues, it was designed to appeal and sell globally. Topics such as inequality among social classes are contemporary and have international resonance but, because the local details are just right – in this case Mexican details – the film earns its credibility abroad: foreign audiences are able to recognise authenticity and hence substitute the local colour for their own, creating wider empathy.

Other universal calling cards include the breakdown in communication between the generations and the sexual anxiety of teenagers. While working on the film, Cuarón consulted his son who, though Mexican, lives in New York, and discovered that the boy's friends had exactly the same obsessions and insecurities as boys in Mexico – most of them about sex.

García Tsao, one of Mexico's foremost film critics, rejected the film as a 'Beavis and Butthead' caper with a storyline straight out of *Penthouse* magazine. This is hard to refute: the plot is pure schoolboy fantasy. Nevertheless, sex is integral to the story – the boys contrive the trip to the beach as a seductive device – as well as spurring on the emotional development of each character. While Luisa becomes liberated through exploring her sexual power, their liaisons with both the older woman and themselves force the boys to grow up.

Whether the film's nudity is fundamental to the movie's realism or unnecessarily inserted to court controversy is also open to debate. The film begins with a frank and forthright sex scene, announcing the movie's daring credentials right from the off, and there can be little doubt that Cuarón and the gang had plenty of fun breaking taboos. One of the film's more notorious scenes is of the boys masturbating on the diving board of a swimming pool, a close-up finally showing a drop of semen splashing into the water. Although not outright explicit, the sequence inevitably drew protest.

Cuarón argues that they simply strived to show sexual situations among the young as they really are and it is true that the movie's erotic episodes are never titillating or prurient. But we are invited to see Mexico as an adolescent country, so Julio's and Tenoch's immature and macho attitude towards sex, versus Luisa, the mature European who shocks the boys with her directness, cannot help but have alarm bells ringing. The sex in the film is quite explicit by any country's cinema standards but especially so for a Mexican film. Cuarón must have known he was heading for trouble with the Mexican censors.

In the end, *Y Tu Mamá También* was given a C classification (adults only) by the RTC (Secretaría de Radio Televisión y Cinematografía – Ministry of Radio, Television and Cinema), a government body. Cuarón and his team accused the authorities of censorship and immaturity and even lodged a lawsuit citing the violation of their freedom of expression.

What made them so cross was not just the fact that the film's target audience was being excluded but also the hypocrisy of the ministry. The '18' certificate was initially awarded due to the film's explicit sex scenes but then remarkably the sex-education lobby backed it – in fact said *Y Tu Mamá También* would not be out of place in school sex-education programmes – and so the RTC changed its tune and said the rating was due to images of drug use. They claimed that drug use depicted in films had to show the users being punished, although the drug use in the film is hardly outrageous: a fair bit of weed, plenty of beer and tequila.

Most outrage, however, arose from a suspicion of political censorship. Cuarón was in no doubt: 'The Mexican government thinks that we should make films to encourage tourism to our country but *Y Tu Mamá También* doesn't quite do that because as well as the beautiful things it shows some horrible ones too: misery, corruption, human degradation – and hotels of the lowest quality. I wanted to make something honest, truthful and direct.' He did, though, end with an optimistic point: 'Ten years ago it wouldn't have been possible to show it in the country at all.'

Atypically, *Y Tu Mamá También* was made entirely without government funding. It may have been producer Vergara's first movie venture but he gave Cuarón complete autonomy, a freedom the director may not have enjoyed had he gone down the more traditional avenue of securing partial government sponsorship.

Given the picture's allegorical elements, Carlos Cuarón made an interesting point: 'I feel that Mexico is still a teenage society. The difference, I believe, is that the society is more mature than the government. We are sixteen, seventeen, and pimply and in the middle of the teenage years. And my feeling is that the government is about thirteen and just starting with the hormonal thing.'

In backing their case, there were calls from the *Y Tu Mamá También* team for the government-affiliated RTC to be replaced by a civic classification body, and forums were held in Cancun to discuss freedom of expression and sexuality. In the town of Fresnillo, in the northern state of Zacatecas, a group of adolescents staged a protest outside a cinema and threatened to strip nude if they weren't allowed in to see the film – they soon were – while in the more provincial and puritanical areas of the extreme north, the sex scenes were played at high speed. When the film premiered at a packed Teatro Metropólitan in Mexico City, Cuarón prewarned the audience of scenes likely to disturb and advised the easily offended to either close their eyes or go to the toilet at such moments. In fact, each such scene was enthusiastically applauded.

The last Mexican film which had run into such problems with the authorities had been the anti-establishment *La Ley de Heredes*, which proved to be a box-office smash, and the government accused Cuarón and his team of stirring up the storm in a similar bid for publicity. Certainly García Tsao saw it that way.

When accused of kicking up a censorship fuss, Cuarón's usual retort was that in France the film had been classified as a '12'. (The response even neatly echoed the film itself: Tenoch is allowed to sleep over at his girlfriend's house because the girl's French mother allows it while Bernal's Julio is up against conservative Mexican in-laws and such an indulgence is beyond question. It is lucky the Cuaróns didn't script Tenoch's mother as British: in the UK, *Y Tu Mamá También* was rated '18'.)

Perhaps the Cuaróns did allow the spat to boost interest in their film but it is hard to contest the fact that the rather archaic Mexican ratings board didn't deserve to be challenged. Many observers highlighted the pointless contradiction of preventing a group of people from seeing a film about themselves. How can you censor adolescents from their own reality? Others pointed out that teenagers would inevitably eventually see the film on video if not immediately on pirate copies. Was the aim of the RTC to promote piracy?

Whatever the rights and wrongs of the matter, the high-profile dispute inevitably generated quite a buzz and anticipation was high by the time the film opened in Mexico in June 2001. It was distributed in Mexico by Twentieth Century Fox. Although it wasn't the first time that a major international studio had done so for a Mexican production – *Demasiado Amor* (*To Love Too Much*), *Crónica de un Desayuno* (*A Breakfast Chronicle*) and *Sexo, Pudor y Lágrimas* had all enjoyed the same treatment – it was still uncommon. This meant that instead of showing in only a handful of cinemas, as is usually the case with a domestic production, there were 230 copies of the film distributed throughout the country. Some 400,000 people passed through cinema turnstiles on its first weekend, translating to almost 12 million Mexican pesos (US$1.1 million) revenue, a Mexican box-office record.

And yet *Y Tu Mamá También* wasn't even the biggest draw of that weekend: that honour fell to *The Mummy Returns*. Of course, *Y Tu Mamá También* came up against classification restrictions that its US rival did not, but the fact that a fairly run-of-the-mill Hollywood sequel could still easily outperform a domestic production that had been hyped so much only went to show what Mexican film-makers were up against.

But, as a home-grown product, *Y Tu Mamá También* did a roaring trade and posted incredible numbers, grossing over US$9.5 million, not bad for a movie made on a US$2 million budget. Producer Vergara was at pains to remind everyone that production and investment costs had been covered before the film even premiered through selling the foreign distribution rights. Abroad, a similar success story emerged. It is rare for unclassified subtitled films to pull in the punters north of the Mexican border but *Y Tu Mamá También* did great US business and proved a surprise hit, as it did in the UK and the rest of Europe.

Despite the pride and affection the cast and crew all felt for the film, its success still caught them by surprise. Bernal has told of how, during the filming of *Y Tu Mamá También*, he asked the producers to send him a VHS of the movie so he could show his family because, used to the ups and downs of Mexican cinema, he couldn't be sure it would actually make it into the cinemas. Little did he realise that it would be lighting up the international circuit, gaining plaudits at the Venice, San Sebastián, Toronto, Río de Janeiro and New York film festivals.

Venice came first and its showing proved a spectacular success. The oldest festival in the world, in its 58th edition, rewarded the Cuarón brothers with Best Script honours while Bernal and Luna were jointly recognised in the Best Newcomers category, collecting the Marcello Mastroianni prize. Collecting their award from Peter Fonda, Luna thanked his own late mother while an emotional Bernal, on the point of tears, thanked Mastroianni for establishing a prize in his name, Luna for being his best mate and everyone who dedicated themselves to the struggle of making films in Mexico.

The film ended up picking up both London's and Los Angeles' Critics Award for Best Foreign Film, but the situation back home couldn't have been more different.

Y Tu Mamá También was not involved in any capacity at the Ariel Awards, organised by Academia Mexicana de Artes y Ciencias Cinematográficas. Anhelo did not submit *Y Tu Mamá También* for consideration in protest at the fact that the academy had not selected the film to compete at the 2002 Oscars. (Guillermo del Toro's *El Espinazo del Diablo* (*The Devil's Backbone*), also an Anhelo film, was likewise not put forward.)

The Mexican Cinema Academy had instead elected to enter *Perfume de Violetas* (*Violet Perfume*) as the country's representative at both the Oscars and Spain's Goyas. Cuarón and the team magnanimously declared their support for the nominated production but pointed out that, if the aim was to secure a statue for Mexico, surely he and his crew's US repute, along with the distributor's publicity machine, would have given them a better shout in Hollywood. (In the event, *Perfume de Violetas* didn't even make the five-film shortlist.) Given *Y Tu Mamá También*'s festival successes and international acclaim, it was hard not to view the non-selection as a snub connected to the censorship tit-for-tat.

Then the following year, something unprecedented happened: the Hollywood Academy itself nominated *Y Tu Mamá También* in the Original Screenplay category, the first time a Mexican film had ever been thus honoured.

The Oscar nomination was something of a premonition on Bernal's part. After leaving the 2001 Oscars empty-handed with *Amores Perros* and making reference to *De Tripas, Corazón*, which had likewise come close but got no cigar at the 1997 ceremony, he quipped that it would be third time lucky next year. So, he was a year out and not quite right, *Y Tu Mamá También* ultimately losing out to Pedro Almodovar's *Hable Con Ella* (*Talk to Her*), but being invited to the party was recognition enough and marked a fine closing chapter to a remarkable success story.

With flair and conviction, *Y Tu Mamá También* had pulled off the rare feat of being acclaimed by critics and doing the business at the box office.

Cuba Libre

While not quite qualifying as method preparation, Bernal's job mixing cocktails at Cuba Libre in London did prove something of an appetiser as he shot two films in 2000 based around the Cuban revolution. One even ended up adopting the restaurant's name: originally called *Dreaming of Julia*, numerous title changes meant that the film hit Mexican cinemas known as *Cuba Libre*.

Dreaming of Julia, to use its original title, is set during the days leading up to the 1959 revolution but takes place in Holguín, a small town at the opposite end of Cuba to Havana, so, far from the heat of the overthrow itself. The plot focuses on a boy who loves cinema and becomes perplexed at the town's sudden loss of electricity halfway through a screening of the Doris Day movie, *Julie*. The youngster, known simply as 'the boy', is desperate to see the film's conclusion and naive to the fact that electric power has been cut at the behest of rebels loyal to Fidel Castro. Here Bernal enters the fray as the local guerrilla leader.

As the rebellion grows in scale and violence, the boy and his circle of friends and family try to hold on to the routines of their everyday lives. It is not a political picture but rather a whimsical portrait of the effects of the revolution on a typical family. Typical, perhaps, but one hardly the model of family unity: the boy's grandfather, played by Harvey Keitel, is having an affair with Julia, the only US citizen in Holguín (although portrayed here by Danish actress Iben Hjejle): the boy's grandmother, played by Diana Bracho, stoically tries to ignore his infidelity. Given that it his grandma who has nurtured his love of cinema, the boy is devoted to her, but he himself develops a crush on the blonde North American, in part due to her charm and beauty but equally as a consequence of her resemblance to Doris Day. The grandmother thus begins to lose the two main men in her life to Julia.

Dreaming of Julia is a nostalgic picture recalling the director's own infancy: Juan Gerard González left Cuba as a youth and went on to become a successful architect in the US, all the time retaining a love for cinema and developing a script based on his own childhood as a pet project. He wrote the screenplay with the help of his wife, Letvia Arza-Goderich, and through bloody-minded deter-mination strove not only to get it made but to be able to direct it himself.

Convinced that Harvey Keitel would be perfect for the role of his grandfather, he sent the actor the script. Keitel liked what he saw and pulled a few strings to get the funding required to make the movie, securing a US$3 million budget. Having previously worked on the debuts of the likes of Martin Scorsese, Keitel was happy to take a chance with Gerard as first-time director, particularly given the personal nature of the project.

Gerard and Arza-Goderich were regulars at the Guadalajara Film Festival and so were familiar with the work of Bracho, whom they wanted for the part of the grandmother, and they had heard the buzz about Bernal who, interested in the subject matter, climbed aboard. Fellow Mexican Claudia Suárez was recruited to play the boy's mother, whose husband (the boy's father) had fled to the US at the first sign of revolution. A truly international cast featured the likes of Cuban Reynaldo Miravalles, Spaniard Gabino Diego, Chilean Aline Küppenheim and Puerto Rican Daniel Lugo.

Keitel's involvement may have ensured the film got made but it also forced certain fundamental changes. In order to better aid international distribution, the film would have to be made in English. What's more, given that Keitel was a distinguished US citizen and the movie was being backed with US cash, there was no way the shoot was going to take place in Cuba itself. In the end, Santo Domingo in the Dominican Republic would have to do as a substitute.

Diana Bracho recalls a fairly torturous film-making process: 'It was a difficult shoot, simply because it was the director's debut. Then there was Harvey, who kept himself to himself. His method of acting is to shut himself off and he had no interest in discussing character chemistry with the others – that is just his way.'

Nevertheless, says Bracho, 'there was a great spirit amongst cast and crew, especially the Spanish-speaking members'. In fact, one of the most pleasing aspects of the shoot, she says, was the friendships made. Especially poignant were those between Cuban Cubans and Miami Cubans: having initially viewed one another with suspicion, they became the best of buddies by the end of filming.

Bernal's is very much a background role and indeed the subplot of his scheming and conniving for the cause does sometimes distract from the central premise. That said, it is an important part given that Bernal represents the revolutionary fervour which is raging elsewhere but is already impacting on almost every element of Holguín's existence. He does not get much screen time and doesn't even make it to the end of the picture. 'It was a small role but a lovely one too,' says Bracho. 'He is a subversive boy who is in communication with the rebels. My character tries for a while to save him, providing him with refuge in the house, but in the end, when he realises he is done for, he commits suicide.'

Despite his brief appearances, Bernal was involved throughout the shoot and actually filmed many more scenes than the ones shown. His character ended up falling prey to a ruthless editing process.

Gerard's first edited version of the film was very long at three hours plus. On such a personal work, cutting the picture down is never easy and the give-and-take between director and producers would contribute to a four-year delay between the film being shot and its release. *Dreaming of Julia* finally hit the festival circuit in 2004 as a pared down, 109-minute feature.

It seems that Bernal was not only happy to be a victim of editing zeal but positively encouraged it. 'Gael appears so little because he himself suggested it be so,' claims Gerard. 'He asked me to take out some of his dialogues and draw back certain other things. In the end, everything he proposed was accepted because it made for a more interesting part.'

Despite weighty chunks of the director's initial vision ending up on the cutting-room floor, the movie managed to retain its personal nature. The writer/director's sense of nostalgia was still evident in lingering exterior shots, in the colourful character portraits and in the fondness of tone used by the narrator. It is somewhat sentimental but the movie has a strong sense of innocence lost as a child's dreams are shattered in a world of adult politics and passions. The loss of light, meanwhile, takes on metaphorical properties, not least with regard to the boy, who is kept in the dark as to why his life is being turned upside down.

Bernal's appearance may have ended up as minimal but that didn't stop those distributing the film banking on his box-office draw. When he made *Dreaming of Julia*, *Y Tu Mamá También* had already been filmed but had yet to be released. Given the delay in *Dreaming of Julia* hitting cinemas, Bernal was quite the global star by the time of its screening, especially in Mexico, where it came out in January 2006. Despite the fact that his participation is no more than special-guest material, Mexican posters advertising the film suggested he was the picture's lead.

'According to my contract I was supposed to be third billing,' says Bracho. 'Harvey Keitel, Iben Hjejle and then me. But by the time it came out here it was "GAEL", in big letters. Harvey Keitel and Gael. Then Iben Hjejle,' recalls Bracho, laughing at the tricks of the promotional trade – Keitel's appearance is likewise supporting at best. 'These things really don't worry me because I am well aware that the quality of acting has nothing to do with your status in the system.'

Nevertheless, she adds, 'I do think that these things are terrible for the actor because it creates expectations amongst the public which can't be satisfied.

Everyone thinks, "Oh, a new Gael film." They go and he appears for two minutes and they feel cheated and it has nothing to do with Gael but with the distributors. It shouldn't be like this.'

Another piece of marketing trickery proved even more misleading. While the movie's original title – *Dreaming of Julia* – relates both to the boy's longing to see the end of the Doris Day film *Julie* and to his infatuation with the character Julia, it also conveys a sense of the movie's nostalgia. In Mexico (as well as in Brazil) the picture was released as *Cuba Libre*, suggesting a political film tackling the nitty-gritty of the revolutionary struggle, which it patently is not.

Even worse, for its DVD release in the US, after a limited theatre run as *Dreaming of Julia* it was renamed *Cuban Blood*. This conjures images of violent warfare or even of a gangster flick set amongst the Miami underworld, not a sweet-natured film about provincial childhood. (Incidentally, the picture got no distribution whatsoever in the UK.)

Something major might have been lost in the film's transition from big screen to small, but something even more significant was lost in translation due to the film having to be made in English. Bracho describes a surreal set-up whereby the non-English-speaking locals simply memorised their lines with no sense of their meaning as Keitel struggled to meet them halfway and adapt his Brooklyn drawl to make it sound like a Cuban speaking English. Meanwhile, Bracho (who had lived for several years in Oxford, England) and Bernal, then still based in London, were instructed to ignore the strong English they both spoke and abandon their polished accents in favour of a faux pidgin offering. Just why it was thought that the audience could suspend its belief enough to accept that the inhabitants of Holguín might speak a faltering Hispanic-flavoured English amongst themselves but not a clear and crisp version remains unclear, but the curious decision did the film few favours, least of all to any claims of credibility.

Bernal's other Cuban-related film that year also insisted on its Spanish-speaking cast playing their roles in English: *Fidel* was an epic chronicle of the Cuban revolution but one made for US television. It had more than just dodgy accents in common with *Dreaming of Julia*: Bernal's part was also of the supporting kind and again he played a rebel leader. At least this time that rebel leader was Che Guevara, a precursor to Bernal's portrayal of the great revolutionary in *The Motorcycle Diaries*.

Another factor that linked the two Cuban projects, and one that provided a very significant plus as far as Bernal was concerned, was the involvement of

Cecilia Suárez: the pair were romantically linked for some time thereafter. In *Fidel*, Suárez played her near-namesake, the militant Celia Sánchez.

Bernal's old mucker Diego Luna took a minor role. Curiously enough, so did Bernal's younger brother Darío, then aged but ten. Bernal and his clan had further Mexican company: the lead role of Castro himself went to Víctor Huggo Martín, an established theatre actor who had appeared in *Sexo, Pudor y Lágrimas*, while Alejandra Gollás played activist Haydeé Santamaría.

As well as the Mexicans, the film's British director, David Attwood, born in Sheffield, united an international cast, which included Venezuelan Patricia Velásquez as Castro's wife Mirta, and the Colombian Margarita Rosa de Francisco as Naty Revuelta, Castro's lover and accomplice.

Produced by US cable television station Hallmark, this biopic of Castro was filmed in Mexico rather than Cuba, in studios in the capital and on location in Veracruz and Morelos. This did at least add authenticity to some scenes, given that Castro prepared his invasion force at a camp in Mexico. For Víctor Huggo Martín, the shoot was tough, lasting for four months and requiring him to make several changes in weight and appearance as the movie spanned Castro's sixty years.

For Bernal, the project was less of a serious undertaking. As he himself has admitted: '*Fidel* I did for the cash. It paid very well and I needed the money.' He had already shot *Amores Perros* but the movie had yet to be released and Bernal was still scratching around for work. 'It was this or go back to soap operas,' he has since explained. That so, the irony of playing the role of one of history's most committed moralists in order to make a fast buck is not lost on Bernal: 'Che was the antithesis of what I did: he had ideals in which he believed very deeply.'

Although Bernal is unlikely to have been too concerned about the finished product, it has to be said that the film is very far from marking his finest hour: he looks absolutely ridiculous in his quite obviously fake beard, like a boy at a fancy-dress party or performing in a school play. His acting responsibilities involve little more than sitting around tables smoking cigars and nodding at the melodramatics of Martín as Castro. Once it is time for Che to abandon the Cuban project and lead the struggle in Bolivia, Bernal does at least get a chance to engage his English. The shoot-out scene in 'Bolivia' that follows is particularly am-dram.

While the film's US transmission reportedly caused something of a stir among the country's Cuban community, Bernal noted that trying to tell such a complex and epic tale in so short a time frame (a four-hour piece screened in two parts) was an impossible task. He preferred to focus on the story itself rather than its depiction: 'It is incredible to think what a crazy thing it was they embarked upon and yet despite everything, they managed to change the (rule of the) country.'

Bernal also drew attention to the fact that it was a US project. 'It is a shame they have not told this story in Spanish. Our cinema hasn't had the courage to tackle these issues: for us, these people are untouchable. But the gringos come along and film whatever they like. If we don't apply ourselves, they are going to tell us all our stories in English.'

As someone with the courage of his convictions, such comments are put into proper context when he committed to the role of Che in *The Motorcycle Diaries* just a few years later. His second crack at Che, therefore, came in a film made in Spanish with Latin American talent and which was a project of rather more integrity. Perhaps the slight embarrassment of his performance and motivation on *Fidel* spurred Bernal into doing Che justice next time around.

Vidas Privadas

Expectations were high for Argentinian film *Vidas Privadas* (*Private Lives*). Bernal joined the project in early 2001, with *Amores Perros* having been released in several Hispanic countries and Bernal already considered to be quite the rising star. By the time *Vidas Privadas* hit cinemas, *Y Tu Mamá También* had done the rounds too and his reputation as a major talent had been cemented. His growing status added to the considerable buzz already generated by the fact that *Vidas Privadas* would be Argentinian rock star Fito Páez's debut feature as director.

Páez may never have been a household name in the English-speaking world but in the Spanish one he was hot stuff. Páez had more than twenty years of hit records behind him and was fresh from Best Artist and Best Rock Song accolades at the 2000 Latino Grammy Awards. Indeed, Bernal has said that one of the main reasons he came on board the *Vidas Privadas* project was that he had grown up listening to Páez's songs.

Cecilia Roth being cast in the lead role opposite Bernal added further to the excitement: the distinguished actress, star of many a Pedro Almodóvar movie, was Páez's real-life partner and the role was to be a complex one, potentially controversial both sexually and politically.

Roth stars as Carmen Uranga, a woman of a certain age who returns to her native Argentina having been forced to flee in exile to Spain some twenty years earlier after upsetting the military dictatorship. She journeys home to visit her ailing father and ends up having to face many a ghost from her past. One of them is Gustavo, played by Bernal, a young model and part-time gigolo whom Carmen recruits to satisfy her somewhat unorthodox sexual appetite: she gets her kicks by listening to couples make love or by men talking dirty to her from the other side of a door without her ever seeing them. This fetish has come about as a consequence of time spent imprisoned in a dark cell before her exile, and so the movie's main theme, that of Argentina's need to face up to its unsavoury past, reveals itself.

Before the movie's release, Páez was aware that as a rock star he would be exposed to accusations of the film being a vanity project and he spent much energy justifying both himself and the project. For one thing, movie-making was not so alien to him, given that in 1996 he made the medium-length *La Balada de Donna Helena* (*The Ballad of Donna Helena*), also starring Cecilia Roth. More importantly, he repeatedly stressed that making a film about the dictatorship years was not so much something he wanted to do as something he felt obliged to do: 'I come from a country where terrible and tragic things have happened, so I couldn't emerge from this period without telling the story.'

After the death of popular president Juan Perón in July 1974, power in Argentina was transferred to his third wife, Isabel Perón. Her government was pushed ever more to the right until finally she was overthrown in a coup in March 1976. A military junta took over with Lieutenant General Jorge Rafaél Videla as president. They closed Congress, outlawed trade unions and initiated a reign of censorship and terror, the so-called Dirty War, in which thousands of political opponents were killed, frequently after imprisonment and torture. The dictatorship lasted until 1983.

Roth herself went into exile with her family in 1976 when she was in her late teens. Her father had worked for *La Opinión* newspaper with Jacobo Timerman, a renowned crusading journalist who brought international attention to the atrocities of Argentina before being thrown in jail himself: her mother sang protest songs and many of Roth's college friends were 'disappeared'.

Páez's family, meanwhile, were actually anti-Perón but the musician formed his own opinions and soon grew to loathe the military regime. 'We have many unresolved problems in Argentina. You can't kill thirty thousand people and then say they just disappeared. We suffered state terrorism and they think it can all be resolved by decree,' he explained. 'Without wishing to be moralistic, we hope that our film will get people talking about the matter.' Páez's determination to tackle the subject was unflinching: the film took eight years to develop from the original concept to the finished product.

The idea came about when Páez and Roth were in Italy and read a story in an Argentine newspaper about two brothers, sons of 'disappeared' parents. Under the dictatorship, it was common for children born to those imprisoned to be handed over to military personnel for adoption. The newspaper piece related that, on discovering this to be their case, the brothers opted to stay with the family who had raised them rather than join their biological relatives. This triggered a train of thought and discussion that led them to realise that the consequences of the actions of the dictatorship were still very much being felt, that they remained ingrained and integral to contemporary Argentina. Páez decided that he had to tackle the subject and that there was too much to say to fit into a simple song, so the idea of a film came about.

Páez recounted the germ of his idea to the Argentine writer Alan Pauls and the pair of them began to collaborate on the script in late 1994. Pauls was then fresh from success with his book *Wasabi* but had done screenplays before, notably *Sinfín* in 1988. (Bernal would also eventually star in an adaptation of another of his novels, *El Pasado* (*The Past*), in 2007.)

Shortly after starting on *Vidas Privadas*, Pauls went to see a production of Oedipus by Pasolini and the idea of incorporating the theme of Sophocles' Greek tragedy took root. As Carmen's sexual games with Bernal's Gustavo lead to a more physically conventional and platonic relationship between the pair, terrible secrets and unfortunate coincidences reveal themselves: while in captivity, Carmen had given birth to a boy who was taken away from her; Gustavo would be that boy's age; Gustavo's father is ex-military; father and son are so dissimilar that one imagines that Gustavo could have been adopted. Oh dear.

So, a fairly intense role for Bernal to take on in what was only his third feature film. Apart from his fondness for Páez's music, it is easy to see how a picture tackling Argentina's dictatorial past might appeal to the politically conscious Bernal. He would go on to play many multi-layered characters (indeed there are several parallels between Gustavo and his part in *The King*), almost specialise in them, and he was evidently on the lookout for parts offering depth of character. 'So many things happen to him [Gustavo]: after falling completely in love for the first time, he is told that his destiny lies elsewhere, that his life is another. And he reacts instinctively,' he told *Fotogramas* magazine.

In truth, the role of Gustavo was written with another actor in mind, Juan Diego Botto, a young Argentine whose father had been killed in the Dirty War when he was two, resulting in his mother taking him into exile in Madrid. Botto had worked on a number of Spanish films, most notably *Sobreviviré* (*I Will Survive*) in 1999. The role of Carmen, meanwhile, had been intended for Spanish actress Marisa Paredes, another of Almodóvar's divas. But prior commitments and delays in the project coming to fruition brought about a change of plan.

During casting, Páez was invited to the Argentine premiere of *Amores Perros* and knew immediately that Bernal fit the bill. 'I loved his beauty, his look, his strength. I called some friends in Mexico to put me in touch with him and the next day he returned my call.'

Bernal himself said: 'I grew up with Fito Páez's music and considered it a great privilege when he called me for the role of Gustavo.' It was also the right role at the right time: 'After *Amores Perros*, I wanted to leave Mexico, to try and do a new accent and that was just when the film with Fito came about.'

So the challenge of the accent was part of the pull but it was the role too, actually somewhat paradoxically: 'It is a character that appeals to me because he thinks a lot and speaks very little, which I appreciate because in cinema there are often too many words.'

Few words there may have been but mastering the accent was Bernal's main task in preparing for the part. He worked with a voice coach solidly for a month, practising all his lines.

Getting the funding together to make the movie was no easy task. It seemed to Páez that many people didn't like, or at least didn't dare touch, the themes the picture raised. Even once everything appeared to be in place it proved not to be: in early March 2001, just two weeks before the start of the shoot, all the film's producers pulled out. These were testing times for Argentina, with the country's purse strings feeling the strains which would eventually lead to outright economic breakdown by the end of the year.

At the eleventh hour, Mate Cantero and Stéphane Sorlat of Mate Productions in Spain came to the rescue and combined with an Argentine consortium called Circo Beat (named after one of Páez's records and comprising money from both the musician and Roth) as well as funds from the Argentine Cinema Institute, to back the film.

On 19 March 2001 in Buenos Aires, the cameras finally began to roll. Páez has described the shoot as pure pleasure. 'Actors are like musicians, each one a specialist, unique. I had to discover them, seduce them, love them. It was like we were all in a room with just one toy, arguing, laughing, hurting one another, giving shape to something none of us really knew what was but that we all loved. Carola, Dolores, Ceci, Luis, Gael, Lito, Yasmín – we were bringing a puppet to life bit by bit: its face, hair, clothes, make-up, feelings and defects.'

The film-making was evidently an enjoyable and collaborative process. Roth has since said, 'Fito was very generous as a director. It was his first film and he was very attentive to detail and open to any suggestion from his actors. Because of the theme and everything surrounding it, the work was also very difficult and intense.'

It is not hard to imagine that a husband-and-wife team making a movie about a woman who masturbates to the sound of hired strangers making love on the other side of a wall might throw up the odd awkward moment. Páez has described working with Roth as very complex, noting that the personal-professional boundaries become stretched to the limit.

The 'sex' scenes themselves were handled with extreme care. 'He was very delicate with all of this. We rehearsed a lot,' said Roth, 'there was a great relationship with Gael, who is a genius.'

The feeling was mutual, according to Bernal: 'I really liked working with Cecilia, a great actress and a great person who didn't try to overwhelm me with her professional pedigree. Here is an example of an actress whereby, the more she works, the more humble she becomes.'

The romantic leads worked so well together that for a while Bernal was pencilled in to star opposite Roth in a new film to be shot in Buenos Aires, *Kamchatka*; Roth did make the movie but Bernal's priorities eventually lay elsewhere (his proposed role went to Tomas Fonzi, younger brother of *Vidas Privadas* co-star Dolores).

Vidas Privadas wrapped in mid-May and was ready for release by the end of the year. However, Argentina, home to the film's core market, had plunged deeper and deeper into economic meltdown: it would have been commercial suicide to launch a film in an atmosphere of record debt defaults, spiralling inflation and currency devaluation; many people were struggling to buy the basics, never mind go to the pictures. The film ended up premiering in Spain, where it was released in November 2001; its release in Argentina was postponed, eventually finding its way on to screens there by April 2002.

However, despite the extra anticipation, the star names and the added resonance of an Argentina in crisis, the film was not well received and reviews of the movie were poor. That is not to say that critics were unkind: many clearly recognised that the film had noble intentions and tried to find the positives. They praised its bravery in tackling taboo subjects and trying to spark debate; Páez's ambition in attempting such a complex topic for his debut also drew acclaim; many even tried to overlook the film's sense of self-importance by focusing on its honesty. The consensus was that a movie grappling with the different levels and consequences of repression in Argentina deserved the benefit of the doubt.

Nor was there much appetite for attacking the film for being made by a rock star unfamiliar with the medium; in fact, from a technical point of view, the film is accomplished enough. Nevertheless, there was no hiding the fact that the movie just didn't work.

The script was too uneven, never finding its feet and allowing the audience to settle in and go with the flow. It flirts with being a thriller then drifts towards drama but never looks comfortable with its identity, and it becomes increasingly

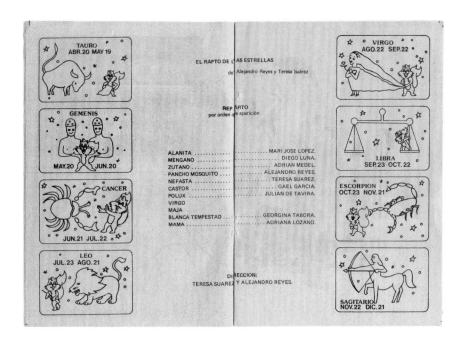

EL RAPTO DE LAS ESTRELLAS

de Alejandro Reyes y Teresa Suárez

REPARTO
por orden de aparición

ALANITA	MARI JOSE LOPEZ.
MENGANO	DIEGO LUNA.
ZUTANO	ADRIAN MEDEL.
PANCHO MOSQUITO	ALEJANDRO REYES.
NEFASTA	TERESA SUAREZ.
CASTOR	GAEL GARCIA.
POLUX	JULIAN DE TAVIRA.
VIRGO	
MAJA	
BLANCA TEMPESTAD	GEORGINA TABORA.
MAMA	ADRIANA LOZANO.

DIRECCION:
TERESA SUAREZ Y ALEJANDRO REYES.

Above: The programme cast list for theatre production *El Rapto de las Estrellas (The Kidnapping of the Stars)*, Bernal's first significant acting role. Bernal, here credited simply as Gael García, played the part of Castor, the beaver seen in the graphics alongside the stars of the Zodiac. Lifetime friend, and co-star of *Y Tu Mamá También*, Diego Luna took a lead role as Mengano while Teresa Suárez, the play's director, played Nefasta, the witch.

Left: The cover of the programme for *El Rapto de las Estrellas*, which played at the Poliforum theatre in Mexico City from summer 1988 through to late 1989.

Above: Vanessa Bauche (as Susana) and Bernal (as Octavio) in a scene from *Amores Perros*. The film propelled both Bernal and Latin America to the forefront of the global cinematic consciousness. It is one of the movies of which Bernal is most proud, although the actor had to lie to his London drama school teachers in order to appear in it.

Right Top: Bernal in his first turn as Che Guevara, for US television biopic *Fidel*.

Right Bottom: Bernal as an Argentine soldier asleep as sentry in *The Last Post*, a British short film dealing with the Falklands War.

Above: Bernal (as Julio), Diego Luna (as Tenoch) and Maribel Verdú (as Luisa), on the road in *Y Tu Mamá También*. Bernal has spoken of the movie's making as one of the most enjoyable experiences of his life, the shoot as full of incident as it was collective creative endeavour.

Above: Bernal as Father Amaro in *The Crime of Father Amaro*, a hugely controversial role and film in his native Mexico.

Above: Matthew Parkhill directs Bernal (as Kit) and Natalia Verbeke (as Carmen) in British feature *Dot the i*.

Above: Bernal and Verbeke get intimate in *Dot the i*, the London-set thriller.

Above: Bernal plays with a camcorder in *Dot the i*, in the company of Charlie Cox (as Theo) and Tom Hardy (as Tom). The three actors became firm friends off-set.

Below: Bernal in his second stint as Che Guevara, this time in *The Motorcycle Diaries*. Rodrigo de la Serna (as Alberto Granado) is in the hot-seat as the pair recreate the revolutionary's legendary journey across the continent. The filming experience would have a profound effect on Bernal.

frustrating for the viewer to figure out what the film is trying to say. The first half tries to build a sense of suspense as a fundamental absence of explanation forces the audience to ask themselves why each of the characters is behaving so mysteriously: why, given that she will only be in Buenos Aires for two weeks, does Carmen rent an apartment and pay a couple to have sex in the next room? What are the secrets that everyone is hiding?

A generous reading of this initial tone of untold intrigue would be that it reflected the mood of an Argentina failing to cope with its dreadful recent past: that secrets reigned as people tried to look to the future, horrors of the past deemed to be best left unsaid. However, as the plot ticks on and begins to fill in the blanks, the film falls flat. Some developments manage to be both brazenly far-fetched and utterly predictable at the same time; others are explained unsatisfactorily with major holes in the narrative. Most problematic of all, given that the film's dramatic thrust depends upon it, is the idea that the 47-year-old Carmen and the 22-year-old Gustavo have fallen in love, on either side of a wall without seeing one another – and all of a sudden. Undoubtedly love works in mysterious ways and there is the little matter of the Oedipus complex sub-theme, but belief in this romance asks a lot of the viewer.

Part of the problem is the characterisations. The movie relies on the concept of secrets and repressed emotions but there are none of the moments of warm tenderness or vulnerability that an audience requires in order to feel for the characters, to care what happens to them. Carmen comes across as a cold, passionless, overly pragmatic shrew: Roth is a fine actress, her work in *Todo Sobre Mi Madre* (*All About My Mother*) helping Almodóvar to the Best Foreign Language Film Oscar, but she is given little to work with here. She undoubtedly tries her damnedest and just about manages to carry the movie through sheer professionalism and force of will.

Bernal may have been drawn to his character's lack of dialogue but a lack of meaningful action too makes it impossible to gauge what makes Gustavo tick. He commands significant screen time, first in bed as a gigolo then at his modelling agency, but all devoid of poignancy. The scenes he shares with his supposed father, in which his padre chides him for appearing semi-nude in a poster campaign and refuses Gustavo's offer of money, begins to paint a picture of family dysfunction but tells us more about the dad than the son. There is a promising discussion with Carmen in which Gustavo explains that the only two places he knows in the world are Buenos Aires and the small rural village he grew up in, yet it fails to deliver: there is no mention of him having always felt out of place, of a sense of not belonging or of loss. Without properly laying the foundations and colouring in the background, the revelations, when they come, seem slightly absurd.

Minor characters, such as Carmen's mother (played by Chunchuna Villafañe, who bizarrely got an Argentinian Film Critics, Association nomination for her performance) and sister (Dolores Fonzi), are equally opaque. As if aware that the story is falling apart, the cast, strong actors almost one and all, double their efforts in an attempt to save the day. Unfortunately, after all the concealed under-statement of the first half, this leads to the impression of overacting and melodrama. This might even have worked: after all, Cecilia Roth is an Almodóvar veteran and he is the king of melodrama. But Almodóvar's skill lies in an ability to structure his everyday calamities and convey a sense of knowing in such a way that he dares the viewer to dismiss them as unimportant. In *Vidas Privadas*, it is difficult to care, indeed occasionally even difficult not to laugh.

Part of the problem is the film's score. As a musician, Páez clearly had grand ambitions of making the soundtrack a dynamic component of the movie's momentum. Unfortunately, sudden crescendos of piano and string build the tension to unnecessarily high levels and a correspondingly grand climax never follows. Cruel reviewers suggested that these sudden bursts of music were perhaps intended to keep the audience awake. They disappear almost as soon as they have peaked and in this they reflect another poor element of the film – that of the powerful dramatic scene being followed by one which seems utterly dispensable.

Despite its many faults, the film takes itself very seriously and it is this unflinching conviction of integrity that proves the movie's unlikely saviour: its defiance of appearing ridiculous actually lends the film its charm. In conclusion, the film is certainly flawed but nevertheless interesting and appealing.

The conclusion of the picture itself is also worthy of a mention. The scripted ending, which was filmed, saw Bernal's and Roth's characters meet up for an emotional farewell. However, once in the cutting room, another idea floated in and the film ended more abruptly, with a death. The DVD's launch in Argentina featured the original ending as a special feature; this ending then replaced the one initially favoured for cinemas for the movie's US DVD release (it never played in theatres in the UK or the USA). Páez denied that this was for commercial reasons: despite getting a critical kicking, the picture played at twenty festivals worldwide and enough people went to see the picture for it to more than recoup the cost.

The ending cinemagoing audiences were faced with saw Bernal's Gustavo confronting and then taking revenge on the man whom he had believed to be his father. As the climactic scene, it is laced with dramatic resonance but was actually one of the scenes most highlighted by those critical of the film's melodrama. Yet it must be said that few blamed Bernal: the fault lay more with the paucity of material at his disposal.

Páez was pleased with the actor's work, likening Bernal's performance to that of Alain Delon in Luchino Visconti's *Rocco e i Suoi Fratelli* (*Rocco and his Brothers*); it would not be the last time Bernal was compared to Delon.

For Bernal's part, the film may not have turned out as well as hoped but the experience of making *Vidas Privadas* had certainly been worthwhile. Having first talked of how moving the story was, Bernal told an interviewer from Argentine daily *La Nación* that actually the best thing about making the film was meeting his then girlfriend during the shoot. When asked to reveal her name he winked and said, 'No, no – leave it so that they all think I'm referring to them.'

However, the girl in question was co-star Dolores Fonzi: the two were an on-off item for some time after the film and remain more than just good friends.

La Nación heaped praise on the young Mexican: 'Gael García Bernal again demonstrates that he is one of the best young Latin American actors and not only by bringing credibility to the troubled Gustavo but also by pulling off a convincing job in imitating the difficult *porteño* accent.' Mastering the *porteño* (as Buenos Aires locals are known) patois was no hardship. Enthusiastically recalling his time in the city, Bernal told the same paper: 'Ay *cabrón*, what women you have there; it is paradise,' before adding, 'and I'll tell you, *güey*, there is no better way of learning the lingo than by having a girl whisper sweet nothings in your ear.'

Latin American New Wave Part II: Argentina

Although ready to go by late 2001, the release of *Vidas Privadas* in Argentina was postponed until April 2002. Given Argentina's giant debt-default in December 2001 and the currency devaluation, hyperinflation and near anarchy that followed, it wasn't the only film to suffer such a delay. Despite the fact that several had already picked up prizes on the international festival circuit, more than twenty films made in Argentina in 2001 ended up in launch limbo.

The economic meltdown caught many by surprise, not least investors holding Argentine assets. Yet, if they had studied the films emerging from Argentina at the time, the impending collapse could perhaps have been foreseen.

Fabián Bielinsky's 2000 film *Nueve Reinas* (*Nine Queens*) proved an international smash hit. It told the tale of a group of Buenos Aires con artists out to trick one another and painted a picture of a country insecure about what the future held and swamped by corruption.

Another successful production was even called *The Swamp* (*La Ciénaga*). Lucrecia Martel's early 2001 movie portrayed a middle class that was complacent but also resigned to its fate, sitting around getting drunk while waiting for the government to lead them to their doom.

Bolivia, meanwhile, by Adrián Israel Caetano, also released in early 2001, was a film about an immigrant from South America's poorest country who had moved to Argentina in search of a better life. Of course, all proves not to be as hoped for in the promised land. The newcomer does manage to find work in a Buenos Aires bar but is hardly welcomed by the locals, themselves mostly unemployed or broke. The film's title suggests that Argentina could no longer justify holding a superiority complex towards its neighbour: Argentina was becoming just another Bolivia.

Things had not always been thus. The superiority complex was based on the fact that, at the turn of the twentieth century, Argentina was the richest nation in Latin America and one of the richest countries in the world. Its strategic location, shipping having to pass the Magellan Straits, had made Buenos Aires into an important trading port.

Argentina's cinema history is equally as rich. In much the same pattern of development as was seen in Mexico, there was immediate interest in the invention of the moving image and a film industry began to develop in the 1920s. Next came the struggle to compete with Hollywood's output, heightened by a downturn in the country's fortunes linked to an export slump following the Great Depression. A boost then came with the arrival of sound in the 1930s, Argentina churning out tango musicals starring the likes of Carlos Gardel.

By the 1940s a significant studio system took hold with its own domestic star system: in 1942 there were as many as thirty studios operating in Argentina, but after World War Two Hollywood regained its poise and again dominated the scene. From then on, Argentinian cinema lost its commercial viability and became more of an artistic pursuit.

Always more inclined to take a cultural lead from the Old World than its own continent, Argentina closely observed European film trends. Torre Nilsson gained international attention in the 1957 with his Cannes success *La Casa del Ángel* (*The House of the Angel*), which borrowed heavily on European realism techniques.

Argentina was plagued by a series of military coups throughout the 1960s: there were no elections between 1963 and 1973. A particularly authoritarian regime ruled the roost from 1966, meaning that cinema was heavily censored. In 1968, the film-makers behind *La Hora de los Hornos* (*The Hour of the Furnaces*), Fernando Solanas and Octavio Getino, were careful to dismantle their film as they made it so that, if interrupted in the process, before the film was complete, its subversive nature would not be uncovered. The resulting four-hour documentary was shown at underground meetings of dissidents.

Democracy was restored in 1983 but Argentinian economics were in such dire straits that even the paltry support the state had previously provided was cut and film production fell: from forty-six films being made in 1982, just four were realised in 1989.

But state support would return with a vengeance and in the most unlikely of circumstances. Carlos Menem came to power in 1989 and put in place a series of free-market reforms that would eventually lead to the events of December 2001, but which did at the time provide a brief economic boost. The peso was pegged to the US dollar, public institutions were privatised and industry deregulated. Yet amidst all these market-friendly (read US-friendly) liberal economic policies came a protectionist law for Argentine cinema.

Quite what inspired this remains something of a mystery: Argentina's film-makers kept quiet and simply set about making the most of the new support. The law, pushed through in 1995, stipulated a 10 per cent levy on cinema tickets and video rentals that would go straight back into film production. At the same time, the television industry was forced to divert some of its profits into making movies. What's more, the incentive helped both commercially minded cinema and art-house fare: one scheme filtered back a fixed sum to cover losses on artistic features while another rewarded box-office successes; everyone was a winner.

Money poured into film schools via the Instituto Nacional de Cine y Arte Audiovisuales (National Institute of Cinema and Audiovisual Arts – INCAA). The Mar del Plata Film Festival was re-established in 1996 after a 25-year break and a new capital-based festival, the Buenos Aires Festival Internacional de Cine Independiente (Buenos Aires International Festival of Independent Cinema – BAFICI), was set up.

Menem's reign ended in 1999. With the benefit of hindsight, his critics view the administration's strategy for cinema as just another example of fiddling the figures and living beyond its means, leading the country to ruin, but it did make fertile ground for film-making.

What's more, although some cinema made under Menem did reflect the government's spirit that business was booming and the country thriving, the new wave of film-makers was not so sure. As students, their professors were often former film-makers who had lived through the dictatorship years, experienced the rule of terror and censorship and recalled the 'disappearances' that occurred under the junta. They couldn't shake their distrust of authority and believe in the apparent economic miracle.

Lucrecia Martel, a film-school graduate herself, spoke of the mood of the times in the *Guardian*: 'There was a euphoric period just after the dictatorship but many people could see a big crisis was coming. The 1990s were a very false period. There was a lot of money around in a country that wasn't growing. This feeling of a menace that was coming was very clear for many years. All these films are of course related to the situation.'

As well as her own *La Ciénaga*, she is referring to the likes of *Mundo Grúa*, *Sólo Por Hoy* and *Bolivia*, which all debuted at the 1999 BAFICI. *Mundo Grúa* (*Crane World*), the debut feature of Pablo Trapero, was a black-and-white piece portraying a crane operator in Buenos Aires who loses his job and heads to Patagonia for work, only to find bleak misery. *Sólo Por Hoy* (*Just For Today*) by Ariel Rotter concerned disaffected youth in dead-end jobs, never finding the time to reach for their dreams.

Bolivia was Caetano's first solo project after being co-director on *Pizza, Birra, Faso* (*Pizza, Beer and Cigarettes*) with Bruno Stagnaro in 1997, the film that really got the ball rolling for what became known as *Nuevo Cine Argentino* (New Argentine Cinema). Having premiered at the Mar del Plata Festival in 1997, *Pizza, Birra, Faso* generated the most excitement any national film had since *La Historia Oficial* (*The Official Story*), a drama looking at the children of the 'disappeared', which had won the Oscar for Best Foreign Film in 1986.

Pizza, Birra, Faso told the story of a gang of streetwise youths who try to pull off a robbery to get them out of their impoverished, prospectless lives. It was stylishly fresh with unpolished camerawork, featured natural performances from mainly non-actors and showed an appreciation for street slang that was advertised in the title: no Castilian *cerveza* for beer here but the more Argentine *birra*; *faso* was a word for cigarette but more popularly meant joint.

All these New Argentine films bore common traits: they favoured realism and were committed to displaying social and economic ills and suggestions that the country had lost its ideology. Stories were small in scope but used personal dramas to highlight wider problems. Solutions were rarely proposed and there was very little preaching. In fact there was a general lack of passion; little love or despair but rather apathy and resignation.

Despite being acclaimed on the festival circuit, Argentines themselves were less enthusiastic about some of these pictures. The INCAA ran its own chain of cinemas, which ensured domestic productions were distributed, but the locals generally proved resistant to their charms.

The box-office smash of the time was Juan José Campanella's *El Hijo de la Novia* (*The Son of the Bride*), a film financed by television and which played more to popular tastes. Released locally in August 2001, it is a family drama about a forty-something man, Rafael (Ricardo Darín), with a lot on his plate, not least a much-loved mother suffering from Alzheimer's in a home and a father who, before she dies, wants to give her the full-blown church wedding she never had. It is a warm, big-hearted film, not afraid of a splash of sentimentality. *The Son of the Bride* was even nominated for a Best Foreign Language Film Oscar.

Nevertheless, social woes are ever present: Darín's Rafael manages a popular Buenos Aires restaurant established by his parents as Italian immigrants but now struggling in the face of unreliable suppliers, unhelpful bank managers and a larger chain trying to buy him out.

In much the same way Bernal proved a lucky mascot for Mexican films, Darín was proving quite the talisman for the Argentine industry, topping the billing in Bielinsky's *Nine Queens*. After graduating from film school, Bielinsky spent several years earning his crust as an assistant director on several features and hundreds of commercials. In 1998, he entered his script for *Nine Queens* into a competition run by the Patagonik Film Group and beat the other 350 entrants to win funding to make it.

Nine Queens concerns two con men, the elder of the pair, Marco (Darín), showing the younger, Juan (Gastón Pauls), the tricks of the trade. After a series of small-fry scams on unsuspecting old ladies, they get wrapped up in a scheme to sell a very valuable set of stamps – the nine queens of the title – or, better still, sell forgeries.

Of course, both men try to double-cross one another; in fact they try to double-cross everyone they meet; actually, everyone they meet tries to double-cross everyone else. It is a portrait of a society rotten to the core and any character of any substance in the film is tainted in some way.

This effect is only amplified when you realise that despite all their efforts and energies our two 'heroes' are minor league; the real crooks are the politicians, businessmen and bankers who are swindling the big bucks and taking the country to the cleaners.

Back on the lower rungs, all this chicanery is not solely motivated by greed. The majority of people believe they are bending the rules merely to reap rewards which would rightly be theirs anyway were it not for such a mismanaged society. The audience is likewise fooled into cheering for the criminals, never considering their victims.

The sense of local colour is vivid, the camera-work flash and showy but rough around the edges. The pace can be relentless but the change in tone, from good, dishonest fun to more sinister and serious fare, is skilfully transmitted.

In keeping with the spirit of things, Bielinsky deceives the audience time and time again, not so much providing a twist in the plot as a whole twister of a movie. Viewers should take nothing for granted, which is quite possibly the wider message.

Released in August 2000, pre-crisis, *Nine Queens* was hugely successful in Argentina and then did good business in the US and UK when released in 2002, post-crisis. That it could be both prophetic and emblematic is a testament to its depth of substance.

While *Nine Queens* looked at crooks by profession, Trapero followed up *Mundo*

Grúa with *El Bonaerense*, a gritty portrait of the machismo, violence, corruption and gun culture at the heart of the Buenos Aires police force.

An altogether tamer affair was *Historias Mínimas*. Along with the streets of Buenos Aires, the flatlands of Patagonia were proving a recurring setting for new films. Carlos Sorin had been making pictures in the area for several years earlier, not least the curious *Eversmile, New Jersey* in 1989, starring Daniel Day-Lewis as a dentist on a motorbike. For his first film since then, Sorin returned to the region to make *Historias Mínimas*, a low-key and charming piece which looks at three characters on quirky journeys across the plains: a woman heads off to take part in a television game show; a travelling salesmen delivers a birthday cake to the son of a woman he has fallen for; an older man goes to retrieve his dog.

Both *El Bonaerense* and *Historias Mínimas* had, like *Vidas Privadas*, been made before the crisis but were released afterwards. Given that the entire economy had been crippled, post-crisis film-making was far from a priority as new governments formed. Subsidies disappeared in the aftermath of the meltdown and yet an incredible 156 films were shot in Argentina in 2002, double that of 2001. How could this be?

For one thing, foreign producers were tempted by the sudden cheapness of the peso and the chance to make the most of the good facilities and abundance of talent available. There were said to be 10,000 film students in Argentina at the time, many persuaded to read film by a lack of employment prospects generally. As Lita Stantic, producer of *Mundo Grúa*, *Bolivia* and *Ciénaga*, would say at the Rotterdam Film Festival: 'The economy is so bad that students just choose what they like to study, not what they expect to get a good job with.'

Times were hard but the tradition of going to the cinema was strong in Argentina and, once people managed to get back on their feet, they returned to the picture houses. What's more, they did so with a new appetite for seeing their lives reflected on the big screen. This had been the case with *Pizza, Birra, Faso* and *Nine Queens* too, but trying to decipher what was happening in Argentina had become more relevant than ever.

For film-makers, the crisis proved an inspiration. Driven by anger or a cathartic need to make sense of things, they rushed to document the here-and-now. And rush they did, spurred on by a sense of urgency that circumstances might get worse still.

Juan José Campanella came up with another popular hit, *Luna de Avellaneda* (*Moon of Avellaneda*), again starring Ricardo Darín. As with *The Son of the Bride*,

Campanella managed to weave serious issues into a crowd-pleasing narrative – a community centre is battling to save itself and weighing up the pros and cons of being turned into a casino, a move which would at least create jobs. The twist is that the social club itself had been founded by Spanish immigrants back in the day when Buenos Aires was prospering. Following the recent crisis, Argentines were moving to Spain in droves.

Sin Noticias De Dios

Bernal very nearly missed his gig as Davenport, the Chief Executive of Hell, in the Spanish film *Sin Noticias de Dios* (*No News From God*). For one thing, a much older actor was originally sought, with rumours placing Mick Jagger in the role. Even once the idea of a younger man took root and Bernal became the favoured choice, prior commitments appeared to rule him out until the film's true star, Penélope Cruz, was delayed filming *Vanilla Sky* in the US, postponing the *Sin Noticias de Dios* shoot by three months. Bernal could make it after all.

And there is no reason for him to regret it. All concerned seemed to have a rare old time making the film. What's more, although the movie itself is certainly flawed, Bernal's performance is entertaining and the role an interesting one to add to the canon. It even earned him a Best Supporting Actor nomination at the Goyas, Spain's top cinema awards.

Sin Noticias de Dios features Cruz alongside compatriot Victoria Abril in the two principal roles. These leading lights of Spanish cinema were actually making their first film in their native country for many years: Cruz had been building up a reputation in Hollywood with movies such as *Blow* alongside Johnny Depp while Abril had been dedicating her time to European features. But Agustín Díaz Yanes, the film's writer and director, had penned *Sin Noticias de Dios* with both actresses in mind and so he was prepared to wait until both were available.

This perhaps goes some way to explaining why six years passed between Yanes' debut as director, the promising *Nadie Hablará de Nosotras Cuando Hayamos Muerto* (*Nobody Will Speak of Us Once We Are Dead*), and *Sin Noticias de Dios*, his second film at the helm.

Previously, Yanes had worked as a screenwriter on several films, some of which starred Abril. The actress grew frustrated that his good scripts kept on failing to reach their potential and finally persuaded Yanes to call the shots himself on *Nadie Hablará de Nosotras Cuando Hayamos Muerto* by making it a condition of her involvement. A sort of action thriller, often quite violent, it also touched upon various contemporary social issues and was well received.

The original script for *Sin Noticias de Dios* took around a year to write and seemed to develop its own direction: initially similar in tone to his debut, the new project ended up a comedy almost of its own volition. Yanes then approached

Cruz and Abril, both of whom loved the story, their parts and the idea of starring opposite one another, and they agreed right away. Two years later, with the project's US$6.5 million budget secured – a hefty figure for a Spanish movie, which would typically come in at around a third of the sum – the crew was finally assembled in April 2001 to begin the shoot.

Yanes cited Buñuel's *Nazarín* as an inspiration: 'I wanted to do a film about good and evil but in which both concepts get confused so that every time the good angel tries to do right she ends up causing a terrible confusion.'

Traditional spy stories also played a part in the concept's germination. Yanes is a big fan of spy thrillers and he imagined the tale of two agents, one CIA, the other KGB, on rival missions; as the story evolves, it becomes clear just how essentially similar both characters are once team loyalties are forgotten. From there, the idea evolved to transferring the dynamic to a much higher plane.

Ordinarily when writing a script Yanes would immerse himself in subject material and, not least, watch any other film which tackled similar themes. However, when writing *Sin Noticias de Dios* he was careful to avoid any other movies with angels in, believing that you always inadvertently borrow ideas and, for something so fantastical, it was better to give his imagination a blank page to start on.

The title of the film comes from a dedication Yanes found in a book written by ultra-Catholic French writer León Bloy. The dedication was to Yanes' own father, the bullfighter Antonio Díaz Michelín. *Sin Noticias de Dios* (*No News From God*, or perhaps even *No Word From God*) is an ambiguous title, suggesting that all is not what it seems, and thus suits the picture well. Bizarrely, when released in Spanish-speaking Mexico, the film's distributors, in their wisdom, changed its name to *Benedito Infierno* (the rather lame *Holy Hell*). For its US release, the movie took the equally uninspiring title *Don't Tempt Me*.

That Bernal was offered a role is perhaps no surprise given the high regard in which Yanes holds Mexican actors. At the press conference held in Madrid to mark the film's launch, he expounded: 'Mexican actors are for Spanish-language films what English actors are for US ones: the best. They demonstrate this in every film in which they appear; they are the best-looking and they know how to pull off the more difficult stuff and that is why, whenever I can, I put them in my films.'

He certainly did so in his first film: the Mexican contingent on *Nadie Hablará de Nosotras Cuando Hayamos Muerto* numbered six and included Demián and

Bruno Bichir, both of whom returned for *Sin Noticias de Dios* (Demián was also in Mexican smash hit *Sexo, Pudor y Lágrimas*. As if to prove Yanes' point, in order to portray Manny, a boxer, Bichir went to the extreme lengths of training for months with Ricardo 'Finito' López, a Mexican boxing legend. Yanes himself would later comment, 'We were hardly making *Raging Bull*.')

Yanes' love of Mexico went further than thespians and embraced food, music, culture – and back to his childhood when he would spend several months there with his father, the bullfighter, who would travel there to perform during Spain's winter season. Yet despite his affinity for all things Mexican, Yanes had never met Bernal when he cast him: a promo video had been enough to convince.

Initially, Yanes had pictured a distinguished Briton or American as the Chief Executive of Hell but, in a flash of inspiration, he suddenly struck upon the notion of him being a young Mexican. He rewrote the part and contacted Bernal, who liked the role and accepted.

In the 'Making of' feature on the film's DVD, Yanes explains how pleased he was with his choice: 'Gael had everything I needed: he speaks English perfectly, is fantastic at imitating accents – and we were lucky because by the time he came to make our film, *Amores Perros* had come out everywhere and, because he was so good in that, everyone fell at his feet.'

As well as a post-*Amores Perros* Bernal and the headline names of Cruz and Abril, other high-profile cast members included French screen legend Fanny Ardant and Spanish actor Juan Echánove, perhaps best known for Pedro Almodóvar's *La Flor de Mi Secreto* (*Flower of My Secret*), all of which made for an on-set atmosphere of much mutual respect.

The shoot itself took place in Madrid and Paris, lasted twelve weeks, was trouble-free and evidently plenty of fun. 'I am still hung over from the whole experience,' Bernal would later say, and the director was evidently the main reason for the off-screen bonhomie. 'Yanes is charming, lovely, intelligent, a true gentleman and a tremendous seducer. He is the best-looking director I've ever worked with and one of the most generous. I have always said that, due to his character, I consider him an honorary Mexican.'

Bernal was obviously a popular colleague too: Abril invited him to visit and stay in her house in Paris and a long-lasting friendship took root with Spanish actress Elena Anaya, who played a supermarket checkout girl in the film, although she never actually shared a scene with Bernal. Meanwhile, he already knew Cruz, whom he had met at a post-Oscar ceremony party thrown by Salma Hayek.

Sin Noticias de Dios itself is rather hit and miss. The central premise is that God is depressed and tired of dealing with humans and has all but given up trying to help them. In God's absence, heaven is in crisis as it loses out to hell in the chase for human souls. The Head of Heaven (Fanny Ardant) tries to regain the initiative by sending an angel (Victoria Abril) down to earth to save the soul of a boxer named Manny, a rough character with a troubled past. The Head of Hell (Bernal) learns of the move and so sends his own dark agent (Penélope Cruz) to deliver the boxer into temptation and thus ensure his soul is hell-bound. The two leading ladies move in with Manny in the roles of his wife and cousin, presumably in the case of Abril by inhabiting the body of his actual wife, although this is not made particularly clear.

In fact, there is much that is not made particularly clear. The soul of this boxer, an especially charmless and unsympathetic character, is the plot's MacGuffin: we are never told why it is so important although the issue is touched upon (thus drawing attention to itself) several times and explained away by both Ardant and Bernal with curious references to Cleopatra's Needle. Both Cruz's and Abril's characters also take jobs in the local supermarket but, again, quite why this should be remains something of a mystery.

Despite the religious theme, the film is a comedy and really doesn't involve itself with the sticky issues of Christianity; it is much more of a light-hearted debate on the balance of power between good and evil. Bernal captured the mood when he told reporters: 'My parents are atheists but I try to believe in heaven and hell. It amuses me that dealing with sacred issues turns into such a taboo . . . which makes it ideal material for a comedy. But we Mexicans are culturally Christian and we always use religion, whether it be to pray or as a reason to celebrate and party.'

Although essentially a Spanish film, *Sin Noticias de Dios* is multilingual (indeed, in order to maximise distribution potential, it was very nearly made entirely in English) and attempts to present itself as something of a globalised project with actors from several different countries. The sequences set in heaven were shot in black-and-white in Paris: heaven is a place eternally stuck in the 1950s and run by a patient and caring woman; they speak French in heaven. In hell, English is the lingua franca: it is an apocalyptic futuristic nightmare and a slightly crazed man (Bernal) is in charge. Meanwhile, back on earth, Spanish is the preferred tongue.

The real point of the film is to cast Cruz and Abril against type; after all, the script was written especially for them. Cruz, usually a delicate, feminine figure, plays a devilish tomboy with bizarre lesbian tendencies who walks with a swagger and cries when watching *Goodfellas*. Abril meanwhile, who in Spain is known for her tough roles, such as those in Almodóvar's *Tajones Lejanos* (*High Heels*) and *Kika*, is the saintly housewife, a kind and caring mother figure.

This worked well in Spain, where both actresses are extremely well known and popular and such role-reversal fun could carry the movie. However, such a heavy reliance on one joke doesn't quite cut it elsewhere when that one joke doesn't really mean much to anyone. They loved it in Spain, where the film notched up no fewer than thirteen Goya nominations (in the event, the movie failed to collect a single gong as Alejandro Amenábar's *The Others* swept the board) but the film got a very limited release in the US and didn't hit cinemas in the UK at all.

The film's other primary problem is that it lacks a central identity. It tries to plant a foot in so many different genres – there are musical numbers, moments of social realism and violence, of fantasy and comedy – that ultimately it stands firm in none of them.

The movie throws up many gags, such as the director of the International Monetary Fund being declared an illegal immigrant at the gates of hell, and Bernal's devilish character is said to carry a Swiss passport. Spanish actor Javier Bardem even performs a cheeky little cameo at the end as a reincarnation of Cruz. As regards the British element, an armed robbery at the start is performed using caricature masks of the Queen, while there are various references to Margaret Thatcher; then when Bernal and Cruz, two residents of hell, meet up on earth they use the Shakespeare line, 'Now is the winter of our discontent,' as their password code. The British winter of 1978/79 became known as 'The Winter of Discontent' after a series of trade union strikes severely disrupted public services, leading to Thatcher grabbing power from Labour at the 1979 General Election. Is somebody trying to say that the dawn of Thatcherism put all us earthlings on a high road to hell?

As with most points raised in the film, this concept is no more than suggested at, as the picture steadfastly sticks to its light-hearted tone. This is sometimes frustrating because the problem with taking on the big and serious issues – and the film does present itself varyingly as a critic of globalisation, xenophobia and corruption – is that they are better confronted with passionate counterargument, while harmless teasing sometimes rubs the wrong way.

In fairness, at no point does the movie claim to be either controversial or subversive and so such criticism is perhaps unwarranted, but it does highlight the picture's identity crisis. There is nothing particularly dislikeable about the movie and, if taken as a harmless bit of nonsense, there are moments to enjoy, not least whenever Bernal is on screen. He doesn't exactly play the Chief Executive of Hell as evil incarnate but rather camps it up, even hams it up. He approaches the role as a sort of older Julio (his character from *Y Tu Mamá También*) on drugs, either hyperactively high as a kite or twitchingly in need of a fix. In fact, there are several references made to the fact that hell's head honcho has an alcohol problem. When he and Ardant share a scene at the dinner table (at one point the respective heads of heaven and hell, along with their good and evil angels, have to negotiate a truce of sorts) the Frenchwoman suggest he has perhaps had enough to drink.

Bernal's outfits for the part are as over-the-top as his performance: shiny blood-red suits; garish disco shirts; even a Maradona T-shirt with the Argentine footballer teasingly labelled '*Dios*' – God. His wardrobe makes him look like a dodgy nightclub owner or at least the Mexican equivalent: Bernal himself said that he based his interpretation on a dodgy bullfight promoter.

His other point of reference was Mexican politics, as he explained when publicising the film: 'My character is the director of hell in a heaven and hell where everything is very bureaucratic. The film has a dark and absurd sense of humour, very similar to politics because if you take a step back it is funny and absurd. Jack is a bit of a crook, the same as most of the politicians in our country.'

His character even gets to make a political speech of sorts: at the afore-mentioned supper, he explains that he fears that his position in hell is in jeopardy and that a plot to overthrow him is brewing; his rivals feel he is antiquated. His ousting would be disastrous for both heaven and hell, he explains, because the pretenders to his throne don't respect traditions and the long-established rules. Hell and heaven have to co-exist side by side, he argues, in order to ensure there is a choice between good and evil; that being able to choose between acting honourably and dishonourably is a basic human right. Watching the scene, it is easy to picture a drunken Bernal making the same semi-serious argument at a dinner table among friends.

Of course, this exploration of ethics is all done slightly tongue-in-cheek and its logical conclusion – that Earth and its freedom to be good or bad offers the best of both other worlds, so make the most of it and quit complaining! – is likewise not supposed to be taken too seriously as the moral of the story.

When in hell and speaking English, Bernal's language skills are impressive, and even raise the odd smile to the British viewer. None of that 'American' nonsense here: his English is peppered with sounds and phrases clearly honed during his time in London. He leaves one scene with the parting shot: 'See yuz later.' Meanwhile, when visiting earth and speaking his native tongue, he retains his Mexican slang with plenty of *güeys*.

Bernal clearly has plenty of fun with the part, not least with his scenes opposite Ardant. In one sequence the two of them share a taxi and flirt: there is clearly a history between the respective directors of heaven and hell. But the celestial one naturally has stronger willpower than her devilish counterpart and resists his advances, saying, 'We are too old for this, Jack.' Clearly, in the afterlife a Frenchwoman of a certain age and a young *chilango* buck are of one and the same generation.

Then again, we are talking about Fanny Ardant, an iconic screen diva of everlasting beauty, as Bernal was quick to acknowledge: 'What I shared with her was incredible – I mean I have seen her yawn, she has heard me sneeze, we travelled around in the same car together. These details are very important to me because she is the most beautiful woman I have ever had the chance to do such things with.'

As well as enjoying the overall experience, working on a Spanish film, especially one that combined a Mexican and Spanish cast, gave Bernal a first-hand introduction to the advantages of linguistic collaborations. When promoting the film he would say, 'Hispanic film-makers should work together in a block, like the Asian ones do, even though they speak different languages.' It is a message he has been repeating ever since.

He picked up a Goya nomination as Best Supporting Actor, and the fact that he didn't walk away with the prize was considered by the Spanish press to be a massive oversight.

The Crime of Father Amaro

After the back-to-back successes of *Amores Perros* and *Y Tu Mamá También*, Bernal chose to work on a series of low-key projects outside Mexico. *El Crimen de Padre Amaro* (*The Crime of Father Amaro*) marked a high-profile return to home territory, and what a return: *The Crime of Father Amaro* broke Mexican box-office records, enjoyed good worldwide exposure and ended up nominated for an Oscar.

Bernal played the eponymous Father Amaro, a fresh-faced young priest recently released from seminary school. A bright future in the church awaits him and he is posted to a small parish where he is to be inducted into the practicalities of day-to-day priesthood by the experienced Father Benito.

As it turns out, his mentor doesn't exactly run things by the good book. Benito keeps up a curious relationship with the local drug lords, baptising their children in return for hefty alms donations, and conducts an inappropriate affair with Sanjuanera, the village bar's landlady.

Sanjuanera has a sixteen-year-old daughter called Amelia (Ana Claudia Talancón) and it isn't long before Amaro, himself only twenty-four, has fallen in love, or at least lust, with her. Amaro soon breaks his celibacy and Amelia falls pregnant, to which the young priest's solution is to take her to an underground abortion clinic.

Despite such indiscretions, Amaro is seen to be making excellent progress in his chosen career, proving a good apprentice to the unconventional Benito and another priest, Father Natalio, who supports the local guerilla fighters.

Unlike *Amores Perros* and *Y Tu Mamá También*, which were both entirely privately financed, *The Crime of Father Amaro* went down the more traditional route, receiving a donation from state institution IMCINE. Its producer was Daniel Birman, the son of auteur director Arturo Ripstein and the grandson of Alfredo Ripstein, a legendary producer who had been making films in Mexico since the 1940s. Alfredo had tried and failed to get *The Crime of Father Amaro* made in 1970. He then renewed his efforts in 1995, handing the baton on to his grandson as the funding gradually fell into place six years later. In the end, a conglomeration involving production companies in Spain, France and Argentina provided the backing, with IMCINE then supplying the final top-up.

The Crime of Father Amaro was the first novel of the great Portuguese writer José Maria Eça de Queiróz, penned in 1875. Ripstein senior had long wanted to adapt the book but transpose the action to contemporary Mexico. Given that Arturo Ripstein cut his teeth working with Luis Buñuel (on *Exterminating Angel*), the family clearly had a taste for making anti-clerical cinema.

Mexican writer Vicente Leñero was charged with transforming the novel into a modern screenplay. Leñero had scripted *La Ley de Herodes*, the film that so upset the government for its portrayal of political corruption, so it was unlikely that he would shy away from a wrangle with the church either. Directors proved less gung ho, several turning the project down, finding the subject matter too hot to handle.

Carlos Carrera, previously a Cannes Palme d'Or winner (for his short, *El Héroe – The Hero*) and highly rated in Mexico after making the acclaimed *Sin Remitente* (*Sender Unknown*), proved different. Carrera was keen to give *The Crime of Father Amaro* contemporary gravitas and so he and Leñero decided to work in some of the main Mexican issues of the day, not least drugs alms, guerilla freedom-fighting and abortion.

The other major structural changes from novel to screenplay involved switching the name of the village, from the Portuguese-sounding Leiría to the more Spanish Los Reyes, and shaving several years off Father Amaro. In the book, Amaro is in his thirties but the fact that Ripstein's pet project was finally receiving financial backing was thanks to Bernal's involvement: Bernal was then in his early twenties, so Amaro would have to be too.

Bernal's box-office appeal may have excited the production executives but Carrera was drawn to the ambiguity he could bring as an actor; in the case of Father Amaro, his ability to appear both angelic and manipulative at the same time. Indeed Carrera felt compelled to emphasise that Bernal had been chosen for his acting abilities: 'Gael was making *Y Tu Mamá También* when he was cast. It took us four years to secure the financing to make *El Crimen* so he had read the script some time before he became such a big star.'

As for Bernal, *Amores Perros* resulted in a flood of offers to play Latin lovers or boys from the barrio, so *The Crime of Father Amaro* stood out. 'Carlos gave me the script and I really liked the idea of exploring the character of this priest who is riddled with moral complexities,' Bernal would explain, 'someone who places the fear of God above anything else, and yet his personal ambitions and goals compromise that fear.'

What's more, if the Julio of *Y Tu Mamá También* was like the real Bernal, part of Amaro's appeal was that he really was not: 'It is a challenge to interpret someone you don't understand. He is a man with a profound fear of God and a profound fear of himself and his sexuality. It is the story of a child who loses his innocence.'

To prepare for the role, Bernal attended Mass and consulted priests. As the son of liberal-thinking parents he was not raised a strict Catholic, but any kind of upbringing in Mexico includes a brush with the church and creates baggage. While promoting the movie, Bernal made use of Buñuel's infamous quote, saying, 'Thank God I'm an atheist.'

Filming took place over seven weeks in late 2001, starting in November. Interiors were shot in Mexico City while the church scenes took place in a tiny village near the town of Texcoco, forty kilometres east of the capital. Exteriors were filmed in Xico in the state of Veracruz, on the eastern coast.

Mariestela Fernandez was in charge of wardrobe on *The Crime of Father Amaro* and is one of Mexico's most respected costume designers. She is known in the trade for her all-round commitment to films, for going far and beyond her job description: if you want your wardrobe department to be hands-on involved in all elements of the production, Fernandez is who you call.

She fondly remembers her time on *The Crime of Father Amaro*. 'It was a good shoot, without any major delay, although one also characterised by a lack of money. But there was a good atmosphere amongst cast and crew, many meals on set and a couple of really good fiestas. The crew numbered about eighty and we were all staying in the same hotel.' This included the star actor. 'Gael always mixes with everyone off-set, chatting away and generally being very outgoing.'

He may have been just another member of the team to his colleagues, but he certainly wasn't viewed that way by the public. 'Gael by then was like a rock star,' recalls Fernandez. 'Loads of girls from the village and its surrounds or having even travelled from DF came to catch a glimpse of him. He was very accessible, posing for photos and signing autographs. It is not something he particularly enjoys or is comfortable with but he understands it is part of the package.

'When we were in Texcoco, the church was closed off. By the time word had spread and too many people might show up, we were ready to move on. Then in DF we were filming in a *colonia* where people didn't tend to go. But Xico, where we were for the longest, that was where most people ended up. There were a few males but the vast majority were women.'

Bernal, Carrera and Fernandez talked long and hard about just who Father Amaro was. Says Fernandez: 'Not only is it very distinct to his other parts but also to he himself: Amaro is really not like Gael, which is why we did so much discussing at the start. The first thing was to decide quite carefully what religious training he had had. We concluded, not much – you might say deficient.'

His level of priestly qualification was important to establish given that they had made Amaro younger than in the book but it was also deemed fundamental in shaping his character. 'So he didn't have a thorough training and study in religious practice – more like an express course – because the important thing is that Amaro comes from a poor background and is driven by ambition. His priestly vocation is less a religious calling and more about opportunity,' explains Fernandez.

Costume brought about further debate between Bernal and Fernandez. 'It may sound silly but we had long discussions about what sort of jeans Amaro would wear. This sort of thing is very important in getting the character right,' she says. 'In the end we went for something simple, not from the market but from, say, a modest shop. He is lower-middle class and not very worldwise, had never been abroad, for example. In the end, his main motivational force is power.'

Of course, there were limits to the bounds of creativity in terms of wardrobe. 'In terms of the religious clothing, there are rules to be observed regarding what you wear for each discipline so that largely took care of itself, but there are still different styles of priest garb, from full-length cassock to short-sleeved.'

People commented on how good Bernal looked in the vestments, although that seems to have been more through an accident of nature than design. 'The idea was not to make him look handsome. Not at all. It was to be realistic. When working with a star it is even more important to be precise and realistic with the clothing – in order for people to forget it is Gael and concentrate on the character.'

By now, Bernal certainly was a big star in Mexico. That he was filming a new movie in the country became news and hence the hordes of fans who arrived on set. Similarly, as the movie's release date approached and preview copies did the rounds, a buzz began to surface about the new Bernal vehicle. Given the topics tackled in *The Crime of Father Amaro*, the movie was going to upset someone sooner or later.

The first organisations to speak out against the film were ultra-right groups such as Pro Vida (Pro Life), whose outrage had been awakened by word of the abortion issue. Jorge Serrano, president of Pro Vida, was so incensed that he took out a lawsuit against Government Secretary Santiago Creel for not censoring the film and against the Minister for Culture, Sari Bermúdez, for authorising its finance.

This reflected the mood of the religious right, who were appalled that, in a country where church and state are so closely linked, the movie had received funding from the government-sponsored IMCINE. Of the film's total budget of 18 million Mexican pesos (US$1.6 million), the final 20 per cent had been provided by FOPROCINE (the cultural wing of IMCINE). Mexico has the second-biggest Catholic population in the world (after Brazil) with some 74.6 million people said to be followers: according to the movie's critics, this meant that the taxes of upstanding God-fearing citizens were effectively being used to attack the Catholic Church.

For her part, Sari Bermúdez was not overly concerned, saying that the film had been backed due to its artistic merits and that Mexico was a free country. Fellow defenders of the government made a virtue of the fact that taxes were being used to guarantee freedom of thought, speech and expression. Others noted that, if the church was such an important concern for such a large section of the population, it was proper and appropriate that a film broached the subject, as very few had done so before.

The church didn't see things that way and its leaders were soon wading into the furore. Bishops and cardinals lined up to attack the picture, urging the authorities to stop the film's distribution for the good of the people. The Archdeacon of Morelia wrote: 'It really is a work charged with hatred towards our saintly church.'

The Conferencia del Episcopado Mexicano (Mexican Catholic Bishops' Conference) released a formal statement claiming that the movie 'constituted an offence to the religious beliefs of Catholics and mocked what were considered to be the most sacred symbols of the Catholic community'. This was in reference to the two scenes causing the most outcry – Amaro seducing Amelia by placing a blue robe over her head, saying she is more beautiful than the Virgin, and a woman feeding a cat the Host, the symbolic Body of Christ to believers. The former was always likely to prove sensitive in Mexico where the Virgin of Guadalupe – the Virgin Mary is believed to have appeared on a hillside in the sixteenth century – is so revered; the Virgin of Guadalupe is perhaps the country's most beloved religious and cultural image.

Carrera argued that the scene was taken from the book and that it was important in that it perfectly defines Amaro's psychology. For her part, Fernandez says that the scene was not considered especially risqué when they shot it. 'We filmed it just like any other. Carlos treats the shoot like a game and that day was the same. Neither Gael or Ana were especially nervous as neither saw it as anything other than another scene. It is just a piece of cloth. If anything, we thought how beautiful Ana Claudia looked.'

Fernandez remembers it being a particularly good day's shoot with cast and crew being especially satisfied with how the scene had gone when it wrapped: 'It was the look in Gael's eyes during that scene that made it.' She considers the fact that it caused such a stir rather ridiculous. 'It is remarkable that what offended most people was not the shooting scene or the abortion scene but the Virgin scene. A true reflection of the society we live in with its macho veneration for the virgin.'

But offence it certainly caused. In Guadalajara, young members of Catholic groups handed out leaflets at shopping centres and cinemas and issued T-shirts featuring the image of the Virgin of Guadalupe and the phrase 'If you love me . . . you decide'.

What you were supposed to decide, of course, was that the Virgin of Guadalupe would not want you to go and see the film; seeing it and deciding what all the fuss was about for yourself was not part of the equation. As well as the fliers, posters were put up in towns and on church doors warning people away from the cinemas. Some groups even took out full-page adverts in newspapers urging people to boycott the film. Religious leaders joined in and called on the faithful not to be tempted by curiosity and to abstain from watching the film. All of which rather highlighted a key point: despite the hysteria, the film had yet to be released and hardly anyone, least of all those purporting to be so utterly offended, had even seen it.

Bernal remembered the period with shame. 'What happened in Mexico was a bit obscene. I was putting myself on the spot to defend a film that people hadn't seen. The people who were protesting against the film hadn't seen it, so there was no basic point of discussion, no common denominator. It was a very stupid confrontation.'

Carrera, reacting at the time of the storm, made the same point but also emphasised that the film wasn't a simple attack on the church. 'I cannot see why there is such offence: firstly, nobody has yet seen the film; secondly, although through certain characters it touches upon topics of celibacy in the priesthood and drugs alms, there are others [in the film] who are honest and follow their religion to the letter.

'Obviously I'm not saying that all priests are corrupt. This is the story of just one character,' he continued, then adding for perspective, 'although we can easily find many more like him throughout our land.'

The director tried to highlight the film's broader themes: 'It is a story that interested me for its human reach, for the possibilities it gives me in showing human motives, which are always complex, never unanimous. And it is this contradiction between obligations and desires which is the key to the film.'

Exasperated by the whole affair, Carrera also tried to remind people of Mexico's movie-making heritage. Was *The Crime of Father Amaro* any worse than Buñuel's *The Milky Way*, he asked? Although this satire on the church was actually shot abroad, it was made while Buñuel lived in and worked out of Mexico. In a memorable scene from the movie, Buñuel himself plays the role of the Pope who is placed before the firing squad.

Speaking of the Pope, by a delightful coincidence, *The Crime of Father Amaro* was scheduled to launch in Mexico slap-bang in the middle of a visit to the country by the pontiff. This was considered to be a provocation too far and so the movie's distributors decided to postpone the release until a week later, 8 August 2002. Another concession made to the protesters was that the film and all its posters would carry a public warning that some viewers might be offended.

Thus the distributors, Colombia Tri-Star, played the role of sensitive pacifiers, but they weren't stupid and knew that the whole controversy had stirred up massive interest. *The Crime of Father Amaro* was released on 365 screens across the country, an unprecedented number for a domestic film (*Amores Perros* opened on 220; *Y Tu Mamá También* on 230).

Some people tried to keep calm. The governor of Baja California, Eugenio Elorduy Walther, for example, declared that he had yet to decide if he would go and see the film but added that it was unlikely to be on opening weekend: 'If I do go it will be on a Wednesday when it is two-for-one.'

But, for most, the movie had become a cause célèbre: whether interested in the story or not, going to watch it was like registering a vote for the freedom of expression, a two fingers up to the religious right claiming to represent ordinary Mexicans. On opening weekend alone, 862,969 people went to see it. The previous record for a Mexican film had been held by *Y Tu Mamá También* – itself aided by the publicity of a censorship scandal – which at 355,646 had been less than half as many. Three weeks later, *The Crime of Father Amaro* had already become the most successful Mexican box-office film of all time, taking 119 million Mexican pesos (US$11 million). The previous record holder had been *Sexo, Pudor y Lágrimas* with 118 million Mexican pesos (US$10.9 million), followed by *Y Tu Mamá También* at 103 million Mexican pesos (US$9.5 million) and *Amores Perros* at 95 million Mexican pesos (US$8.75 million). *The Crime of Father Amaro* went on to make 162 million Mexican pesos (US$14.9 million) domestically.

Referring to the before and after, Carrera commented, 'On the one hand we saw a living Mexico that we thought no longer existed, a very conservative Mexico, from the dark ages, a Mexico we thought no longer participated in national life. On the other hand surged the reaction of the Mexico who went to the cinemas, that of a mature society, sane, with sound judgement.'

The whole scenario of going to the pictures as a stance of protest worked well in terms of the new cinemagoing demographic, that of the middle classes, who liked to see the church criticised. The working classes, the more faithful section of society, could no longer afford to go to the movies in any case. That said, the overriding conclusion was that Mexicans generally may well be Catholics but their rebellious streak is stronger than their religious conviction: they don't like being told what to do.

The nature of the box-office success sat uncomfortably with some, not least Bernal. 'Maybe the film is not that good. Maybe we're just talking about an event. That's what made everything feel a bit obscene because it wasn't about the actual film,' he told *indieWIRE*.

Given the circumstances, as a gesture of liberal solidarity, reviews of the film were inevitably supportive. Some people felt that the media had generated much of the fuss in the first place, manipulating the far-right and church leaders into making ever more idiotic statements. Bernal certainly thinks so, as he told the *Observer*: 'It was generated by the media. It was journalists ringing up the clergy and saying, "Hey, did you know there's a film about such and such?" And they'd say: "What! We must censor it!" It makes sense. We lived through many years when journalists didn't have that kind of freedom. And they got their own back – big time.'

On seeing the film, many commentators were genuinely surprised that the movie was not an out-and-out aggression against the church and praised its balance and humanity. Everyone agreed that it should never have caused such a furore.

But given the hype, the lack of a shock-factor left many observers in a flux of anticlimax. The whole hoo-ha had built the movie up but it had also diverted many from a balanced appraisal. Casting aside issues such as freedom of expression, *The Crime of Father Amaro* was an accomplished and well-acted piece but nothing much more than that.

As the dust settled and the box-office figures had put the intolerant sectors of society in their places, critics began to lament that the movie had promised much but delivered little. Bernal had said that one of the reasons he became involved in the film was his interest in exploring the question of whether fear of God was the same as love of God and which of the two sentiments motivates Amaro, but in truth the film never quite pursues the theme. The plot touches on issues such as the corruption of office and the relationship between the church and those in power, yet never explores them thoroughly, instead concentrating on the more obvious sexual element. Some people felt that the film's eagerness to shock had been at the expense of the original novel's weightier themes.

In most places outside Mexico, a film depicting church corruption is less of an event movie and so *The Crime of Father Amaro* was judged on its own merit. Furthermore, far uglier tales of paedophilia in the church had made headlines across the globe, rendering *The Crime of Father Amaro*'s story fairly tame in comparison. The film garnered fair praise and did respectable business, although it has to be acknowledged that many viewers overseas went to see *The Crime of Father Amaro* on the back of *Amores Perros* and *Y Tu Mamá También*, a sign of Mexico's and Bernal's growing cinematic recognition.

Bernal's star status was decidedly a factor in Mexico too. The scandal may have raised the film's profile but Bernal's pulling power certainly helped people decide to go and see it. Some wags suggested that it was in Bernal that the church had lost the battle: if he really had been a priest, everyone would have been rushing to confess instead.

Yet there were also those who felt the film suffered for Bernal's involvement. The cash to make the movie may have come thanks to his presence but many in the audience found Bernal too young to be taken seriously as a priest.

Nevertheless, most people praised his performance. Certainly Fernandez was impressed with his work: 'Gael does the role very well as he is quite cold and calculating, very good at showing that Amaro knows what he is doing, knows how the system works.'

She also believes that Ana Claudia Talancón was deserving of more credit than she received, slightly lost as she was in Bernal's shadow: 'Gael's character develops and reaches its height and stays there but Ana's is more in constant development.'

As far as developments were concerned, behind-the-scenes goings-on may well have helped actor and actress get into their roles. 'There was an off-screen romance between Gael and Ana, which always helps,' says Fernandez. 'Then we could see that they were beginning to break up off-screen as the characters were about to do so on camera and so we were quite pleased,' she laughs. 'They remain good friends today. It was not perhaps a very serious romance, more the natural process of what they were going through as actors. This sort of thing often happens.'

As a stand-alone role, Fernandez thinks Father Amaro one of Bernal's finest: 'Gael is very different in Amaro than to, say, *Amores Perros* or *Y Tu Mamá También*. His character in Amaro is not quite so brilliant – it is darker, more complex – but in his body of work, Amaro stands out as a completely different role.'

Latin American New Wave Part III: Brazil

The Crime of Father Amaro played at the 2002 Toronto Film Festival but was overshadowed by another movie from Latin America, *Cidade de Deus* (*City of God*).

In much the same way that *The Crime of Father Amaro* (and *Amores Perros* before that) became a social event in Mexico, *City of God* transcended the film world to become the topic on everyone's lips in Brazil in 2002.

In October 2002, the former shoeshine boy Luiz Inácio 'Lula' da Silva won the general election, making him Brazil's first-ever socialist president. A mood for change was in the air. One of Brazil's most pressing problems was urban crime. Millions of citizens dwell in favelas, areas controlled by armed drug gangs with a complete absence of state-backed law and order. Periodic police raids achieve little more than converting the favelas into authentic war zones. For so long, the favelas had been Brazil's inconvenient truth, brushed aside and ignored, as if the problem didn't exist. *City of God* told the story of life in the favelas and, in a no-holds-barred fashion, forced the reality into everyone's faces.

Lula campaigned on a promise to represent Brazil's downtrodden and to tackle social problems from the base. In the build-up to the ballot, Lula urged incumbent president Fernando Henrique Cardoso to see *City of God* in order to better comprehend the urban issues at play. Cardoso took his advice, as did many others. The film was becoming a must-see movie in Brazil and became a smash hit.

City of God was directed by Fernando Meirelles, who would direct Bernal in *Blindness*, and co-produced by Walter Salles, who would direct Bernal in *The Motorcycle Diaries*. Salles then was becoming the figurehead of a revival in Brazilian cinema. In 1998, his *Central do Brasil* (*Central Station*) had awoken a dormant industry, which had fallen into decline since a creative heyday in the 1960s.

Cinema had always been a popular pastime for Brazilians. Rio played host to the first demonstration of the *cinématographe* contraption in Latin America in July 1896. Brazilians were quick to embrace the latest form of diversion and started to make their own films, so efficiently so that the period from 1908 to

1912 would become known as the *Bela Época* (Golden Age) of Brazilian cinema with up to one hundred films, mainly news-based but some fiction too, made locally each year.

As with Mexico and Argentina, Hollywood then wrested the initiative away from Brazil but the advent of sound provided the impetus for renewed domestic energy. A popular Hollywood formula had been to shape a film around a star and a show with musical numbers and in Brazil this led to the *chanchada*, carnivalesque musical comedies. *Chanchadas* dominated the Brazilian cinema scene from the 1930s through to the 1950s and even produced an international star in Carmen Miranda.

The *chanchada* phenomenon helped form a studio system, Rio's Atlântida studios churning them out, and proved instrumental in forging a sense of multicultural identity in Brazil.

Of course, *chanchadas* were fairly dreadful from an artistic perspective and young film aficionados had begun to take cinema seriously with a new magazine, *O Metropolitano*, proving influential.

A conceptually artistic yet technically basic cinema was emerging from Europe in Italian Neo-Realismo, whereby hand-held cameras were used to shoot films on location. This appealed to Brazilian film-makers not only in terms of its approach to social commentary but also as a cheap and practical way to make movies. Nelson Pereira do Santos applied the principles to impressive effect with *Rio, 40 Graus* (*Rio, 40 Degrees*) in 1955, showing everyday folk at popular locations such as the Corcovado, the Maracanã, the favelas and the town squares. He then repeated the trick with *Rio Zona Norte* (*Rio North Zone*) in 1958.

The French Nouvelle Vague was born the following year, following the Neo-Realismo template and then using slipshod editing. This allowed a certain rebellious streak to be added to what Pereira do Santos had been doing. The result in Brazil was a new film movement called Cinema Novo (New Cinema), which announced its arrival in 1963 with a string of acclaimed movies. Pereira do Santos upped his game with *Vidas Secas* (*Barren Lives*), the tale of a desperate family coping with drought; *Os Fuzis* (*The Guns*) by Rui Guerra told of a group of soldiers defending a food store from the starving locals. The next year, *Deus e o Diabo na Terra do Sol* (*Black Gold, White Devil*) by Glauber Rocha appeared and exposed hopeless agrarian conditions in the interior.

A coup d'état changed the political landscape in 1964. The authorities banned *Barren Lives* as part of its clampdown on dissent. Nevertheless, the military rulers established a National Film Institute and funding platform in Embrafilme, hoping to show Brazil off to the world through its sophisticated cinema. Rocha managed to sneak through his seminal, anarchic *Terra em Transe* (*Land in Anguish*), about a corrupt politician who forever switches allegiance, before a change of regime brought more hard-line generals to the fore in 1968, bringing an end to the fun.

In the 1970s, government-sponsored institutions such as Embrafilme and Concine kept a tighter rein on output, ensuring a steady flow of approved productions of zero cultural value. *Dona Flor e Seus Dois Maridos (Dona Flor and Her Two Husbands)* managed to rise above the mediocrity in 1976 to become Brazil's biggest ever box-office hit after *Jaws*, released the previous year. Otherwise, *pornochanchadas*, an erotic spin-off of the popular musical genre, dominated the scene.

An economic recession hit Brazil in the 1980s, hampering domestic production. Television took off and the national addiction to soap operas began. Matters went from bad to worse for politics and cinema with the coming to power of President Collor de Mello. Immediately on taking office in March 1990 he downgraded the Ministry of Culture to a secretariat and shut several state-backed cultural institutions including Embrafilme, which had been in charge of film distribution. Embrafilme may have been struggling to underpin Brazilian film but it had been the last stronghold of former Cinema Novo practitioners.

Between 1990 and 1992, no more than two Brazilian films reached national cinemas annually. The industry was in crisis but so was the government: in 1992 Collor de Mello was impeached on corruption charges. Itamar Franco completed Collor de Mello's mandate and proved more sympathetic to cinema: he brought in the Prêmio Resgate do Cinema Brasileiro (Brazilian Cinema Rescue Reward) which reallocated Embrafilme assets and resuscitated film production.

The turnaround then truly began under Cardoso's presidency. He encouraged privatisation and provided incentives to business: one such initiative was the Lei do Audiovisual, the Audio-visual Law, which linked tax breaks to film production. The law basically allowed businesses to pay lower taxes if they donated a portion of their profits to the film industry. Other incentives followed – screen quotas for domestic films, government grants and co-productions via state-backed institutions such as Petrobras (Brazil's largest oil concern). In 1996, the tax discount offered to companies investing in film was then raised from 1 per cent to 3 per cent, the decisive sweetener.

Production immediately started to pick up (between 1994 and 2000, Brazil produced nearly two hundred features) and the boom became known as the *retomada do cinema brasileiro*, the rebirth of Brazilian cinema.

The first indication that Brazilian films were winning back Brazilian audiences came via *Carlota Joaquina – Princesa do Brasil* (*Carlota Joaquina – Princess of Brazil*) made by Carla Camurati in 1995. After being released only at art-house venues, it proved to be a grower and went on to pull in more than one million punters.

Critical acclaim was building too with a string of Oscar nominations. *O Quatrilho* (*The Quartet*) was nominated for a Best Foreign Language Film Oscar in 1996; *O Que é Isso Companheiro* (*Four Days in September*) pulled off the same trick in 1998; Salles' *Central Station* did likewise in 1999 but went one better, picking up a Best Actress nod for Fernanda Montenegro, too. What's more, whereas *O Que é Isso Companheiro* achieved only a limited international release and *O Quatrilho* practically nothing at all, *Central Station* did the business everywhere.

Salles grew up the son of a diplomat and he says that jumping about from country to country made him more curious about his own and led to his becoming a documentary film-maker. He made documentaries for ten years before his break into fiction with *Terra Estrangeira* (*Foreign Land*) in 1996. The movie concerned the plight of a family following a major event in recent political history, namely when Collor de Mello (him again) froze all assets. This leads the son on an adventure to Portugal. Critically acclaimed, the film scored modest box-office success.

His follow-up, *Central Station*, was a huge hit, first in Brazil and then around the world. It tells the story of a young boy, Josué, who turns to a tough old woman, Dora, for help when his own mother is killed. Dora eventually takes him on a journey into the interior of Brazil's northeast in search of his father. The film, meanwhile, is on a journey into the heart of Brazil, in search of its soul: while the cynical Dora represents the Brazil of the past, Josué, young and full of hope, is the Brazil of the future.

Beautifully shot and paced, the movie is also superbly well acted, with veteran actress Fernanda Montenegro earning her Oscar nomination, a rare honour indeed for a non-English-language film. The delightfully natural performance of Josué, on the other hand, comes courtesy of Vinícius de Oliveira, a non-actor who Salles encountered shining shoes.

Largely on the strength of *Central Station*, in 1998 there was a 50 per cent increase on the previous year in attendance of domestic production in Brazil, with

3.6 million admissions: 1999 continued the progress with 5.2 million and 2000 saw further improvement with 7.2 million, *O Auto da Compadecida* (*A Dog's Will*) by Guel Arraes accounting for 2 million of them.

Buoyed by its success, the government continued to promote national cinema. Overall, his presidency had very mixed results, but Cardoso's two terms were good for film. Conscious of cinema's contribution to the trade deficit, in 1999 Cardoso featured cinema among the thirteen goals of O Programa Brasileiro de Produtividade e Qualidade (The Brazilian Programme for Productivity and Quality), the intention being that it would claim 20 per cent of the country's cinema market by 2003, and he pumped new money into production as part of the Programa Mais Cinema (More Cinema Programme).

Top-quality films kept coming, many securing international releases. Beto Brant had shown promise with the stylish thriller *Os Matadores* (*Belly Up*). *O Invasor* (*The Trespasser*) was even better. Based in the mean streets of São Paulo, it sets forth with the same overflow of adrenaline that marked the likes of *City of God* and *Amores Perros*. Two partners in a construction firm use the services of a hit man but the hit man, sensing his employers to be a fairly feckless duo, decides to stick around and muscle in on the business.

Moving to the mean streets of Rio, *O Homem do Ano* (*Man of the Year*), José Henrique Fonseca's debut movie, relates the fortunes of an everyday guy who reaches tipping point with life's travails and ends up killing a man in a bar who had been giving him grief. As it turns out, the dead man was a nasty piece of work, loathed by both the local community and the police. The murderer becomes a hero and offers of more vigilante work flood in.

Overall, revival cinema was characterised by its variety, although common traits existed. Given the creative void of the intervening years, the influence of Cinema Novo could be traced to the *retomada* films, although there were subtle differences: dismay at state oppression had become dismay at state neglect; revolutionary fervour had been replaced by frustration and a modest wish for personal happiness.

Most films were concerned with questions of Brazil: What is it? Why doesn't it work? Migration was a popular theme for allowing characters, and through them the viewer, to encounter unfamiliar corners of the country, highlighting its contrasts. Films also favoured the margins for settings, the favela or *sertão* (the northeast interior) where the desperate lived life on the edge. The same locations had likewise shaped Cinema Novo pictures.

Given the overriding realist tone of the movement, documentary film-making also made an impact. José Padiha's *Ônibus 174* took a look at the events before, during and after a notorious bus hijacking in Rio, which went dramatically wrong while being played out live on Brazilian television.

In 1998, João Moreira Salles (Walter's brother) and Kátia Lund made *Notícias de uma Guerra Particular* (*Notes on a Particular War*), a detailed look at the various factions and factors bringing violence to the favelas.

Fernando Meirelles had bought the rights to *City of God* the book, a first-hand non-fiction account of life in the favelas by Paulo Lins. In order to make the film, Meirelles, who had never before set foot in a favela, turned to Lund for some expert help. The pair ended up collaborating, although to quite what degree remains somewhat up in the air.

Lund had cut her teeth as assistant director on *Central Station* and asked for co-director credit on *City of God*, which she got, although Meirelles was named outright director. In Brazil, where getting projects off the ground was still a tough business despite the cash injection, co-direction was common (Meirelles' previous two features had been co-directed and Salles' *Terra Estrangeira* was co-directed by Daniela Thomas). Lund is most commonly credited with directing the actors on *City of God*, Meirelles as making the film, although that seems to be a simplification of matters.

What is certain is that Lund helped persuade Meirelles of the need to use non-actors. Her documentary background gave her a preference for real performances and she also saw the opportunity to give something back to the communities they would be portraying. She and Meirelles formed a drama group in the favelas and, over the course of a year, from them plucked their talent for the film and trained them in their roles. The subsequent performances are superb, frightening in their naturalness.

The film tells the story of the City of God, a housing project built in the 1960s which, through state disregard, becomes ever more downtrodden and transforms into a favela. Its inhabitants resort to petty crime to make ends meet but the arrival of cocaine in the 1970s raises the stakes. Turf wars bring guns and soon the violence is completely out of hand.

The film begins with an audacious set piece: a barbeque celebration is under preparation with chicken on the menu, but the chicken escapes and a comic pursuit ensues, with heavily armed gangsters chasing a confused hen. Suddenly the whole party bursts on to an open street to emerge face to face with a police raid.

121

Stuck in the middle is a boy called Buscapé (Rocket) holding a camera. The movie then skips back in time to explain how everyone got to be there.

The opening also announces the film's stylised credentials: there is fast editing, camera swipes, hand-held filming and a rocking soundtrack. We are treated to split screens, fast-motion, slow-motion, even frozen moments in which the action stops but the camera is able to pan around. Colours are bright and brash, the dialogue loose and fast and the violence, when it comes, is cold and shocking.

Far from being a triumph of style over substance, *City of God* backs the technical panache with skilful storytelling and a delicate handling of the overall theme. We are never forced to judge these people, not the most malevolent gangster nor corrupt cop, but simply asked to understand how they came to be. By the end, we have been taken into the reality of their environment, become captives and, like the protagonists, desensitised into seeing their world as the almost inevitable norm.

Dot the i

Although *The King*, on its release in 2006, was billed as Bernal's debut US film and his first feature with an English-speaking lead role, it was neither. The romantic comedy *I'm with Lucy* takes the honour in terms of being the former while British film *Dot the i* can lay claim to the latter.

I'm with Lucy is hardly significant in terms of Bernal's canon of work but it is certainly unusual in being the only Hollywood-style movie he has done and a definite case of take the money and run. What could be more stereotypical than accepting the part of a Latin lover?

In his defence, Bernal told *CloseUp Film* that it was only a one-week shoot and that he managed to keep his credibility intact by being too slippery for the cliché machine, insisting that his Latin lover actually be Romanian. Technically, given that the Romanian language derives from Latin, Bernal was right to argue that Romania is considered part of Latin Europe.

I'm with Lucy concerns a good-looking New Yorker called Lucy, played by Monica Potter, who tells a close friend that she is engaged, revealing only that she met her future husband on a blind date within the last year. Like the friend, we the audience are invited to guess who the lucky man could be. Twelve months earlier, long tired of being a singleton and fast approaching her thirties, the eponymous Lucy had embarked upon a series of blind dates to find her perfect match. The film documents in flashbacks how five such encounters developed into differing relationships, but who eventually popped the question?

Of course, each of the five candidates is distinctive from the rest, each perfect in his own way. John Hannah shows up as the shy intellectual; Anthony LaPaglia plays a former baseball player, slightly full of himself but sensitive too; Henry Thomas is the computer nerd with a sense of fun fighting to get out; David Boreanaz is smart, good-looking and rich but possibly too good to be true.

Then there is Bernal as Gabriel, the Romanian Latin lover, not tall, of course, but certainly dark and handsome. The master seducer, he has Lucy in bed within minutes of them meeting; Gabriel is somewhat addicted to sex and, of all Lucy's relationships, this is the most passionate.

Bernal seems to have plenty of fun in using his remit to provide his character with a sense of mystery as a licence to act eccentricly. 'It's very light, but I'm glad

I made it. My little brother and sister are eleven and seven. They know I'm an actor, but they weren't allowed to see my first two films,' said Bernal, referring to his half-brother and half-sister Darío and Tamara and his first two films, *Amores Perros* and *Y Tu Mamá También*.

As can be seen from the rather formulaic character clichés, the movie is somewhat predictable, although it does try to avoid being so by jumping around from encounter to encounter. Unfortunately, this stunts each relationship's development as a story. The film has its odd moment of charm and provides the occasional moment of humour but all in all it resembles many a straight-to-DVD, which is what it was in the UK.

Sadly, *Dot the i* shared the same fate, despite the fact that it was an accomplished British piece made entirely in London, went down a storm at the Sundance Film Festival and proved popular in other markets.

In many ways, *Dot the i* offers a case study in the trials and tribulations of getting a film released in the UK. Director Matthew Parkhill reflects on the sobering experience of providing what the industry had called for and yet still not getting a launch. 'At the time, the whole idea was to do English movies that worked abroad and, on a small scale, it [*Dot the i*] got released in a lot of places and made money. But it didn't get any backing in its own country and I've always thought it a real shame.'

In essence, *Dot the i* was the victim of an untimely change of personnel at the UK distribution company which owned its rights. Meg Thomson, one of the movie's two co-producers explains: 'It was released in forty-two countries and did really well elsewhere but in the UK we pre-sold it to Momentum and there was a regime change there just afterwards. English distribution is very tough and I just don't think they [the new regime] were fans of the film.'

'They just buried it,' adds Parkhill, still aggrieved at the treatment his picture got at the hands of Momentum's new management, but its non-UK theatre release was just one of a number of ups and downs for the picture. Even Bernal's involvement was an on-off-on affair.

As one of the two lead roles, *Dot the i* offered Bernal the most screen time he had enjoyed since *Y Tu Mamá También*, although his services were secured before the latter film's release. 'The first time I saw Gael was when I went to a preview screening of *Amores Perros* a couple of months before it came out and, like a lot of people, I was like, wow – who is this guy?' explains Parkhill.

Thomson takes up the story: 'Matthew and I saw *Amores Perros* and we were at the time casting the lead role for *Dot the i*. It was written as an English role and we wanted a guy like that [Bernal as Octavio] but English. We told our casting director and she said, "Oh, he lives in London.'''

Parkhill again: 'Everyone afterwards asked how did we get Gael? Really we just sent him the script.'

This was around June 2000, so it was also a matter of being in the right place at the right time, as Thomson concedes. 'It was really good timing. We saw *Y Tu Mamá* at the London Film Festival in the November and still nobody had really heard of him. But we had attached him and we thought, "Oh no – he is going to explode." Then in January, at Sundance, we got the funding from a company called Summit and I ran into Gael at Sundance where *Y Tu Mamá* was playing. He was, like, "I don't know if I want to do the movie any more, I just broke up with my girlfriend, I want a bit of privacy."'

There was a long period between when Parkhill first met Gael and getting funding for the project. 'Obviously *Amores Perros* had come out and it seemed that people around him were advising him to have a good think about what he was going to do next.'

Bernal's participation was very much in the balance. 'To his credit, he had always said he was going to do it and he kept his word, which was a big deal, it meant a lot,' says Parkhill. 'He didn't have to and financially it wasn't a lot of money for him. But he had said he'd do it. Years later I was talking to his agent [Elyse Scherz] and she said, "He did it because he gave his word." I'll always respect that. He has got a lot of integrity.'

Thomson: 'He came through for us, he really did, because there were a few weeks there where we were . . . He had signed a letter of attachment but we knew *Y Tu Mamá* was coming out in April and we were shooting that April. In the end it was very exciting: he signed the night *Y Tu Mamá* premiered in LA, which was great.'

Dot the i could have gone ahead without Bernal: Summit's participation didn't stipulate his involvement. 'It wasn't dependent on Gael, they just liked the business model and the project,' says Parkhill. Nevertheless, Bernal's commitment helped, although securing funding still proved the usual challenge.

'In any independent film, trying to get the money is a nightmare,' explains Parkhill, who tells a good story about the moment he received the news that they were finally up and running. 'At the time, I was teaching a class at the London Film Academy. I ran a course on getting an independent feature off the ground when, of course, there I was not having got one off the ground,' he says, laughing. One freezing-cold Friday night in January, having just come out of teaching another class on the subject, he turned on his phone to see he had 25 messages from Meg Thomson and George Duffield, *Dot the i*'s other co-producer. 'The first one said: "We are at Sundance – Call us." And then the messages got more and more frantic, ending up: "What are you doing? Fucking call us now."'

Parkhill had originally pitched the idea to Thomson and Duffield at Cannes, then worked on the script of what was to become his debut as director. Then came casting, and although bagging Bernal proved quite a coup, his getting the part was no foregone conclusion.

'In the space of one morning in Meg and George's flat, we had Orlando Bloom, Jonathan Rhys Meyers and Gael all really wanting to do the film,' recalls Parkhill. 'Gael had a body of work whereas, although he was lovely, Orlando didn't; I hadn't seen him in anything. Plus my heart was really always set on Gael. So he came in, he did a reading, we had a chat.'

And that was that, though the fact that Bernal was not only not English, as the script had originally stated, but was actually Mexican threw up a few extra problems, given that his opposite number was to be from Madrid.

'I didn't want two Spanish speakers speaking to each other in English; I don't buy that,' says Parkhill. He ended up turning to his Brazilian director of photography, Affonso Beato, for the solution. 'I asked Affonso, "If you were speaking to someone from Argentina would you speak in English?" He said he would, so Gael became Brazilian.' In the film, his character, Kit, an out-of-work actor, is said to be Anglo-Brazilian.

The other lead role went to Natalia Verbeke, who had previously appeared in the Argentine hit *The Son of the Bride*, among other titles. She plays Carmen, an Argentine who has long lived in Spain (as indeed had the actress) but who has fled an abusive lover to move to London. There she meets the perfect man in Barnaby (played by James D'Arcy), rich, handsome, sensitive and devoted to her. She agrees to his offer of marriage, although she realises he perhaps loves her more than she loves him. Then, on her hen night in a French restaurant, she is instructed to honour the French tradition of kissing a stranger. That stranger turns out to be Bernal.

The kiss is full of passion and inevitably sows seeds of doubt in Carmen's mind. For Kit, it is an equally stirring embrace and he becomes determined to win her heart, tracking her down at work and begging to be given a chance. The film continues in this vein, Carmen torn between the unknown adventure that would be a romance with Kit versus the reliable and secure future promised to her by Barnaby.

The shoot took place in London in 2002 from the end of April to mid-June, over thirty days, shooting five-day weeks, and was fairly straightforward. 'Something I was slightly worried about was that Gael and Natalia had never met,' says Parkhill. 'I was casting blind, not sure what the chemistry was going to be like.' Luckily for Parkhill, it was good. In fact the whole ambience on set was positive.

Along with Bernal, Verbake and D'Arcy, actors Charlie Cox and Tom Hardy were making their debuts. Parkhill recalls: 'Bernal got on very well with Tom and Charlie, they hung out a lot together,' as indeed do their characters in the film.

'It was not like a location movie where everyone is in the same hotel for two months. Everyone went home, then we met up again,' says Parkhill. Bernal had his own house in London at the time. 'But it was a very nice atmosphere. Maybe too nice. When you are a first-timer you sometimes don't put your foot down and say you are not happy with something,' recalls Parkhill, looking back with a hint of regret. 'I was a first-timer so it was kind of nerve-racking in lots of ways for me. I was very in awe of Gael because I knew he was a phenomenal talent. Looking back now, with what I have learned since, perhaps I was too in awe.'

Parkhill, who sees a Marlon Brando quality in Bernal, maybe didn't make the most of his improvisational streak. 'He is very instinctive and often he would come up with stuff: he likes to have the room to work and breathe. But because I was a first-timer, I was concerned with making the day, I was concerned with not using too much footage. What I have learned since as a director is to have a more free approach.'

That said, it was an enjoyable process. 'As a director, I learned a lot from Gael, watching him work. It was the first time for me to see someone who came from a very different tradition from people like James and Tom and Charlie. James was quite structured but Gael was just very, very instinctive. He just had this sense of whether it was or was not working.'

Having a cast of mixed origins throws up other difficulties, as Parkhill admits: 'It is hard work with people for whom English is not their first language because, no matter how good their English is, it is different when you act in a foreign language – the subtext, the intonation. It was one of my big concerns: Are we being understood?' Parkhill says that this was more an issue with Natalia, less so Bernal. 'His English is great.'

The cosmopolitan crowd spread from cast to crew, including Parkhill's Brazilian lensman. Beato had shot many of Pedro Almodóvar's movies and Parkhill was looking for a similar sense of creativity. 'It was a reaction,' explains Parkhill. 'When

I grew up I liked movies to take me away rather than remind me how miserable my life was, I liked movies that were a bit of an escape.' Parkhill also felt that British movies tended to fall into one of two categories: bleak and gritty realist or idealised picture postcard. To this end, there was a self-imposed rule of no obvious landmarks, no black cabs, no red buses. Shot in several locations around London, with exteriors in Shoreditch, Borough and Battersea, the result is a beautifully photographed and moody vision of the capital, if one also slightly magical and hard to pinpoint.

As it transpired, Almodóvar's link to *Dot the i* extended further than his preferred cinematographer. The Spanish director was in the process of casting *Bad Education* and was keen to screen-test Bernal in drag, as Thomson recalls: 'Gael was getting ready to do *The Motorcycle Diaries* immediately after [*Dot the i*] and then the Almodóvar movie. We had one night when Almodóvar came to our set to turn Gael into a woman. He used our make-up artist and Pedro stayed until about three in the morning. Basically he wanted to see what Bernal would look like as a woman – and pretty good he looked actually.'

Parkhill found the visit of one of modern cinema's geniuses to the set of his own debut feature all rather daunting: 'I was nervous I have to say. At that point we were shooting up a stairwell and he [Almodóvar] was downstairs. But I was nervous. What I should have done was go up and say, "Hey, maestro, give me some advice." But of course you are too nervous to do that kind of thing.'

Although Almodóvar's picture perhaps operates on a slightly higher plain, there are similarities between *Bad Education* and *Dot the i*: each one plays with the idea of a film within the film and in both there is rather more to Bernal's character than at first meets the eye.

While most of *Dot the i* is concerned with the quirk of fate that was Carmen encountering Kit, leading to her questioning her proposed marriage, fate is soon banished from the scenario. If you would prefer to watch the film and be surprised for yourself, do skip to the beginning of the next chapter.

The audience gradually realises that it is not being shown the full picture. Regular inserted camcorder footage can only partly be explained by Kit's hobby of filming things. Kit also seems to know rather more about Carmen than might be deemed reasonable. Eventually, Barnaby, the supposed perfect groom, proves not only to be too good to be true but in fact something of a mad professor who has engineered the whole thing in order to make the first true-life film. Kit, it transpires, has been hired as an actor to begin an affair with the unwitting Carmen, while Barnaby's relationship with her had been but a charade all along.

Of course, it is all rather bonkers, wonderfully or infuriatingly so, depending on your opinion. Even those viewers happy to embrace the about-turn must spend much of the movie questioning the film's plausibility, and the sense of dissatisfaction cannot entirely be undone by the sting in the tale. For example, that Barnaby is happy with Carmen walking alone down dark streets despite the probability of her having a stalker can be explained away once we know his true motives, but it can't change the fact that the audience has spent most of the movie feeling unsatisfied and thinking 'how stupid'.

Where the film did get released and reviewed, critics were unkind. Most complained of a twist too many and of the film being not nearly as clever as it thought it was. *Dot the i* is certainly open to accusations of overambition. By its very changing nature, it has to try to be several things at once: starting out as a romantic comedy, it then becomes something of a thriller before reinventing itself as a self-reflexive and self-conscious noir. When you add to the mix the very key factor that the picture is not supposed to be taken too seriously, the identity crisis grows deeper. Audiences inevitably end up confused as to what to think.

Part of the problem for reviewers was the impossible task of discussing the film without giving the game away. When a movie's tone changes almost entirely in its final segment, it is hard to direct those who would enjoy the picture towards it; nor is the film quite good enough to be unreservedly recommended to people under the notion, 'I don't want to spoil it: Go see for yourself.'

One of the movie's harshest critics was actually Bernal himself. Parkhill thinks this could have been avoided if they had waited until the final version was ready to allow Bernal a first glimpse, as opposed to letting him see a work in progress. 'I made a mistake because what we showed him was a very unfinished film and I think that combined with the shock of him seeing himself speaking English. I always regret it and I wouldn't show an actor an unfinished piece of work again, because it is not as you intend it to be.'

Thomson and Parkhill had travelled to Buenos Aires, where Bernal was preparing *The Motorcycle Diaries*, to do a looping and Bernal talked them into allowing him a sneak preview. Thomson remains philosophical: 'I don't think *Dot the i* is Gael's greatest movie by any means but it was a not-quite-done cut which we shouldn't have shown him and, although he did get to see it again in LA, he had decided he didn't really like it and he didn't really back it.' Thomson says that they can't complain: they got lucky in securing Bernal's participation and his simply being in the film helped it get released in many places – in Mexico for example, under the title *Obsesión (Obsession)* – but his promoting it could have made a difference too.

Parkhill, on the other hand, isn't quite so sure. In his view, the fact that *Dot the i* didn't find its audience was in part a consequence of Bernal's involvement. 'That was the blessing and the curse about having Gael. He brings a certain kind of audience, which is quite a highbrow audience, and this was very much intended as a fun film. So I think people came expecting it to be *The King* or *Amores Perros* and it's not; it is supposed to be a piece of entertainment.'

All of which is a shame because, taken with a healthy dose of credulity, *Dot the i* is an enjoyable slice of madcap entertainment. Some audiences – such as the voters of the People's Prize at the Deauville Film Festival – loved it. 'It was a hit in crazy places, like in Lebanon and in Russia,' recounts Thomson. 'It has made all its money back and then some and is actually becoming a little bit of a cult hit on DVD.' This makes sense given that, once you know the twist, you can go back and watch the first part again, safe in the knowledge that it is not all intended to be serious. As Thomson recognises: 'Barnaby is not supposed to be a great film-maker, which is one of the flaws of the early part of the film, because it's kind of meant to be a bit shit.'

Parkhill agrees: 'It was supposed to be a crowd-pleaser, not to take itself too seriously, a little bit of a piss-take of very serious films: a lot of French films are love triangles so it was having a bit of fun with that. It was entertainment but when it came out it ended up at art-house theatres.'

He also takes up the cult theme, explaining that a friend overheard drinkers at a bar in a small town in Alaska reciting lines. Parkhill also reveals the rather delightful news that a Bollywood version has recently been made. As regards the latter development, Parkhill doesn't know whether to laugh or cry: 'I have seen the film and it is terrible. Of course, it is amusing really but then again they have completely ripped off our film shot by shot. I mean, the actor in the Gael role – who doesn't much look like him; not nearly handsome enough – must have really studied the film as he copies his every gesture.' A Bollywood Bernal impostor does indeed have great cult appeal.

Latin American New Wave Part IV: El Nuevo Cine Latinoamericano

The international commercial and critical success of *The Motorcycle Diaries*, following on from the likes of *Amores Perros*, *Y Tu Mamá También*, *The Crime of Father Amaro*, *City of God*, *Nine Queens* and *The Son of the Bride*, had the film world abuzz with talk of a Latin American New Wave. Some commentators dubbed the movement La Buena Onda, which literally translates as 'The Good Wave', although in Mexican-Spanish the phrase also means that something is good fun or cool.

The box-office success these films were having, both domestically and on the international stage, was unprecedented yet in many ways the Latin American New Wave was following in the footsteps of an earlier film movement from the region. In the 1960s and early 1970s, what became known as El Nuevo Cine Latinoamericano (The New Cinema of Latin America) caused quite a splash on the international film circuit.

Not that today's film-makers appreciate the comparison. There is considerable friction between the two camps, the newcomers despairing at the pretentiousness of their forebears, the old brigade denouncing the commercialism of their successors. The likes of Alejandro González Iñárritu dismiss the thought of El Nuevo Cine Latinoamericano as being an inspiration or even influence, but there are parallels in the two movements.

Mexico, Argentina and Brazil have always been the traditional centres of Latin American film-making. All three countries attempted to ape Hollywood's winning formula and establish studio systems, but Tinseltown has always aggressively targeted Latin American audiences and has successfully cornered the market. If a country wanted to acquire the rights to show the latest US smash hit, they could only do so by buying it as part of a package of ten other films, most of them mere fodder. Even the advent of talkies couldn't halt California's progress as the US studios shot Spanish versions of films, subtitled them, dubbed them, did whatever was necessary to maintain the hegemony.

Despite all this, Latin American film aficionados were always aware of and

131

more interested in the latest trends emerging from Europe. As the film-making medium developed, so too did the study and appreciation of the art form: magazines, film clubs and university departments were founded across the continent. From them would emerge a restless breed of cine-literate film-makers.

Following World War Two, European directors began to treat film as a serious art form. Perhaps in keeping with the introspective mood of the time, there was a move away from using cinema merely to entertain: film-makers attempted to use the medium to comment on the world that surrounded them. In Italy, this meant movies which captured the everyday reality of a country trying to recover from the ravages of war. A new style emerged that came to be known as Italian Neo-Realismo, typified by films shot on location with non-professional actors, thus infusing them with a documentary edge. Classics of the genre include Roberto Rossellini's *Roma, Città Aperta* (*Rome, Open City*) and Luchino Visconti's *La Terra Trema* (*The Earth Trembles*), both made in 1945; three years later came Vittorio De Sica's seminal *Ladri di Biciclette* (*Bicycle Thieves*).

Latin American film lovers could not only relate to the sense of struggle on display but also thrilled at the back-to-basics approach. Film-making had become a technically complicated and thus financially draining operation, but these were pictures stripped of special effects.

A few years later, François Truffaut's *Les Quatre Cent Coups* (*The 400 Blows* – 1959) and Jean-Luc Godard's *À Bout De Souffle* (*Breathless* – 1960) burst on to the scene and the French Nouvelle Vague was born. These films were likewise shot on location, usually via hand-held cameras and, rather than the smooth and seamless editing of Hollywood, they favoured jump-cut experimentation. Once again, Latin American film enthusiasts could appreciate that this was a cinema they could produce.

While European fashions influenced Latin American film-makers stylistically, political developments closer to home inspired content.

Up until the 1950s, the cultural agenda in Latin America was generally set by the authorities and so was a representation of what governments wanted the masses at home and observers abroad to see, as opposed to a reflection of how circumstances really were. Cinema was also traditionally subsidised by the state, either due to an appreciation of film's almost magical social power or because regimes saw it as a sophisticated and modern form of culture and its advancement something of a badge of honour.

By the dawn of the 1960s, the environment had begun to change. People started to question those in power and film buffs likewise started to react against the formulaic productions of the state-backed studios. Brazil and Cuba were at the forefront of movements for change in both spheres.

In Cuba in 1954, Fulgencio Batista's military dictatorship banned *El Mégano* (*The Charcoal Worker*), Julio García Espinosa's documentary that looked at the miserable lives of charcoal burners. Fidel Castro then led the Cuban Revolution in 1958 and in 1959 the Instituto Cubano de Arte e Industria Cinematográficos (Cuban Institute of Art and the Cinema Industry – ICAIC) was founded. Its main purpose was to produce propaganda documentaries to educate the masses but creative film-making was also encouraged.

In Brazil, Cinema Novo emerged with Glauber Rocha as its chief spokesman. He gave the clarion call: '*Uma câmera na mão, uma idéia na cabeça.*' (A camera in hand and an idea in the head.) The militant imagery of the camera as gun was hard to miss. In 1964, the military took power in a coup and clamped down on subversive cinema, but Cinema Novo managed to survive as part of a wider artistic movement known as Tropicália, the most recognised contributors to which were the musicians Caetano Veloso and Gilberto Gil. A change of rule within the junta brought increased censorship and persecution in 1968, forcing Tropicália leaders into exile. Rocha himself managed to stick around until 1971 before being likewise forced abroad.

Across the world, the 1960s grew more tumultuous as the decade went on. In 1967, Che Guevara was killed in Bolivia; Martin Luther King was assassinated the following year. Student-led protests sprang up in Paris, at Columbia University in the US, in Mexico, Argentina, Germany, Italy, Czechoslovakia and elsewhere, usually met with heavy-handed police response.

In Latin America, protesters primarily denounced authoritarian law in a cry for political and economical freedom. In 1968, Argentina, Bolivia, Brazil, Paraguay, Peru and Uruguay were all under military dictatorships as well as all the Central American countries besides Costa Rica and Belize. Mexico, meanwhile, was in the grip of the PRI, which has come to be called the 'perfect dictatorship' due to it effectively being an authoritarian rule in all but name.

It was believed that cinema could play a key role in the struggle to overthrow or at least undermine the juntas. In a continent where literacy levels were low, its visual power gave it a particular edge. Film-makers burst on to the scene motivated by social rather than artistic – and especially not commercial – concerns. From such origins emerged El Nuevo Cine Latinoamericano.

As an artistic movement, El Nuevo Cine Latinoamericano was unusual in that it had no recognisable aesthetic or formulaic style. It was purely political in concept and politics dictated not what this new cinema should be but rather what it should not: it would oppose the Hollywood model.

While political dissent focussed on the lack of democracy in Latin America, there was also a strong understanding that dictatorial governments were linked to colonialism and imperialism: indeed, most of the military regimes were supported if not sponsored by the US. Underdevelopment was holding the continent back and this came through economic oppression: unfair terms of trade and exploitation were forever preventing society from advancing.

In many people's eyes, Hollywood was the epitome of the way in which US commercial power suffocated its southern cousins. Hollywood may have reached the top of the pile by combining efficient methods of production with populist content, but it had then imposed its star system and cultural brand via aggressive marketing and its capacity to undercut local producers.

El Nuevo Cine Latinoamericano initially took many forms. In Brazil it was Cinema Novo; in Argentina it began as a Third Cinema (Hollywood productions were considered to be First Cinema, Europe's auteur productions Second Cinema) with a manifesto that demanded films that 'the system cannot assimilate and which are foreign to its needs'; in Cuba there was talk of Imperfect Cinema, the antithesis of the polished Hollywood movie.

Despite the different terminology, they were all essentially banging the same drum and when the continent's movie-makers came together at regional film festivals they were able to fuse their ideas and develop a homogeneous identity.

Films emerged to back up the rhetoric. In Argentina, proponents of Third Cinema Fernando Solanas and Octavio Getino came up with the subversive *La Hora de los Hornos* in 1968. Combative in tone and content, it was made in semi-clandestine conditions and then shown underground. In Bolivia, Jorge Sanjinés addressed the country's excluded Andean people with *Yawar Mallku* (*Blood of the Condor*) in 1969.

Creative movie-making had surged in Cuba once it had become commercially isolated by the US. The result was classics such as *Memorias del Subdesarollo* (*Memories of Underdevelopment*) by Tomás Gutiérrez Alea and *Lucía* by Humberto Solás.

Mexico suffered from the complete opposite set of circumstances, being so close to Hollywood and flooded with its produce. Mexico's contribution to El

Nuevo Cine Latinoamericano was slower to emerge but Alfredo Joskowicz provided *Crates* in 1970, Arturo Ripstein made *El Castillo de la Pureza* (*The Castle of Purity*) in 1972 and Paul Leduc came up with *Reed: México Insurgente* (*Reed: Insurgent Mexico*) in 1973.

Chile ended up something of a case apart. The Unidad Popular (Popular Unity) government of Salvador Allende (1970 to 1973) provided fertile ground for film-making, with the likes of Raúl Ruiz and Patricio Guzmán emerging. The latter had been filming a documentary on the Allende administration for the nine months leading up to General Augusto Pinochet's coup on 11 September 1973. After brief imprisonment, Guzmán was able to escape to France with his film stock. The resulting documentary, *La Batalla de Chile* (*The Battle of Chile*), was as powerful as might be expected. Back in Chile, the Pinochet regime put a stop to all forms of film production, viewing cinema as intrinsically dissident.

Come the 1980s, El Nuevo Cine Latinoamericano was hit by a crisis of confidence and identity. The political climate had changed and, with the notable exceptions of Cuba and Nicaragua, revolutionary fervour had died down. Some of El Nuevo Cine Latinoamericano's key players argued that the movement could reinvent itself, change with the times, but many liberals had gone into exile, both in the cinematic world and broader sphere, and the Latin American left lacked a clear vision or structure.

Most military dictatorships had fallen, replaced by a new breed of politicos who had wangled their ways into the seats of leadership via Washington's assistance, so right-wing governments in favour of the free market held sway. Public debt became a major issue and a series of economic setbacks hit the region as a whole, diminishing governmental financial support in film and negatively effecting cinema attendance. TV and video became the default leisure pursuits with even the poorest households on the continent boasting a television and signal, via the tapping of existing communication lines.

The region's governments were far from models of democratic legitimacy but most had managed to manipulate the system in such a way as to give themselves a semblance of credibility, which reduced the sense of urgency for the Nuevo Cine Latinoamericano movement, at least in the eyes of the international film fraternity. The likes of Ripstein tried to hit back by adopting an ever more artistic approach to film-making, which came up against new prejudices: artsy pieces were considered the near exclusive remit of European directors; Latin America 'did' revolution cinema.

Losing the international audience was important because a major reason why El Nuevo Cine Latinoamericano had failed to truly flourish as a theory or practice was that as a significant social movement it never really reached the masses. Abroad, its anti-imperial stance gave El Nuevo Cine Latinoamericano a political credibility that grabbed attention and greatly aided its appreciation. Back home there was no such novelty element to fall back on. Ironically, local spectators remained faithful to the Hollywood productions that the movement was so vehemently opposing.

El Nuevo Cine Latinoamericano's practitioners, as well as being radicals drawn to activism, tended to be artist/intellectuals from the upper-middle classes. Ultimately this meant that they didn't quite understand the people and their seemingly illogical behaviour. In the less fortunate realms of society, escapism has obvious appeal no matter how well intentioned the experimental new-wave cinema might be. Furthermore, in modern art of every form, concept is too often everything; whereas viewing and taking in a painting, sculpture or installation takes a matter of minutes, a film is long and asks a lot of its audience if concept outweighs content.

The battle to be both of and acclaimed by the people has long been a challenge to artists, but several elements within the Nuevo Cine Latinoamericano movement were not only unconcerned with being popular but actively sought to avoid it, as if popularity was incompatible with credibility.

Crowd-pleasing genres such as the melodrama or costume piece were rejected by proponents of the Nuevo Cine as escapist, distracting from the here and now. As if to hammer a nail in the movement's coffin, Argentina's *The Official Story*, a historic melodrama, was released to much acclaim in 1985, going on to win the Best Foreign Language Film Oscar. Horror was another genre dismissed by the old guard as unworthy but Guillermo del Toro brought it back to life with his acclaimed *Cronos* in 1993.

In the same year that *The Official Story* was picking up its statue, Mexican Felipe Cazal remained true to the art-house cause by making *Los Motivos de Luz* (*The Motives of Light*), an exploration of poverty and exploitation at the bottom of the social scale. Alfonso Cuarón has distanced himself from that particular film and others like it, dubbing them the 'cinema of denunciation'.

For his part, Alejandro González Iñárritu has said that something he and Guillermo Arriaga shared right from the beginning of their collaboration was an intense dislike for those films which seemed to follow the maxim: 'If nobody understands us and nobody goes to see a movie, that must mean it's a masterpiece.'

By way of retort, Ripstein, having seen his *Así es la Vida* (*Such is Life*) completely overshadowed at Cannes by *Amores Perros*, said, 'I don't make films for idiots.'

Cuarón answered similar charges in the wake of *Y Tu Mamá También*. 'It's the mantra of the old guard. If you don't have a naked Marxist ideology then you're a reactionary. If you have a strong story and production values, then you're a Hollywood wannabe. And if you enjoy any success abroad, you're a sell-out,' he told the *Guardian*.

In the same paper, Guillermo del Toro waded into the debate. 'Every time you move a structure that's been sitting on its fat ass for too long, there are going to be loud howls of protest. Critics in Mexico are still stuck twenty years in the past. They're revering a culture that's dead, saying, "Well, it's boring as fucking hell but it must be educational". I subscribe to the culture that's happening now, the one that's alive and letting you fondle it.'

A defining characteristic of the Buena Onda was that films tended to be made by young directors with little in the way of track record. Their arrival on the scene signified a generational changing of the guard. In the same way that Ripstein and the gang had been rebelling against the Hollywood-style Época d'Oro films, now Iñárritu and co were rebelling against Mexico's art-house output of the 1970s.

Yet even by violently reacting against something one is acknowledging its influence; feeling inspired to destroy the old system is still being inspired by the old system. And there were direct links between the two movements too. Many of those who made pictures during the Nuevo Cine Latinoamericano years ended up teaching and thus passing on their knowledge to the next generation through the film schools. While Iñárritu and others did arrive via a different path, the likes of Cuarón, and most of the technicians who formed part of the Latin American New Wave, were film-school graduates. This was also the case in Argentina.

Nor must all generational comparisons be negative: Cuarón is a known admirer of Leduc; in Brazil, Salles is happy to acknowledge a debt to his Cinema Novo predecessors. In crisis-hit Argentina, film-makers improvised with digital cameras, and the rough cinema that emerged became known as *cine piquetero* (picket cinema), which revived the traditions of Third Cinema.

There was less generational friction in Brazil and Argentina than in Mexico, a matter of geography, with Hollywood and its production values that bit further away, and a lack of the sort of continuity that would see Ripstein and Iñárritu present films at Cannes in the same year.

Those at the forefront of the Latin American New Wave wanted their films to be seen by as many people as possible, both at home and abroad, and in this they were defying the previous generation. Having lost the limelight, some of the old guard did begin to sound bitter, which encouraged the new wave to oppose them all the more and embrace commercial success. For the newcomers, film-making was still a passionate choice, often still a political one, but they were a more cosmopolitan and well-travelled bunch than their predecessors, wise to the ways of the world and comfortable and confident with market practices. It is no coincidence that the likes of Salles, Meirelles, Iñárritu and Bielinsky all made commercials before feature films.

Of course, there are ethical arguments against the marriage between responsible, creative film-making and big business. AltaVista, the production company behind *Amores Perros*, is part of the Sinca Inbursa group, which is owned by Carlos Slim Helú. He is said to be the world's richest man, a fact considered vulgar by many given how well it epitomises Mexico's vast inequality. In Brazil, film production is principally financed through oil companies.

The defensive argument is that they have no content control and it is true that *City of God* hardly doubles up as a promo to come and do business in Brazil. Besides, the El Nuevo Cine Latinoamericano brigade were making their radical films with funding from a variety of corrupt and tyrannical governments.

These days, private finance is frequently the only way to get movies made and the Buena Onda's leading players might argue that such partnerships are justifiable in terms of the greater good – ensuring the region still has a cinema industry to speak of – and if that means occasionally teaming up with the corporate world and pandering then so be it.

Likewise, they are fully aware that success at the box office brings with it artistic freedom. In order for Latin America to continue riding its wave, a healthy respect for commercial practices is going to be essential.

The Motorcycle Diaries

Come the turn of the millennium, the only major cinematic treatment of one of the twentieth century's most iconic figures, Che Guevara, had been the rather risible *Che!*, made in 1969 and starring Omar Sharif. It was high time somebody put the big-screen record straight. Meanwhile, Bernal's portrayal of Guevara in the television film *Fidel* was hardly something to be proud of. Bernal was desperate for another chance to do the great man justice. For all concerned, it was to be hoped the makers of *Diarios de Motocicleta* (*The Motorcycle Diaries*) got things right.

In December 1951, Ernesto Guevara, then a 23-year-old medical student, set off with his friend, Alberto Granado, a 29-year-old biochemist, on a journey through South America on the back of an old motorbike. They departed the city of Córdoba, Argentina, and headed to Buenos Aires, to bid farewell to Guevara's family, before dipping south in their own country and then on to Chile. From Chile, they journeyed north to Peru, then worked their way to Colombia and eventually Venezuela, which marked the end of the trip in July 1952.

On their travels they made many discoveries and got into all manner of adventures: they negotiated the continent's huge variety of terrain, from snow-capped mountains to desert to jungle, came across signs of its ancient history at Machu Picchu, and most important of all, came into contact with its people. The social realites of everyday folk, from exploited miners to the workers and infirm in a leper colony, had a huge impact on the two impressionable young travellers.

Both experienced a spiritual and political awakening that would change their lives and give them new purpose. Granado decided to retrain to become a doctor and serve the poor. As for Guevara, he came to view the continent as a fractured whole, its downtrodden people the common victims of injustice and oppression. Two years later, he would meet Fidel Castro – and only then acquire his 'Che' soubriquet – and seven years down the line would take part in the Cuban revolution.

Guevara kept a journal of the trip, a logbook that recorded events and his observations and which would eventually be published as *Notas de Viaje* (*Travel Notes*) in 1993, being retitled the slightly flashier *Diarios de Motocicleta* (*The Motorcycle Diaries*) a few years later. This is the film of that book, or rather the film of that journey, incorporating into its fabric the memories of Guevara's companion, Granado, who also penned a book of the adventure, *Con El Che Por América Latina* (*With Che in Latin America*), published in 1978.

The Motorcycle Diaries film was for many years a work in progress. In 1999, Robert Redford's Sundance Institute, which the previous year had been instrumental in helping Walter Salles make *Central Station*, approached the Brazilian director about adapting *The Motorcycle Diaries* for the screen. Salles was interested but sceptical that such a project would ever get funding. He was right to be cautious as the script ended up being rejected by almost all the US studios.

The majors were reluctant to back it for many reasons: they balked at its unconventional structure – no Act One, Act Two, Act Three here – and its absence of conflict. Salles couldn't contest the first point but argued that there was conflict aplenty, only that it was internal rather than external.

Other drawbacks from a US marketing perspective were more difficult for Salles to paper over. Given both Guevara's and the book's near mythic status, Salles felt that there were certain principles which simply couldn't be compromised: it would have to be made in Spanish with a Latin American cast and crew. Redford, himself a passionate fan of the book, understood and agreed.

Progress was slow – in the meantime, Salles made *Behind the Sun* – but Redford was determined and, bit by bit, the financing fell into place. *The Motorcycle Diaries* ended up being bankrolled by an international co-production formed by South Fork and Sound For Films in the US, FilmFour in the UK, and production houses from Argentina, Brazil, Peru and Chile, important in keeping the Latin American spirit alive. The film would cost US$10 million.

While Redford had been busy with the budget, the young Puerto Rican writer José Rivera, a graduate of the Sundance Institute, had been working all the while on the screenplay. Taking Guevara's and Granado's accounts as core texts, he managed to produce a script of structure, while leaving room for manoeuvre. Salles was keen to have the freedom to adapt to the unexpected once on the road.

To research the film, Salles twice retraced Guevara's and Granado's tracks (and steps once the bike conked out). When setting off on the first trip, he still wasn't sure that the film was truly viable, but he quickly realised that not much had changed in Latin America in the intervening fifty years. In a *Guardian*/NFT interview to promote the film, Salles said, 'I didn't go ahead on *The Motorcycle Diaries* before realising that the reality of South America in 2002/03 was very similar to that described by Ernesto Guevara in his book. The structural problems are pretty much the same, of bad distribution of land and wealth.'

Depressing though such a discovery was in the grand scheme of things, it also reassured and inspired Salles in terms of shooting the film. On the very practical side, it made the job of making a period piece spread over half a continent a lot easier. In creative terms, it meant that they could improvise and work into the movie whatever they might discover on the road. This was important to Salles who had, before going into fiction, been a documentary film-maker for ten years. 'Especially on road movies, you have to leave the door open for things to happen and you have to be ready to absorb the people you meet en route: you have to open yourself up to them and allow them to change the film.'

All this was also relevant to their sense of artistic integrity. If they were going to be portraying the journey of discovery of one of the continent's greatest free spirits, applying the same sense of adventure to making the film as Guevara had to the original trip seemed appropriate as a guiding principle. 'I realised that our own adventure within the continent could somehow mirror what happened to them on a very small scale, and that improvisation was possible,' confirmed Salles. 'We wanted to be faithful both to the book that inspired us and to the spirit of the journey.'

That journey had led Guevara to conclude that he and all Latin Americans were one and the same, so to be faithful to its spirit also meant promoting the continent as a block. Right from the word go, Salles, who himself learned Spanish especially to make the picture, had been adamant that the film's actors and technicians would be representative of the new wave of Latin American cinema that had emerged over recent years. The crew he assembled hailed from Argentina, Chile, Mexico, Peru and Brazil and the post-production team included Argentine Gustavo Santaolalla, the brains behind the soundtrack for *Amores Perros*, and Daniele Rezende, editor of *City of God*. Someone breaking the mould was his cinematographer, Frenchman Eric Gautier.

Of course, the main man of the Latin American New Wave in acting terms was Bernal. He was invited to play Guevara even before *Y Tu Mamá También* had been released (June 2001). 'I met Gael in 2001 when I saw *Amores Perros* and I was very impressed, not only by the viscerality [inner depth] that he had but also his maturity as an actor. Everything was coming from within in a very internalised manner, and that's very rare for an actor of nineteen or twenty years of age,' said Salles at the NFT. 'He does have the capacity to hit you with very light strokes, like gentle rain.'

Bernal continued the drizzle theme when discussing his approach to interpreting Guevara: 'He was a man of few words, bittersweet in his behaviour;

we didn't want to create a character that wasn't true, that was the bet. We wanted an intense humanity but with a light change, like a gentle rain that suddenly has you wet through.'

Che had long been a figure of admiration for Bernal, whose own grandfather had fled the Cuban dictatorship. 'Guevara formed part of my life ever since my father talked to me about him when I was a boy and I understood what the Cuban Revolution signified,' he has said. 'Without it, Latin America wouldn't be what it is now. You can't grow up in Mexico and remain unaware of what happened.'

To prepare the role, Bernal threw himself into the research, reading not only everything that had been written about Che but the books Guevara himself had been reading at that time, William Faulkner in particular. Bernal visited the areas in Argentina that the travellers had grown up in and went to Cuba to meet Che's friends and family. He surveyed letters that Guevara had written on the trip to his mother and girlfriend. On the physical side, two months before the shoot, Bernal began to play football and rugby in order to acquire the Guevara physique, and gorged on polenta. In practical terms, he learned to ride a motorbike. Mastering the 1939 Norton 500 proved a challenge – 'all the controls are on the English side, in reverse' – and Bernal trained on it four times weekly for three months. In mastering the accent, he observed that at that stage, Che was still Guevara and so had yet to acquire a Cuban twang; not only that, he worked out that, although Guevara had been born in Rosario and split his youth between Buenos Aires and Córdoba, it was the Cordobese slant that dominated.

Matthew Parkhill and Meg Thomson, the makers of *Dot the i*, met Bernal in Argentina during the actor's period of preparation and his dedication to the task made an impression on them both. 'Gael is incredibly articulate and when we met him in Buenos Aires he had done so much research on Che and had so many opinions,' recalls Thomson. 'We went out for dinner with him and he talked in depth about the background, the politics,' adds Parkhill.

Incredible thoroughness no doubt helped compensate for nerves: Bernal has admitted to being initially overwhelmed by the responsibility of portraying such an iconic figure. At least he didn't have the added pressure of the real figure being alive and well and ripe for comparison, as with Granado's character. As Salles explained, unlike when casting Guevara, 'I needed to find an actor that could bring to life the Alberto Granado that I knew by that time, and it was so difficult because Alberto Granado is so generous and flamboyant and wonderful and he's also got a certain freshness.'

Rodrigo de la Serna was a theatre actor in Argentina who impressed Salles in a screen test, reminding the director of the Italian greats of the 1960s with his gushing humanity. To play Granado, de la Serna also had to learn to ride the motorbike as well as to tango. He had to put on fifteen kilos in weight and he too read everything he possibly could to practise the role, and of course met with Granado himself.

Alberto Granado was 82 when the film was being made, still fit and healthy and living in Cuba. The team interviewed him several times and were astounded by his strong memory. Granado even ended up joining them on the shoot to offer advice and, in homage, Granado appears at the end of the film before the final credits.

The movie also had the blessing of Che's descendants. 'The Guevara family was very close to the project from the very beginning. They opened the doors of the Che Guevara Institute in Havana, we had access to so many photographs which have never been published, and to letters from that period, and that helped a lot to shape what the film is,' said Salles. The director also appreciated the fact that, although supportive, the family never asked to approve or even see the script but trusted in Salles and the project.

Another resource for his actors, indeed for the whole crew, was a series of seminars that Salles began to organise in Buenos Aires three months before the cameras rolled. Subjects included asthma, leprosy and basic first aid, and then the history, politics and culture of Latin America in the 1950s, both from a continent-wide perspective and one specific to the individual countries on the journey; they watched feature films and documentaries, listened to music, engaged in debate. The intention was not only for them to all understand the era they were portraying but also the mind-set of the people of the time. This was pre-television and ordinary folk then knew very little about what their neighbouring countries looked or felt like. Scholastically, the educated would have studied the Classics but be ignorant of the Incas.

Furthermore, at that time in Argentina, those of Guevara's social class looked to Europe for cultural guidance and opinion. In fact, Latin America was regarded as considerably inferior to the sophistication of the Old World. By choosing to travel in Latin America, Guevara and Granado were quite the pioneers, not just going against the grain but doing something extremely unusual. There were no tourists or backpackers journeying across South America in 1952.

The crew didn't immediately warm to these workshops. 'In the beginning, it was four or five of us while others found the idea especially boring,' said Salles.

'But little by little, they all started to come, and something amalgamated prior to the shoot. Therefore, the shoot itself was very interesting because we were bonding more and more as we progressed, but physically it was very, very difficult as you can probably see.'

Guevara and Granado covered some 13,000 kilometres spanning five countries. Salles and his team didn't go over the exact same terrain on their shoot but Argentina to Chile to Peru is still quite some undertaking. In climatic terms, they moved from sub-zero temperatures in the Andes to the tropical heat of the Amazon jungle.

When filming at a lake in the south of Argentina, Bernal feared for his life, believing himself stricken with hypothermia. Guevara has to wade into an ice-cold lake to retrieve a duck they have shot for their supper. 'It was a stupid thing to do. After two minutes you are freezing but after two more minutes you start to feel that freezing actually feels OK and you start to feel that everything is fine and in that moment you are dying. You're getting hypothermia. It's like a narcotic really,' Bernal told *The Action-Adventure Movie Guide*. 'And then they took me out. I felt cold in this bone, the sternum, incredibly cold and as much as I rubbed I was gasping, not able to breathe. It was a horrendous feeling.'

Apparently, it had snowed just two days before the lake scene was shot. They tended to film in whatever weather circumstances presented themselves, not worrying too much about continuity: in Latin America, weather is volatile and changeable so variation in the film is not only realistic but helps highlight the continent's contrasts.

Salles had done the route twice, the first time as a recce, the second scouting for locations. Wherever possible, they filmed in the same locations where the events themselves took place, that is to say, the places Guevara and Granado had visited themselves.

Logically, they tended to film the road-trip in sequence as they the crew made the journey themselves. Starting to shoot in early October 2002, they were in Bariloche, Patagonia, by the end of the month; late November and they had covered Valparaíso and reached the Chuquicamata copper mine in northern Chile. Unlike the original travellers, the crew then swung back to Argentina, Bernal spending his 24th birthday in Mendoza, then down to shoot some street scenes in Buenos Aires before New Year; on 6 January they reconvened in Peru and then the shoot wrapped in Venezuela in February.

The crew varied greatly in size: they numbered from around a hundred and fifty at the leper colony to no more than fourteen for some of the Andean mountain scenes; twelve crew members and the two actors. This is really the bare minimum, although if Salles wanted to seek out some improvisation opportunities, he, his director of photography and the two leads would scurry off on their own.

Such a tactic led to some of the movie's most memorable scenes, as Salles told his NFT audience: 'The little boy in Cuzco, we found him in the streets, or he found us. He came to us and asked if we wanted to know a little bit more about the city and offered himself as a guide. So we said, "Yes, but can we bring the Super16 camera along?" And he said, "Bring whatever you want." And there it was. That scene, everything is Take One. Nothing was repeated.'

In the movie, in a series of short snippets, a local boy shows them the sights of Cuzco and gives them his tourist spiel while Bernal and de la Serna listen and ask questions as Guevara and Granado.

It was only because Bernal and de la Serna were so in tune with their characters that such impromptu scenes could be used. 'Later that same day we found these Indian women who don't speak Spanish but only Quechua, who also started to talk to Gael and Rodrigo. And the two of them were so immersed in their characters that they were able to improvise freely within the framework of the screenplay.' In said scene, after discussing the life and plight of the eldest of the Quechuan ladies, via translation into Spanish from a younger member of the group, the women share their coca leaves with Bernal and de la Serna. The women instruct the boys how to hold the leaves between their two fingers and to dedicate each mouthful to the mountain where they come from, to thank it for providing for their people. Bernal has described it as the scene most special to him.

According to Salles, some 90 per cent of the characters in the film are non-actors. Blending the professional with the everyday person is no easy business: in order for it to work, for performances to be natural, those participating must be made to feel comfortable in front of the camera. Again, Bernal and de la Serna distinguished themselves. 'You have to work with actors with the talent and intelligence and the generosity of Gael and Rodrigo to achieve that, because it's not something that comes immediately,' explains Salles. 'You have to actually create something behind the scenes and not work specifically on the scenes themselves in order to generate a back story between them, so that you can then recreate something later in front of the camera. And again, the less obtrusive the camera is, and the smaller the crew trying to capture that, the better it is.'

Nowhere was the ability to manage non-actors more important than when filming at the San Pablo leper colony. For those scenes, some one hundred extras were employed, including five actual former patients of the colony. Salles allowed everybody to get familiar and comfortable with one another before setting up any scenes: they organised a football match, jammed on musicical instruments, all to forge a sense of togetherness. 'You need the ties, you need that bond before you can actually go and introduce the camera into their midst,' says Salles. 'You have to respect those people, and not try to steal something. The opposite is true, you have to do it in total synchronicity with them.'

One of the most delightful things about filming at the leper colony, the same one that Guevara and Granados had spent time at fifty years previously, was that some of the patients there remembered and recognised Granados, who had accompanied the crew.

The defining scene of the movie is the final scene at the leper colony: during a party to celebrate his 24th birthday, Guevara decides to swim across the river in the dead of night in order to celebrate with the patients, quarantined on the other side. The river is wide, the currents strong and Guevara a serious asthma sufferer, but he makes it.

It was a challenging scene to shoot, not least because there were piranha fish in the water and they have been known to bite. But Bernal was determined to do the stunt himself. 'The take was in the last days of the shoot and I too was at the end of my personal journey. How could I let an extra do the take which shows the birth of the conscience of Che?' says the actor.

In fact, this scene was the last of the shoot. When Salles called 'Cut' for the final time, the whole crew jumped into the water to join Bernal. They swam in silence, embracing one another and reflecting upon what their experiences on the shoot had taught them. All concerned have described it as a very moving moment.

The harmony between cast and crew generally, seems to have been particularly special, except on Saturdays, their day off, when they would play football and national rivalries – not least Brazilian and Argentinian – would suddenly rise to the fore. Bernal has said, 'Rodrigo de la Serna and I became really good friends. During the film we also had fights about stupid things like the motorbike, but friendship is like that.' He also insists that the most pleasing thing about making the movie was getting to know Walter Salles. The Brazilian director was equally taken by Bernal, praising his intelligence and sense of curiosity.

Salles was also indebted to Bernal's dedication to the cause in getting inside the mind of the young Guevara. 'During the days off or after the shoots, Gael was the first one to go to find out more about what kind of life these people [rural locals] were living. In doing so, he was mirroring what Guevara had done fifty years earlier,' says Salles. 'He was reading the same books, Camus, Céline. That kind of predisposition really created a situation which made me consider him one of the co-authors of the film.'

For his part, Bernal felt that, 'It was a film where, if I'd been a bit detached from it, it would have been a useless experience. You had to give yourself and transform yourself as the two guys on that journey transformed themselves.'

That said, he found it tough going at first, doubting he was worthy of the task. Some simple advice from Guevara's travel companion helped him find his feet. 'It helped me a lot that in the break of one scene Alberto Granado said to me, "Do it in your voice," and I realised that in 1952 Ernesto and Alberto were just young Latin Americans aged twenty-three and twenty-nine,' says Bernal, 'therefore, as I was a twenty-three-year-old Latin American, I had the same strengths and platform to tell this story.'

It perhaps helped Bernal identify with this journey towards self-awareness that he arrived on set in a fairly introspective mood himself; he has stated that he was single and going around in circles as far as relationships were concerned, travelling a lot. 'I tried to stay true to the idea of showing the internal geography of Guevara at twenty-three years old, when a boy becomes a man. I have to confess that on finishing the film I felt myself a different person to the Gael who started filming a few weeks before,' he said. 'For me there is a before and after of this film.'

Salles believed the sentiment could be applied to them all: 'This is a film made by people who were not the same at the end of the journey – we were completely transformed by it.'

Of course, going on a trip, discovering new places and tasting different cultures, is an experience that has altered many a young traveller. Yet it has to be acknowledged that so specifically reliving Che Guevara's epic journey is not your average gap-year experience and the significance of the adventure cannot help but have made a particularly strong impression.

What's more, it was not so much the differences but the common ground that seems to have had the bigger impact on Bernal: 'Che invited me on a journey in which I lost myself and therefore found my true self. He helped me to contextualise myself as a Latino. To prove there are no borders. Mexicans, Chileans, Peruvians, Argentines . . . we are all one,' Bernal told *Fotogramas*. 'Right now I, as did he, consider that we all belong to the same mestizo race and the borders seem to me to be fictitious and illusionary.'

Again, Salles made a similar observation about the group as a whole: 'It's a film made by young Argentinians, Chileans, Peruvians, Mexicans, Brazilians . . . so it's really a family effort, a collective effort. And a lot of us didn't know very much about our own continent.'

One of the film's most stirring scenes takes place at the leper colony just prior to Guevara's heroic swim when he gives a stirring speech. 'We believe, and after this journey more firmly than ever, that the division of America into unstable and illusory nations is completely fictional. We constitute a single mestizo race, which from Mexico to the Magellan Straits bears notable ethnographical similarities.'

He goes on to propose a toast to Peru and to a united Latin America.

Bernal concurs: 'We have to get back together, and understand and accept that we are countries that were created out of colonial caprices, we are countries that were not necessarily meant to be. It was the church that decided where the countries' borders would be, so there's nothing we can do but keep on searching and fighting.'

Sounding more and more the revolutionary in his NFT/*Guardian* Q&A he added:

> Throughout our history, there's a sense of cycles repeating – of violence, of people with privileges overthrown by those without privileges who want those privileges for themselves. That doesn't mean justice. In Latin America, we have the same problems everywhere – in some places it's more evident than others. We have the same inconsistencies, we share the same failed, neo-liberalist dreams. And we share the same sense of disgust with what democracy has given us. But we share the same hope as well that things will work out.

That Bernal appeared to have undergone a similar transformation as had Guevara himself was no affectation as part of some marketing wheeze, nor merely a happy coincidence: such sentiments were genuine and evidence that the movie-makers had been successful in their approach.

The film was a depiction of Guevara before he had become Che: that is to say, before he had become the idealistic guerilla that established his legend. Yet the young man who set off on the back of Granado's motorbike was the same man who took part in the Cuban Revolution and who was gunned down in the Bolivian jungle while attempting to launch another militia-inspired overthrow of power. The trick was to balance the one with the other: to show that the young Guevara in the movie would one day become the guerilla leader but not to play on the myth; that his political ideas were emerging but were not yet fully formed.

Salles has said that he would never attempt to make a biography of Che because there is just too much to cover in a two-hour time frame. But he was also fond of quoting the great Argentine writer Jorge Luís Borges, who believed that every man in every single moment of his life is everything that he has already been and everything that he will become. Therefore, Salles strove to show that in the film, 'there was already something in him anticipating the man who would implode the limits of his social class, and play a definite role in our continent, of Latin America'.

For the director, the key was to focus on the human dimensions of the two characters in order to get to the man behind the Che myth. This meant including the humour, which is such a part of both books. It also meant showing a doubtful and insecure side to Guevara, the younger and less mature of the pair. Thus the film makes a virtue of Guevara's honesty – only he is prepared to tell the patient that he is terminally ill, to tell a doctor that his novel is unreadable – but, as Bernal acknowledged, 'he also wanted to screw the mechanic's wife'.

Nevertheless, many critics felt that the movie's attempts to show a warts-and-all Guevara were token at best. Che was a principled man of strong ideals but he was also a violent guerrilla and ruthless military leader. The film regularly shows Guevara's struggles with his asthma but, although the adrenaline shots he would use to treat it are said to have caused mood swings and temper tantrums, this opportunity to explore Che's darker side is not taken. The best we get is a stone thrown by Guevara at a truck.

While latter traits, such as a supposed authoritarian streak and a sense of the egocentric, probably came as a consequence of his rise through the revolutionary ranks, that a fire raged below the surface in the young Guevara is known. In the film and books, for example, the nickname Granado calls him by is not Che but

'Fuser', from 'Furibundo Serna' (Furious Serna – from his full name Ernesto Guevara de la Serna), a moniker acquired as a consequence of the aggressive way he played rugby.

That such aspects of his character were not explored frustrated many who had assumed that the whole point of a serious attempt to understand the formation of an icon was for it to be bold in confronting his less savoury side. This was surely especially the case for a man as complex and contradictory as was Che.

Many commentators wondered why such timidity. Who were they afraid of upsetting? Could it be that the film-makers themselves were wary of getting too close to Guevara for fear of not liking who they found him really to be? In the same way that Che's martyrdom wiped his flaws from memory, allowing him to become a politically-correct fashion icon adorning T-shirts and posters, so too the film pays testimony to the myth, not the man.

Yet most observers gave *The Motorcycle Diaries* the benefit of the doubt. Considering the politics at play, the film avoids being preachy and does its best to steer clear of amateur-psychology hindsight. If the leap from charming young man to live-wire guerilla leader seems a big one, well, we are dealing with one of the most remarkable figures of the twentieth century.

The awakening of Guevara's social conscience is teased out rather than clumsily forced home: in two moments of giving, he hands over his travel budget to a victimised communist couple and donates his own asthma medicine to a dying old lady. The trip to the leper colony then provides the context for his thoughts to finally come together as something tangible. For his part, it is life at the colony that persuades Granado to retrain as a doctor.

Guevara is appalled that the hospital is located on one side of the river, the patients kept on the other. Hence why he plunges into the river to visit them and symbolically reunite them. As we have heard, filming the sequence, or rather finishing filming it, proved a cathartic moment for the crew, but the scene comes across as rather sentimental to the viewer. This is largely because – given our need for Act One, Act Two, Act Three – presented as the dramatic climax to the film, it falls slightly short.

Salles blends images of everyday folk into the movie. Accusations of sentimentalism are again valid, either on the film-maker's part or, perhaps more cleverly, from Guevara's perspective.

A cynic might even look at the overall story and mock the fact that the privileged Guevara and Granado fell into shock when first they encountered poor people. But the pair, the film and the material deserve more respect than that. For starters, the film draws attention to their backgrounds at the outset: they are guests at the well-to-do hacienda where Guevara's girlfriend lives and their observance of social manners here contrasts well with their lack of materialism once on the road.

As for Salles' use of the real-life, it is not a question of exoticism but rather of context. Furthermore, it might reasonably be argued that the very act of using contemporary documentary footage in a film set fifty years ago makes a valid and rather powerful point in itself.

The fact of the matter is, for better and for worse, Latin America is a land of enormous contrasts – in landscape, social strata and history – and this makes for spectacular imagery. The film is also beautifully photographed by Gautier.

Overall, Salles' direction was widely celebrated for its sleight of hand and its patience in letting the two heroes find and prove themselves. Given the Brazilian's admiration for the way his leads were so easily able to slip into their characters, it is little wonder their performances were praised for their naturalness. Their ability to work with and bounce off one another was also appreciated: Bernal brought a sense of naivety to Guevara while de la Serna conveyed the more confident charisma of Granado.

Bernal's work was particularly praised for the way in which he emanated the idealism of Guevara but also allowed a sense of his seriousness to shine through. It was seen as a subtle depiction, appropriately ambiguous. Salles was evidently satisfied: 'I'm not a big fan of "performance" in acting. On the contrary, I prefer what comes in layers, not what is spelled out, and I think that Gael has that quality.'

The movie itself gained many plaudits. It premiered at Cannes, where Salles, de la Serna and Bernal were joined on the red carpet by Celia Guevara (Che's daughter) and Alberto Granado himself. Another guest was Gael's mother, Patricia Bernal, who cried tears of joy after the film received a ten-minute standing ovation. It ended up scooping the Ecumenical Jury Prize, which rewards cinematic achievement along with ethical and deeply human qualities. Elsewhere, it went on to pick up the Bafta for Best Film Not in the English Language, as well as being nominated for Best Film outright and Bernal getting a Best Actor nod, won an Oscar for Best Original Song (*'Al Otro Lado Del Río'* – 'The Other Side Of The River' by Jorge Drexler) and was nominated for Best Adapted Screenplay.

Latin American New Wave
Part V: Buena Onda

With Walter Salles on his travels, it fell to others to keep the Latin American New Wave torch burning in Brazil. Fernando Mereilles and Kátia Lund obviously did so with *City of God*, and *Carandiru*, another crime-ridden flick, kicked up a storm a year later (released locally in 2003 and in the UK in 2004).

Unlike the rest of the movement's directors, Hector Babenco was a member of the old guard. Born in Argentina, Babenco headed to Brazil in the 1960s and, apart from a stint in Spain, has remained there ever since. In 1981 he made the acclaimed *Pixote*, about a Brazilian boy living by his wits through petty crime on the streets of São Paulo. Over twenty years later, the criminals are behind bars in *Carandiru*, Babenco's portrait of life inside one of Latin America's most notorious prisons.

Structured as a series of vignettes, *Carandiru* tells the stories of how its prisoners arrived inside and the survival instincts they cultivate once there. It ends with a re-enactment of the 1992 massacre, when police officers stormed the jail to break up a riot and killed 111 inmates in the process.

With a US$5 million budget, *Carandiru* was then the most expensive Brazilian film ever made. Babenco managed to get permission to film inside the real Carandiru prison, in north São Paulo. Not long after filming and before the movie was released, Carandiru was knocked down, the better to defuse the furore about its administration, policing and overcrowding.

It is at once very different and very similar to *City of God*. At times as colourful and energised as its predecessor, *Carandiru* is slightly more measured although less a complete work. Both tackle the same issues of crime and violence in unflinching fashion.

Other Latin American films were also keeping the movement ticking over. From Argentina, a number of directors who had caused a splash with first films had similar success with their next offerings: Lucrecia Martel's *La Niña Santa* (*The Holy Girl*) combined religion and sexual awakening to great acclaim; Carlos Sorin's *Bombón: el Perro* concerned a middle-aged man down on his luck until he is donated a stud bulldog; Pablo Trapero's *Familia Rodante* was a road movie wherein the grandma of a family forces the whole extended clan on a journey in a camper van but, rather than draw them closer, the adventure pushes them further apart.

Another key figure, Fabián Bielinsky, sadly died prematurely: after following up *Nine Queens* with *El Aura* in 2005, he had a heart attack and died one year later, just 47 years old.

Out of Uruguay, Pablo Stoll and Juan Pablo Rebella followed up the 2001 festival hit *25 Watts* with *Whisky* in 2004, a downbeat, quirky account of two middle-aged brothers meeting for their mother's memorial service after many years' estrangement. One of the brothers, in an attempt to make his life seem more impressive to his sibling, persuades a female employee from his sock factory to accompany him and pretend to be his wife.

As for Mexican fare, Carlos Reygadas' *Japón* won the New Directors Award at the Edinburgh Film Festival and much praise across the festival circuit as a whole. It is an original piece of film-making with its own cerebral style, far more artsy than other recent film's from the region's canon. A man in his sixties heads into remote and rural Mexico in order to end his life, although the act takes longer to build up to than expected.

His follow-up, *Batalla en el Cielo* (*Battle in Heaven*) was similarly left-field. An unappealing chauffeur to a military general is involved in a series of deaths and has sex with the general's daughter at the brothel she works at for kicks. Reygadas certainly makes love-it or loathe-it cinema but there is no doubt that he is one of the most individual creative talents around.

Reygadas is as eccentric as his films. Of wealthy stock, he was sent to public school in Yorkshire for a year in his teens where he developed a love of cricket and rugby. Then, after graduating in law in Mexico City and studying at the London School of Economics, he worked for Mexico's foreign service in Brussels. Frustrated with the desk job, he decided to pursue his passion for films. Yet he says that most films, at least all those designed to tell a story, bore him. For his own productions, he uses non-actors and refuses to tell them the plot, such as there might be one, or read the script.

Another slightly off-the-wall picture from Mexico was *Temporada de Patos* (*Duck Season*), the debut of Fernando Eimbcke and a slow-burner comedy of a Sunday in the life of two teenage friends in a flat who end up being joined by a female neighbour, who has come to bake a cake, and a pizza delivery boy.

The sheer variety of films bracketed among the Latin American New Wave made many people question whether talk of a movement was justified. Some observers believed the labelling of the Buena Onda to be no more than media hype: the press are always keen to spot a new trend and enjoy pigeonholing artistic works for the convenience of writing a story.

Alfonso Cuarón was one of the sceptics: 'It is not a wave. It is about extremely talented individuals. A wave signifies a movement. A trend. A group of people working together. That is not the case.'

While that is not entirely true – Cuarón, del Toro and Iñárritu consulted each other even before they formed a production team together; Bernal alone has worked with Cuarón, Iñárritu, Salles, Meirelles and Babenco – it cannot be argued that any collective effort went into making *Amores Perros* and *Nine Queens*, both of which surfaced in 2000.

It is true that there was no conscious decision or effort to produce movies as part of an overall strategy or body of work, nor have the *cineastas* involved ever announced the arrival of a new set of film-making principles, let alone declared loyalty to a Latin American movement. Without physical production links or a collaborative manifesto, can it be justified to speak of a Latin American New Wave, let alone call it La Buena Onda?

Iván Trujillo, director of Mexico's UNAM Filmoteca (National Centre of Film Studies and Archives), comes at the question from a slightly different angle: 'On a literary level they had the same discussion as to whether there was a Latin American movement or not a number of years ago. At least then you could argue that readers did consume lots of Iberoamerican literature. But we [in Mexico] don't get to see many Argentinian films nor in Argentina do they watch many Mexican films. There are some co-productions out of obligation but I don't know if really it is a movement or just an abundance of talent.'

Salles made a similar point at the NFT, saying that he was only able to see Argentinian films *El Bonaerense* and *La Ciénaga* outside of Brazil. But Salles did get to see them. If it is true that consumers are being denied the chance to participate in a potential movement, film-makers travel to festivals and usually eventually catch up with the movies that are out there. Indeed Salles was quoted in *O Estado do São Paulo* saying: 'Alejandro Iñárritu and Alfonso Cuarón have said that *Central Station* influenced *Amores Perros* and *Y Tu Mamá También* and I can say that both those films helped with *The Motorcycle Diaries*.'

While *Amores Perros* is more commonly cited as ushering in the Latin American New Wave, in part because it burst off the screen and on to the scene, it would perhaps be fairer to give the credit to Walter Salles' *Central Station*, released two years earlier. After becoming a rare domestic smash hit in its home market, the movie pulled in the punters the world over. In terms of the British market, *Central Station* arrived in 1999 but *Amores Perros* didn't surface until May 2001. There was then a Latin American film of huge impact each year: *Y Tu Mamá También* in 2002; *City of God* in 2003; and *The Motorcycle Diaries* in 2004.

Those films were connected in that they fed off one another, making the most of the momentum and interest in Latin American cinema that other movies had caused. They were able to do this because, despite their differences in terms of origin, common traits could be detected by audiences.

That they are all in some way politically engaged is perhaps the most obvious link. As Mexican producer Rosa Bosch is quoted as saying in the opening lines of *The Faber Book of Mexican Cinema*: 'Sometimes these things are just moments in time, linked to specific political, social or cultural situations. It's not only that there were a bunch of film-makers.'

That many of the principal and pioneering films cited triumphed in their domestic markets was certainly to do with particular moments in time: *Amores Perros* was released two weeks before the PRI lost its seventy-year stranglehold on power; *City of God* hit screens as Brazil prepared to elect Lula, its first-ever socialist president; *Nine Queens* anticipated the on-coming drama of an Argentinian economic crisis.

Audiences were eager to embrace local films examining local issues because these were times of introspection. What *Amores Perros*, *City of God* and *Nine Queens* have most in common is their unflinching and very immediate depiction of reality.

The realities tended also to be at life's margins. The likes of *Historias Minimas* and *The Motorcycle Diaries* showed depressed rural areas, the latter highlighting the disgraceful lack of progress in the last fifty years. Elsewhere, Fernando Mereilles has told of how he made *City of God* for an urban middle-class audience, to shock them into facing the truth of favela life on their doorsteps. It is also interesting that *Amores Perros* and *Y Tu Mamá También* were the first Mexican films to fully embrace *chilango*, the coarse slang spoken on Mexico City streets. Buena Onda films like to look at life on the edge, the most downtrodden parts of an underdeveloped continent.

Inequality is such a part of the fabric of Latin America that it is reflected in almost every element of daily life. Therefore inequality and, by extension, its causes cannot but help find their way into the region's films. In this way, seemingly personal stories almost inevitably become allegorical: what motivates characters to act will be linked to their personal circumstances which, for better or worse, will be a product of an imperfect society.

A near uniform theme in Buena Onda cinema is the failure of the state to assume and manage its responsibilities, be it through neglect, incompetence or corruption. This is often reflected by the absence of a father figure. In *Central Station,* young Josué goes in search of the father he has never known but fails to find him; in *Amores Perros*, papa is either conspicuously missing or making a mess of things; in *Y Tu Mamá También*, there is a complete lack of engagement between padres and their children. In each such case, the metaphor is likely intentional but in *City of God* it is more straightforward: zero state support in the favelas creates a desperate environment in which young men without hope end up shooting each other; fathers are absent because they are dead.

The missing father figure can often be equated to economic factors too – a lack of opportunity leading to migration, family tension or crime – and the same can be said for corruption, another fundamental of Latin American daily life and film. That the police are not policing the favelas as they should do in *City of God* (or especially in its successor *Tropa de Elite* – The Elite Squad), or are mediating between hit men and clients in *Amores Perros*, is emblematic of a society in which officers are poorly paid and where inequality and limited prospects either force people into desperate measures or create a climate in which fear of losing what you have got trumps standing up for justice.

This appetite for tackling meaty topics is perhaps unsurprising. Latin American countries may still not always be (arguably rarely are) governed by those with their people's best interests at heart, but oppressive military dictatorships are now a thing of the past. Restrictions on civil liberties and censorship have all but been discarded and, in a manner that might be compared to post-Franco Spain, the continent's cultural commentators are embracing their right to criticise, making up for lost time.

Y Tu Mamá También and *The Crime of Father Amaro* may have run into trouble with the more conservative elements of Mexican society but there was never any real suggestion that their releases would be prohibited.

At his talk at the NFT, Salles addressed the theme: 'We live in a freer society. You have to realise that twenty years ago part of the continent was living under horrible military dictatorships. If cinema has burgeoned, it's also thanks to the fact that democracy – not economic democracy but at least political democracy – has returned to a great part of the continent. And this allows us to express what we're feeling as film-makers and to try to provide a reflection of that on the screen.'

Despite new-found freedoms, Brazilian films *City of God*, *Carandiru* and *Ônibus 174*, as well as recent Latin American pictures generally, are all careful not to offer a definite message. While it is hard to think of a triumphant Latin American New Wave film, they rarely judge the state of things, preferring simply to show social injustices and communities breaking down. They trust their audiences to reach their own conclusions.

By avoiding being preachy, these films have forced viewers to think through the complex problems facing these complex countries. Unlike in the days of the dictatorships, enemies are harder to define. Arguably the films offer no real solutions because they can't come up with any – or because there are none.

Latin American New Wave films managed to engage domestic audiences only by regaining their trust. This has been achieved by telling it like it is but also by raising the bar in technical terms too. Until recently, domestically made movies were considered inferior products. Choosing foreign fare in Latin America is sometimes snobbishly considered a sign of refined taste, but sometimes it is merely an act of consumer choice, an acknowledgement that, in many matters of industry, the region lags behind.

Bernal touched on this in his appearance at the NFT. 'I feel that in Mexico there's an absurd perception [of conservatism]. We're only conservative until we realise we're not. You know, Mexico really isn't. *Amores Perros* and *Y Tu Mamá También* are not films you'd think of as big box-office and yet they were huge hits in Mexico. And so I think that in many ways society there [Mexico] is much more advanced than it's thought to be.'

Latin Americans have long been told to embrace the modern and reject the old in order to progress: modern usually meant all things US. Increasing local pride and an understanding of the globalised world have been married with growing resentment towards the US and multinational companies generally. This has led to increased loyalty for local products and, in terms of cinema, has helped bring audiences back to watching Latin American films. This sort of mobilisation against the Hollywood flick is precisely what El Nuevo Cine Latinoamericano strove for but failed to achieve.

The region's films have not only begun to match the production values of their Hollywood counterparts but the most successful have surpassed them. Both *Amores Perros* and *City of God* were accomplished pieces of film-making, slick and stylish visually but also innovative in format and with pumping original soundtracks to boot. They could and would hold their own against anything being made anywhere.

Buena Onda pictures played well at home and abroad because they were able to shape specific national realities into universal themes. The colour and flavour may be local but topics such as animal instincts in human behaviour (*Amores Perros*), sexual awakening (*Y Tu Mamá También*) and coming of age (*The Motorcycle Diaries*) are perennial, understood and related to the world over. Drug-gang warfare in the favelas (*City of God*) is undoubtedly a problem specific to Brazil but lack of opportunity as a cause for crime is an issue that transcends borders.

It is universality that co-producers look for when considering whether to support a project. Placing local problems in a universal context plays well with domestic audiences who are comforted by the fact that their troubles are not unique. Meanwhile, foreign audiences enjoy being able to relate to issues as they gain entry into a so obviously alien world. And they do look for a touch of the alien, or at least the exotic, from Latin America. Ignorant clichés should not be encouraged but the continent is a fantastic mix of landscapes, customs and people and can't help but project a sense of mystery for the outsider.

The Latin American New Wave brigade also understood that international audiences – and thus international producers – expected Latin American films to follow the original El Nuevo Cine Latinoamericano blueprint and be radical and rebellious. The political climate had changed and so it was no longer appropriate to make films as a call to arms, but there were still injustices to draw attention to, shocking realities that could be revealed.

'A lot of Latin American movies succeed because we have so many real social issues to deal with and, because we have to address these problems, our films will always kick you in the balls,' said Iñárritu. 'Our films are more relevant because, even though our work might not be so technically perfect, it comes right from deep in the gut. I sweat and bleed my country and no matter what I do I cannot escape that and even though Mexico can give me a lot of pain it is in everything I do.'

In so-called developing countries, the business of film-making, just like any number of other non-fundamental sectors of the economy, is unlikely to flourish. The Buena Onda players may have understood the commercial workings of cinema but making a fast buck was never the attraction of getting involved. 'In Mexico everybody makes movies for all the right reasons, none of which are to get rich,' said Alfonso Cuarón. 'In [the United States of] America there is so much money and it is a film industry. In Mexico it is not. In Mexico we make cinema because we love it.'

Speaking in the *Independent*, Bernal agreed: 'We tend to make films because we believe in the project and not the pay cheque. Money has never been there so it is not a consideration. And that is why we make films that mean something or say something worthwhile. It is not only about the box office.'

What all these observations reveal more than anything is that, rather than specifically in the film-making, it is the Latin American countries themselves which have a great deal in common. Sadly, this too often means sharing the same problems. As trying to make sense of problems is a basic principle of any art form, it is only natural that films in Latin America have been thematically similar.

Bielinsky recognised such links: 'We are all Latin American. We share similar problems and a similar heritage. We've all suffered under colonialism. We're all little industries trying to connect with the wider world. Artistically, I think we share the same social smell, too.'

That these films have been so darned well made is more a matter of coincidence. Across the region, film schools have churned out a generation of extremely talented individuals in all aspects of film-making, acting and directing most evidently but in many other technical areas too, not least photography.

Those involved in the continent's film industry have never sought to develop a common approach, and cross-border collaborations such as there have been are probably a by-product of globalisation more than regional film-making unity.

Yet the Latin American New Wave's movers and shakers are close, regularly interact, support and remain loyal to one another and, although they may never have come together officially to discuss them, their concerns and aims are invariably the same. Therefore, although it may have been a happy matter of chance, it is fair to talk about a Latin American film movement of the past decade – and the Buena Onda seems as good a name to give it as any.

Bad Education

In *La Mala Educación* (*Bad Education*), Bernal was presented with the opportunity of a lifetime: the lead role in the latest offering of one of modern cinema's true auteurs, Spanish director Pedro Almodóvar. And what a juicy role it was – or rather several roles, such was the complexity of Bernal's part.

He plays Juan, an out-of-work actor who pretends to be his own brother and ends up scooping the part of a transvestite in a film within the film. Such is the intercutting and overlapping nature of *Bad Education* that these distinctions take time to emerge.

The story starts in 1980. Madrid is in the midst of the *movida*, its hedonistic heyday, catching up on all the fun that had been missed out on under General Franco's dictatorship (he died in 1975). A twentysomething actor (played by Bernal) enters the office of film director Enrique Goded (Fele Martínez) claiming to be Ignacio Rodríguez, Enrique's long-lost former school chum and first love. This supposed Ignacio, now going by the stage name of Ángel Andrade, hands Enrique a script called 'The Visit' based to begin with on the true story of their schooldays at a morally corrupt Catholic college then imagining what might have happened to the protagonists in later life.

As Enrique reads the script, he starts to visualise it as a film with Ignacio (Bernal) as the lead: in the story, Ignacio has become a transvestite who performs in cabaret clubs and who returns to their former school to take revenge on Father Manolo, the priest who became infatuated with him, sexually abused him and, in a pique of jealousy, arranged for Enrique's expulsion all those years earlier. Before deciding to make the movie, Enrique learns that Ángel is not in fact Ignacio but Ignacio's younger brother, Juan: Ignacio had died several years earlier. Intrigued by the enigma that is Juan, Enrique starts to make the movie anyway. Once filming ends, the plot thickens yet further when Father Manolo, now a publisher called Berenguer, shows up to explain to Enrique what really happened to Ignacio in later life and how Juan is implicated in his death. This tale is told in flashback, with Bernal as Juan alongside Francisco Boira as the real Ignacio.

So Bernal's part is effectively three roles: he starts off as Ignacio, or at least Ángel pretending to be Ignacio; he is then Zahara, the transvestite portrayed by Ángel in the film, 'The Visit'; finally he is Juan, Ignacio's brother. Given such intricacies, it is little wonder that casting the part initially proved problematic.

Almodóvar has something of a reputation as a perfectionist when it comes to getting the vision in his head up there on screen. What's more, he was particularly loath to compromise on this one, given that *Bad Education* was such a personal work: it was based on a short story he had written as an angry young man. Like Enrique, Almodóvar was a successful director working out of Madrid in the 1980s (Almodóvar's first feature, *Pepi, Lucy, Bom y Otras Chicas del Montón* (*Pepi, Lucy, Bom and Other Girls Like Mom*) was released in 1980); Almodóvar also attended a Catholic college where the teachers took advantage of the boys, although the director has said that he himself was not abused.

So everything had to be just right, especially as regards the lead role or three, one of which required a sex change. Finding the right man for the job inevitably proved taxing.

Of the hundred-plus actors Almodóvar screen-tested in drag (essentially every Spanish actor who fell in the right age bracket), Eduardo Noriega, who had worked with the director previously on *Carne Trémula* (*Live Flesh*), came closest to fitting the bill. El Deseo, the production company Almodóvar heads with his brother, even released publicity shots of Noriega as a transvestite. However, Almodóvar wasn't completely satisfied and his perfectionist streak won out. Though Noriega's face fitted – 'the prettiest of them all', Almodóvar would later say – his shoulders were too broad, making him just too damn masculine. Exasperated by his fruitless search, Almodóvar shelved the whole idea and made *Hable Con Ella* (*Talk to Her*) instead. Not a bad idea as it turned out: it scooped him an Oscar for Best Original Screenplay.

Then Bernal arrived on the scene. 'He was very attractive as a boy and a girl and this was essential in order to understand the relationship his character has with everyone else, the intensity with which everyone obsesses over him,' Almodóvar said when publicising the movie. 'The advantage of Gael is that as well as being *guapo* [good-looking] he is very small. He is one of the most photogenic people I know. I studied his face millimetre by millimetre and I discovered that one side was more coarse, one more feminine, depending upon where you positioned the camera. This asymmetry served us very well given the man–woman nature of his character.'

The other advantage to Bernal was that, given his experiences on *Y Tu Mamá También* and *The Crime of Father Amaro*, he was unlikely to flinch when making a film which some might consider controversial because of its themes of homosexuality and child abuse within the church.

Indeed, a dream opportunity, but what a complicated part. In one particularly multidimensional scene, Bernal is actually Juan (going by the stage name of Ángel) passing himself off as Ignacio, who is performing in a film the role of a transvestite called Zahara, who is herself impersonating Sara Montiel (a Spanish silver-screen star of the 1960s). Tackling so many layers was no easy task, as Bernal wryly told *Fotogramas* magazine when they asked if it was the strangest film he had ever worked on: 'Well, I had to play a multiple character, put on an accent, change sex without it seeming forced and place myself inside characters whose cultural baggage I don't share.'

Few roles can ever have required such levels of preparation. For starters, although Bernal fitted the bill, he wasn't guaranteed the part until he could prove himself capable of imitating a Spanish accent: Almodóvar was adamant that the character had to be unambiguously Spanish; the character was complex enough without adding any nationality confusion to the mix.

In terms of cracking the accent, Bernal worked from February 2003 until the start of the shoot in June with several different voice coaches to help ensure that his words tripped off the tongue in Castilian as opposed to *chilango*.

But it wasn't merely a matter of perfecting the lingo: his body language had to be Spanish too. Bernal took flamenco dance classes, not because there is a *gitano* musical number in the film but to help him learn to walk the Iberian walk.

Once he had fully acquired his Spanish airs, the next stage was to learn how to camp them up and to turn his attention to becoming a woman. To this end, Bernal studied the films of Barbara Stanwyck, a true Hollywood *femme fatale*, as well as Almodóvar's previous leading ladies, Carmen Maura and Victoria Abril, with whom Bernal had worked on *Sin Noticias de Dios*. Bernal also looked for inspiration from Alain Delon's sexually ambiguous performance in the 1960 film *Plein Soleil* (*Blazing Sun*).

However, Bernal's primary point of reference was the aforementioned 1960s' screen star Sara Montiel, whom he would have to impersonate. In a flashback sequence, Ignacio and Enrique go to the cinema as boys to watch Montiel in the 1969 film *Esa Mujer*; later on in *Bad Education*, Bernal (as Ángel acting in the 'The Visit') has a scene in which he gives a drag-queen performance singing '*Quizás, Quizás, Quizás*', a musical number from *Esa Mujer*. Bernal took classes from Sandra, a transvestite Montiel impersonator from the Babylon gay cabaret in Madrid; in *Bad Education*, Bernal (as Ángel preparing for 'The Visit') likewise goes to a cabaret to observe and ask for help from Sandra, who plays herself.

Bernal has compared the difficulty of mimicking a Spanish icon like Montiel in a Spanish film as akin to someone not from Mexico trying to tell him about tequila. A lack of cultural insight was a major barrier: 'Maybe I could play a Caribbean transvestite or one from Veracruz [in Mexico], but a Spanish drag queen from 1977 – I didn't have the slightest idea how to do it,' Bernal would later explain.

Factor in Almodóvar's stubborn high standards and the whole charade becomes harder still. 'I had to create the character from nothing and in front of Pedro Almodóvar. The bastard won't compromise his vision; you have to manage it exactly as he wants it, which is part of his genius,' added Bernal, before highlighting one of the contradictions of playing the role: 'I needed to act more freely in the role in order to do justice to what Pedro was asking for but I didn't know how to; it is almost impossible to act spontaneously when you have to play something as specific as a Spanish drag queen from 1977.'

Practice makes perfect and over time Bernal learned what worked best for him. 'The secret of being a man or a woman is in the hands and the Spanish move their hands in a very distinct way to Mexicans. That was the key: how was I going to do gestures and touch things?' He began to turn his attention away from drag queens and watch the hand gestures of every woman who crossed his path. 'The problem with transvestitism is that sometimes you try to demonstrate that you are a woman with every gesture. The trick is to feel so much like a woman that you don't have to show it.'

To get inside the female mind, he started some interesting method experiments, such as going to a nightclub dressed as a woman with a group of friends. 'It was great fun. I realised the power women have over men. It was a liberating experience and, as an actor, an exceptional opportunity.' Friends recount that while in their company, Bernal would often slip into character and croon songs by popular Mexican singer Juan Gabriel, in the manner of Zahara.

Bernal also noticed the way people on set acted differently around him when he was dressed in drag. 'They'd move things a little closer so I could reach them, ask me if I wanted anything . . . They'd do whatever I asked them. All because I was a woman.' This despite the fact that they couldn't help but have seen the transformation process, given how long make-up took. 'I would have to arrive four hours before filming, shave until I had perfectly smooth skin – and the high heels killed me.' Wearing high heels wasn't the only new fashion experience. 'The thong – that was the most extreme situation that I have gone through. That was the biggest stunt that no double would do, getting that thong in place.'

Despite the difficulties, Bernal's performance as a woman is one of the movie's triumphs. We first see him as her in a sumptuous scene in which the camera slowly pans up the shiny Jean-Paul Gaultier dress he is wearing to his painted face and golden wig, his head in halo from the stage lighting behind. Certainly Almodóvar pulls out all the stops to introduce the character with tremendous affection.

In Almodóvar's diary of the shoot, he wrote:

> There are moments when Gael, in character as Zahara, resembles Marie Tritignant. He has her melancholic eyes, full of determination, eyes which inhabit a place you don't know about, full of mystery. But Gael reminds me of her not just because of the stare but also the clean outline which marks the shape of his jaws. That said, the one person Gael really resembles when in drag is Julia Roberts, with the big smiley mouth, like a little boat floating on the face.

Regarding Tritignant, she was clearly on the mind of cast and crew, who were shocked during the shoot to learn of the French actress's death at the hands of her boyfriend; as for Roberts, Bernal has said that, as his character was quite trashy, he did try to play it a bit like *Pretty Woman*, and in any case, he was more alarmed by his resemblance to his own mother.

Another condition of Bernal being offered the part related to certain physical-shape commitments, a scene subsequently echoed in *Bad Education* itself when Ángel promises to Enrique the director that he will be able to lose weight in order to play Zahara. Bernal had to buff up and put on some seven kilos for the start of the film, when he rocks up as the bearded Ángel, meaning a regime of constant workouts and feasting began five months ahead of the shoot. Then, once it was time for Bernal to transform into Zahara, he was expected to shed ten kilos.

This was crucial to Almodóvar's single-mindedness. While filming a scene at the school in Alella, a sequence in which Bernal as the transvestite Zahara returns to confront Father Manolo, it became clear that Bernal hadn't slimmed down enough: he couldn't fit into the tight trousers he was supposed to wear; Almodóvar went spare and shut down filming for a week until Bernal had lost the required weight. As Almodóvar insists on shooting in chronological order, the whole movie had to pause until Bernal had shed the extra pounds. He was forced on to a strict diet and kept under medical supervision, finding himself back in the gym, this time to sweat off the excess pounds he had worked hard to put on. The whole process was not appreciated by Bernal, who told *Fotogramas* that, though he didn't mind shaving himself to become a woman, 'I am not in favour of harming my body. After all, it is just theatre, a game, a joke, fiction.'

Bernal described it as an intense shoot, eight long weeks with barely time to think of anything other than the film, never mind actually to rest. Almodóvar is very specific with regard to what he wants, to achieving his vision. 'He is always looking for what he already has in his head and it is hard work getting there. We had a difficult relationship but only in working terms and that is positive because often conflicts generate better results,' said Bernal philosophically.

When discussing Almodóvar a few years later, at the NFT, Bernal said: 'He's very specific – he tells you how many steps to take from here to there. If he says it's nine steps, you have to make it in nine. So that creates a tension but it also creates a world. He's one of the few directors in the world who do that – he creates a very specific world.'

Living up to Almodóvar's expectations makes for much repeating of scenes, take after take until everything is just right. It was also the first time Bernal had ever made a set-based film, which makes for a particular intensity and claustrophobia, especially after the wonderful experience of making *The Motorcycle Diaries* (he had just a fortnight's break between the two films). There were times when Bernal said he felt like surrendering to his homesickness and heading back to Mexico, just throwing in the towel and walking away from *Bad Education*. But it was a tough shoot for all concerned: even before Bernal's weight issues had come to light, filming had been postponed due to Almodóvar injuring himself right at the start of proceedings, and the heat was said to have been infernal throughout.

The shoot itself began in mid-June 2003. Bernal's scenes were mostly shot in Madrid, where he rented himself a flat in the Los Austrias neighbourhood, a pretty bohemian barrio. He became a regular in the district's bars and restaurants, particularly Café del Nuncio on Calle Segovia and Mexican restaurant La Taquería del Alamillo, where the press spotted him dining on the terrace with then girlfriend Natalie Portman.

The school scenes were filmed on location in Alella, a village near Barcelona, and others in Valencia, where Almodóvar fondly described a moment of street theatre at 3 a.m.: the local residents had all come out on to their balconies to watch the action and when the scene ended (Lluis Homar as Berenguer throws himself into the arms of Bernal for a farewell embrace) a collective intake of breath could be heard from the spectators in the galleries followed by a huge round of applause.

Tough the process may have been but it was evidently a rich and rewarding experience too. Bernal has described Almodóvar as obsessive but great fun with it and stated how privileged he felt to have worked for him, one of the last great geniuses in cinema.

As reports filtered through of on-set tension and the postponement of the shoot, the media delved into the rift between director and lead, but Bernal was keen to downplay tensions when publicising the movie in the US: 'I have had enough of all the sensationalist press. We have not had any difference of opinion and the proof of it is that here I am at the US premiere [with Almodóvar].' *New York Times* reporter Lynn Hirschberg went further and claimed that the two had clashed over the explicit gay-sex scenes. Bernal would not let her get away with that and insisted it go down on record that he had had no such reservations whatsoever.

Almodóvar too tried to lay some ghosts to rest, thanking both Bernal and Daniel Giménez Cacho (who plays Father Manolo) for their lack of prejudice on the shoot, for the manner in which they had been prepared to strip themselves bare, disposed to try everything he asked of them. Specifically with regard to Bernal, Almodóvar described his role as the most complex character he had ever written, adding, 'He managed to transmit what I was looking for with this story – I want to work with him again and there will be time in the future.'

Nevertheless, even when complimenting Bernal in *Fotogramas*, it is not hard to see how Almodóvar might have rubbed the Latin American up the wrong way:

> His role was very complicated and it was a very hard shoot for him because he had to lose his own accent and camp himself up. There are actors for whom this sort of work is not complicated because they come from cultures with more feminine behaviour; for example, Andalucian, and when I say this I'm thinking of Antonio Banderas. But Mexico has a very macho mentality and, although Gael is a modern boy, you could see this. But he worked hard on his role and I think he is very good, especially in the darker parts of the character.'

When the *Observer* mentioned this point, Bernal's reply was telling. 'They're such wankers,' he said, before elaborating on the hypocrisy of Spaniards denouncing

Mexico as macho given the very serious domestic-violence problem in Spain. As for having to lose his Mexican accent, again Bernal sees it differently. 'What I really did was put on an accent. If I un-Mexicanised my accent, I'd speak like a robot. I tried to put on a Spanish accent – it consists more of putting on than taking off. In Spain they think like this a lot.'

Fotogramas asked Bernal about his reaction to seeing the film for the first time:

> I was very nervous. I had so many doubts to the point that I almost had a nervous breakdown before seeing it, too many expectations. Then I began to relax as I realised that everything had turned out, at least in my case, as I had expected them to. There were no surprises. This has never happened to me before. Always in the past there was always an element of the unknown but Pedro is somebody who doesn't doubt. He knows exactly what he wants.'

When this was mentioned to Almodóvar, the director replied, 'That is the first time an actor has said anything like that about me. Actors usually remember their part but are not conscious of my manipulation during the filming and editing. Gael probably meant something else – I wouldn't give it too much importance.'

All in all, it would seem that the film-making process was hardly a laugh-a-minute love-in but rather a tough and at times laborious slog with two artists working to their limits: given the nature of the material, it could hardly have happened any other way. Certainly Almodóvar and Bernal had their prickly moments and, despite claims to the contrary by the director, it would be a surprise if they worked together again. But mutual respect appears to have remained intact: from Bernal, respect for the genius of the maverick director; from Almodóvar, respect for the actor's application in a very complex role.

In the movie, there is a line spoken by the character Enrique, the director, about the character Juan, the actor, which certainly seems as if it could apply to the Almodóvar-Bernal dynamic: 'I wanted to see how far you would go and how much I could take.' There is no doubt that both Almodóvar and Bernal ultimately gave their all to the endeavour of making the best possible picture and the reaction of most viewers was positive and justified their efforts.

Many critics recognised familiar Almodóvar themes – fantasy, desire, melodrama, selective memory, everything being not quite as comfortable as it seems – as well as the trademark bright and colourful tones, in this his fifteenth feature. But commentators were also quick to recognise the ways in which *Bad Education* differed from the director's more usual fare: his films typically focus on women whereas this is a film all about men and, although the plot is naturally critical of the Catholic Church and touches on homosexual identity, in both cases such topics are merely incidental.

Bad Education is primarily a study of poisonous desires; of how some people consciously give in to their lusts, even though they know they are forbidden and that doing so will be their ruin. *La Mala Educación*, the movie's Spanish title, is particularly smart in that it translates both as 'bad behaviour' as well as 'bad education'. Almodóvar shows sympathy towards those who resign themselves to behaving badly, even seems to admire the way they stay true to themselves, if to no one else.

As Bernal himself said, 'I love how, in his films, he makes a flower emerge from the immorality and moves you.' Almodóvar invites the audience at least to consider the motivations of his baddies: in the case of Bernal's murderous impostor, we see a confused young man trying to escape his elder brother's contaminating shadow; with regard to Father Manolo, we note the tragedy of a man powerless to correct or control his passions.

Giménez Cacho was singled out for special praise for his portrayal of Father Manolo, for capturing the subtle complexity of such a tortured soul, a man who knew that his love for Ignacio was immoral but who was unable to resist all the same. Giménez Cacho himself, a fellow Mexican, preferred to highlight Bernal's work. 'What Gael did was braver than me. The sex scenes made a strong impression on me, I think he does them very well, especially the one where he simulates being a homosexual and lets himself be possessed in order to get some reward, although even he doesn't know what that might be. That scene is a very strong one for me and he does it very well.'

Of course the paedophile priest is the real villain of the piece in *Bad Education* but Almodóvar makes sure that the story's film director (whom he knew the audience would identify with himself) is just as exploitative in his own way; indeed the object of obsession for both characters is the same. Fele Martínez's turn as Enrique is another delicate one, creating a manipulative character but a vulnerable one, resigned to fate.

Bernal's performance was almost universally acclaimed, with most observers appreciating the complexity of the role and how difficult his character was to pin down, given Juan's instability. It was Bernal's skill in bringing a sense of ambiguity, in showing some things and suggesting many others that most caught the eye, along with his effectively playing three roles at once.

Sight & Sound magazine went so far as to describe Bernal's performance as 'miraculous', praising his 'emotional dexterity' and ability to keep the film moving forward when the overelaborate plot threatened to tie it up in knots: 'When the film gets in a spin, Bernal is its compass. Without him, the movie's symmetry and self-reflexiveness could have squeezed the life out of the material.'

Whereas Bernal was highly praised for his multifaceted performance, the main criticism of the movie centred on the fact that it was just too schizophrenic. Some reviewers complained that it wanted to be all things at once – a melodrama with comic undertones that turns into a thriller with ambitions to be a film noir – and ultimately ends up as none of them, less than a sum of its parts. Others felt that the plot was too full of twists and turns and trickery; that for every mystery resolved another opened up and so the film becomes bogged down and too confused.

But, for all those who found the film to be overcomplicated, there were just as many who admired the way the various narrative threads ultimately came together. Several critics made comparisons to Hitchcock, others talked outright of Almodóvar as a master at the height of his powers, making a perfectly controlled and polished piece.

The *Observer* noted that, although all the key characters were either gay, transsexual or bisexual, even a mainstream audience was unlikely to overly dwell on the movie's sexual politics. This, it felt, was not just a tribute to Almodóvar's deft storytelling but also to more tolerant times, to the changing mores of modern Western society. Given that *Bad Education* touches on Spain's growing maturity and liberal conscience and spans the country's transition to democracy, this was an interesting and important point, and one which would quickly and severely be put to the test.

The movie opened in Spain in March 2004, the week after the terrorist train-bombings in Madrid claimed 191 lives. Indeed, its original Spanish presentation in Barcelona was cancelled due to the atrocities. During a press conference, Almodóvar referred to rumours about the ruling party Partido Popular (People's Party – PP) deliberately withholding information and attempting to postpone the forthcoming general election. (The party lost the election after trying to cover up the fact that the bombs had been placed by Islamist terrorists by blaming ETA, the armed Basque terrorists.) When the film finally premiered in Madrid, five days after the attacks, those who queued to see it were greeted by protesters who threw eggs and insulted them: Spain was in a volatile mood and Almodóvar's comments about the PP had struck a raw nerve in some people.

Be that as it may, despite the nationwide trauma some 250,000 flocked to the cinema to see *Bad Education* in its opening weekend in Spain. The movie then kicked off the 2004 Cannes film festival the following month, the first time a Spanish film had done so, and Almodóvar dedicated the opening-night performance to those who had been killed in the bombings.

But more problems were to come for *Bad Education* on home soil: *Mar Adentro* (*The Sea Inside Me*) was chosen ahead of it to represent Spain at the Oscars (and in fact won); at the domestic Goyas, despite being nominated in four categories, *Bad Education* came away empty-handed. Almodóvar and his brother, producer Agustin, promptly resigned from the Spanish Film Academy in protest at what they saw as an unfair voting system. Inevitably, suspicions lingered that Almodóvar was still being punished for his outspoken political comments. Some compensation came the following year when the film was awarded La Navaja de Buñuel (Buñuel's Knife) for best Spanish film of 2004, an award given by the TV programme *Versión Española* and the Sociedad General de Autores y Editores (SGAE).

As for Bernal, he picked up Best Actor nominations from both Spain's Cinema Writer's Circle and its Actors Union. He had missed the controversy at the Spanish premiere – having been away filming *The King* in the US – but was most definitely present in Cannes. As well as *Bad Education*, Bernal was also promoting *The Motorcycle Diaries* at the festival and so was quite the poster boy on the French Riviera.

Sex Mex

'It is one of the strangest jobs in the world but at the same time it is one of the best, because you get to experience all the lives you can ever imagine, travel a lot, meet many friends,' Bernal has said of his chosen profession, 'and most importantly you get to fulfil one of the biggest objectives I had in my life: to meet girls. That was my main reason for wanting to become an actor.'

He has certainly managed to meet girls and some very pretty ones too. The tabloids gossiped of a whirlwind romance with Naomi Campbell and reported that Sienna Miller's post-Bafta bender was spent in Bernal's company, although Rodrigo de la Serna was a fellow reveller. Then there was the former ballet dancer he met in a pub while performing in *Blood Wedding*.

Bernal himself is protective of his privacy, viewing interest in his personal affairs as intrusive and nothing to do with his job as an actor. He is a very sociable type of guy and can party with the best of them, but he's no hell-raiser and tries to keep out of the public eye in this regard. Whenever asked about girlfriends in interviews, he bats the questions away and he is certainly not the sort to turn up at a celebrity party with his latest squeeze on his arm. Quite the opposite: it was speculated that Bernal's decision to take his mother along with him to Cannes in 2004 for the premiere of *Bad Education* and not then girlfriend Natalie Portman caused the US actress to dump him.

What is certain is that Bernal has quite a knack for charming his co-stars. As thirteen-year-olds in soap-opera *El Abuelo y Yo*, Bernal and Ludwika Paleta were sweethearts on and off screen and romance is also said to have blossomed between the actor and his opposite number in *Amores Perros* (Vanessa Bauche), then again with Cecilia Suárez, a fellow cast member on *Fidel*. On *The Crime of Father Amaro*, a behind-the-scenes affair with Ana Claudia Talancón brought a touch of method acting to proceedings.

However, by far the most significant of Bernal's on-set flings was with Argentine actress Dolores Fonzi, initiated during the filming of *Vidas Privadas* in Buenos Aires in early 2001. Bernal admitted to the *Sunday Herald*: 'It used to be a good excuse to evade responsibility and leave things behind. To say to a girlfriend, "I've got to go do this film; sorry".' Thus their partnership fizzled out after the shoot, but Bernal was back in Buenos Aires by mid-2002 to prepare for

The Motorcycle Diaries and the romance rekindled. By early 2003, Bernal was on the move again, eventually bound for Spain to limber up for *Bad Education*, and so the second liaison with Fonzi went the way of the first. Then, at the 2003 Oscars in March, Bernal met Natalie Portman.

His relationship with the *Star Wars* actress lasted over a year, making it his most serious to date, but it was all over by the end of Cannes 2004. They had made a good couple and not just as far as the celeb mags were concerned: Portman, three years Bernal's junior, had likewise been acting and in the public eye since her youth, having made her screen debut in Luc Besson's *Leon* aged twelve, and they had much in common. Even when they had split, they were said to have remained good friends.

Fast-forward to February 2006 and Bernal and Portman being sighted again out and about in public and appearing to be more than just good friends. The consensus was that they were an item once more. Cue Fonzi's untimely re-emergence on the scene. The Argentine was producing a television series called *Soy Tu Fan* (*I am Your Fan*) and wangled an episode in Mexico City, where she inevitably met up with her old flame, and even persuaded him to appear on the show.

What's more, by June 2007 Bernal was back in Buenos Aires to shoot another movie, *The Past*. Appropriately enough, Fonzi and Bernal seemed to be reliving old times, spotted together by the local paparazzi on several occasions despite their efforts to keep a low profile. Matters came to a sudden head with Portman's unexpected appearance on the streets of the Argentine capital. Similarly trying to avoid attention, Portman, already evidently upset, reacted angrily to being discovered by photographers. Sadly for her, a rolling camera was on hand to record the whole episode, which subsequently played out on Argentine television. The gossip columns had a field day, speculating that Portman had flown in to reclaim her man but been sent packing.

Doubtless many women would agree that Bernal was worth fighting over, certainly the legion of screaming female fans who welcome him whenever he makes a public appearance. Be it in a small Mexican village for the filming of *The Crime of Father Amaro* or on the banks of the River Thames ahead of his talk at the NFT, Bernal has had to become accustomed to being greeted by hordes of excited women.

It's not exactly a mystery what makes women swoon about Bernal: he is strikingly handsome. But the fact that he has such broad appeal, gets pulses racing in women of all ages and has the crossover appeal to attract the boys too, both gay and straight, proves there is more to the Gael magic than just a pretty face. As with his acting, he is able to project a certain ambiguity that means admirers are able to shape him to meet their own particular tastes: there is something very boyish about his good looks and an innocence in his smile that has led the French press to label him 'Angel Face', while the sincerity and passion with which he talks about issues can make women of a certain age melt and want to mother him.

On the other hand, the French media's second nickname for Bernal is 'Sex Mex' and there is certainly a more manly, sexy side to his persona. That angelic smile can quickly become devilish, sweet but at once suggestive and naughty. Matinee-idol looks bring success but sex appeal makes a star. The fact that Bernal's early films were fairly sex-charged helped, and he was hardly shy about getting his kit off.

He is dashing in his handsomeness yet his tussled hair and unkemptness give him that bit-of-rough rawness or boy-next-door earthliness, depending on what rocks your boat. For foreign admirers, there is undoubtedly something mysterious in his Latino looks, while an everyman quality attracts Mexicans.

Measuring in at just five foot seven inches, he's not the archetypal tall, dark and handsome. His shortness rarely comes across on screen and is of little consequence either way. Certainly Bernal doesn't seem to care: 'A lot of leading actors are small. Maybe you have to be small to fit into the TV.' Clearly he is comfortable in his own skin and he carries himself with a quiet confidence that helps create his aura.

That he has a screen presence is really the key, that unknown quality which you either have or haven't got. The camera loves him and that's just the way it is, although it seems clear that the magnetism has much to do with his eyes. Commentators have noted that they change colour from grey to green depending upon the light and many a director has praised the way Bernal can use his eyes to say a hundred different things. Herein lies his ability to be all things to all women.

His brooding image has seen him labelled the Latin James Dean, although Bernal is more a rebel with than without a cause. Others have called him the new Marlon Brando. Ignoring any Latino link, comparisons with Brando do at least pay homage to his body of work as an actor. Brando too, at least in the early part of his career, was careful with the roles he went for, preferring to take on the challenge of a conflicting personality than play it safe as a classic hero. Bernal himself dismisses such bracketing as no more than the media conveniently building up its latest flavour of the month.

Nevertheless, as with Brando, Bernal has the acting talent to match if not outweigh the poster-boy posture. In this regard, some see Bernal as a throwback to the 1960s and a golden age of cinema when European actors and actresses became international icons without having to serve Hollywood. The likes of Brigitte Bardot, Sophia Loren, Jean-Paul Belmondo, Marcello Mastroianni and Alain Delon had universal silver-screen appeal but retained firm roots in their homelands, lending them a certain otherwordly sense of cool. Certainly Bernal appeals to the art-house crowd in the US and UK. *Paste Magazine*, the US entertainment glossy, even placed him second to Philip Seymour Hoffman on its 2006 list of most important stars of independent cinema.

Other publications have been quick to sing his praises too. In evidence of that movie-star magic whereby women want to be with him while men want to be like him, *Esquire* magazine named Bernal one of their Best-Dressed Men of 2004, the same year *GQ* featured him in their Men of the Year. The *Gay Times*, meanwhile, ranked him fourth in its Sexiest Movie Stars of All-time list.

Apart from his big-eyed, boyish sexiness, the gay crowd will have warmed to the fact that in *Y Tu Mamá También* and *Bad Education* he has made films tackling homosexuality. Many actors avoid gay roles but Bernal not only takes them on but embraces them, getting stuck into some quite explicit scenes too.

Furthermore, Bernal publicly promotes gay rights. In November 2006, he lent his support to a new civic law which allowed couples of the same sex living in Mexico City to register their cohabitation and thus be entitled to inheritance and other benefits previously denied them.

Bernal's dedication to good causes plays well with females too: 'Wow – not only is he good-looking and a damn fine actor but he's out protesting as well, speaking his mind. He seems clever.'

Given Bernal's cross-sector appeal, he is the marketer's dream ticket yet his forays into advertising have been minimal. Alejandro González Iñárritu originally came across him when making a promo for MTV but since then Bernal has only shot one commercial, for Levi jeans.

Night has fallen on an unidentified port city and Bernal is at the wheel of a clapped-out car with a young lovely there for a ride. But they are not out on a romantic pleasure cruise: Bernal races his motor through the dockside streets as a serious-looking wagon gives chase. Our hero gives his pursuer the slip, turns to his belle and smiles. They get out of the car and push it off the quay and into the deep blue yonder.

In the roll of an eye, Bernal's look of satisfaction turns to one of anguish: he has left something important in the car. He launches himself into the drink and, underwater, manages to penetrate the car and retrieve the lost item, stuffing it into the back of his jeans. Back on dry land, his girl asks him what it was he had forgotten: *'Qu'est-ce que tu as oublié?'* Bernal smiles and puts his arm around her. As they walk away, the camera focuses in on the treasure tucked in the back of his denims: a French phrasebook. In tune with the Gallic mood, 'Playground Love' by Air provides the soundtrack.

It is a curious one-off venture into commercial sponsorship but it is a stylish advert with a creative heartbeat. Perhaps he was trying to jeopardise sales and pull down capitalism anyway, by demonstrating that the pockets on the new Levi's are not fit for purpose.

He could undoubtedly do more commercial sponsorship work but, given his fair-trade anti-capitalist stance, it does go against what he stands for. It is this integrity, the way he handles himself off the big screen, that wins him even more admirers.

Bernal can match his on-screen persona by being quite the charmer off it too: at the start of press junkets, he is well known for greeting reporters one by one, shaking the hands of the males and offering a kiss on the cheek to those of the fairer sex, reducing most of them to quivering wrecks before they have even had a chance to ask a question. And he can be cheeky with it: when an Irish journalist asked Bernal if he thought he would be able to master an Irish accent, the actor replied that 'you pick up accents quickly in bed'.

But Bernal earns the respect of journalists by speaking openly and intelligently about his films and ensuring that the reporters leave with some decent material with which to write their stories. He gives an interviewer his full attention and engages on a personal level. They will often later find that they have been fed the same lines as others, but he has an ability to make tried and tested stock replies sound someway refreshing. What's more, reporters are generally impressed with the way Bernal seems to believe in what he is saying, actually to care about what he is doing.

There is a genuineness to Bernal that is unusual in film stars and is a quality near impossible to fake, even in the acting community. When Bernal talks of politics, of social and cultural issues, it is because they are matters that concern him and his enthusiasm rubs off on to those listening.

As an actor, Bernal lends charisma to whatever part he plays. Off-screen, he has that certain star quality but also comes across as being down-to-earth, something fans respond to well. Fame doesn't appear to have gone to his head. He tries to keep things in perspective. 'Things have gone well for me but there are no limits to this and you can never say, "I've made it"; wherever you look, there is always something you have not done.'

He is careful to try and take the positives from stardom and not to let it change him too much, as he told Mexico's *La Jornada* newspaper, 'It should only affect you in a good way. It has its downsides, like having to get used to seeing yourself in magazines, but that has nothing to do with who you actually are. The immediate surrounds change quickly but in the end you realise that you are the same,' he says, adding that keeping a sense of 'why' it is all happening is key. 'There is something more integral: the work, something that doesn't belong to you but rather one belongs to.'

Celebrity status is a curious thing, he says. 'Fame is like getting on a bike, it doesn't come with an instructions manual.'

And who could have prepared him for a Mexican backlash?

Things began to take a turn for the worse when he returned to Mexico to promote *The Motorcycle Diaries*, having spent the best part of the previous two years out of the country on various film projects. The local media got a little overexcited about the return of the prodigal son and Bernal didn't much appreciate all the extra attention, especially not all the prying into his private life. The press became spikey with him and Bernal would be short back. Mexicans were soon accusing him of acquiring the diva characteristics they associate with Salma Hayek.

Of course, this is all part and parcel of building someone up only to knock them down again, a media game played out the world over. Bernal himself has acknowledged that it is connected with putting yourself out in the public realm. He has no problem with anyone who might not like his work, that being a matter of opinion, but finds it hard to deal with criticism of the way he acts in public, such as when being disturbed in the middle of eating at a restaurant. 'That's something that in Mexico they pick up a lot on – "Oh, he didn't give me an autograph, he's lost it." And it's funny because it's so ephemeral and so trivial.'

Some people who have known him all his life note that Bernal can be a bit *mamón* these days, slightly dismissive of others if not quite stuck up his own backside. Given fame and fortune, that being recognised on the streets has been part of his life since soap stardom aged thirteen, acting somewhat aloof towards

Above: Bernal as Leonardo in a stage production of Federico García Lorca's play, *Blood Wedding*, alongside Thekla Reuten (as 'the Bride') performed at the Almeida Theatre, London, May-to-June 2005.

Above: Bernal (as Stéphane) and Charlotte Gainsbourg (as Stéphanie) in one of many fantastical scenes in *The Science of Sleep*.

Left Top: The role was complex and the shoot fraught with tension but Bernal's performance in Pedro Almodóvar's *Bad Education* was ultimately considered a triumph. In this scene he plays transvestite Zahara, alongside Javier Cámara (as Paca).

Left Bottom: Bernal (as Elvis) and Pell James (as Malerie) share a tender moment in *The King*, the actor's only lead role in a US feature thus far – and a bold one to have chosen at that.

Above: Bernal is at the forefront of a boom in creative cinematic talent in Mexico. Here he lines up alongside the country's leading directors, Alejandro González Iñárritu, Guillermo Del Toro and Alfonso Cuarón. Nicknamed 'The Three Amigos', here they celebrate the launch of their Cha Cha Cha production company at Cannes, May 2007. The first film out of the stable is *Rudo y Cursi*, starring Bernal.

Above: Bernal in another surreal sequence from *The Science of Sleep*.

Below: Directors rave about the expressive way Bernal uses his eyes. Here he provides a piercing stare as Santiago in *Babel*.

Above: Canana is a production house set up by Bernal and Luna to help get unconventional film projects off the ground and inspire budding film-makers with a can-do attitude. Leading by example, Bernal directed himself in *Déficit*, his debut behind the lens. Here his character (Cristobal) is chauffeur-driven to the family's country villa.

Above: As something of an ambassador for Latin American cinema, Bernal has appeared in films throughout the continent, with the region's best directors. Here he can be seen (as Rímini) with Moro Anghileri (as Vera) in Hector Babenco's Argentine production *The Past*.

Above: Away from acting, football is Bernal's main passion. He and best friend Diego Luna play together for a Saturday team in Mexico City and even star as footballing brothers in *Rudo y Cursi*.

mere mortals is perhaps understandable. Most people praise his humbleness and that he has managed to remain so modest in spite of everything.

Misunderstandings with the Mexican press are much less frequent these days. For starters, his commitment to Mexican cinema and social projects make a mockery of accusations of him having sold out or disappeared into snootyness. Furthermore, being once more based in the country, Bernal is a more regular feature on the Mexico City scene. He is frequently seen without minders in the bars and restaurants of Condesa, a fashionable DF *colonia*, and he plays football every Saturday just like any other *chilango*.

Football-mad, whenever work commitments allow and Bernal is in town, he turns out for Sinaia, a team cobbled together with actors and other film-industry cast and crew. They play every Saturday at El Rancho Viejo, a series of pitches tucked inside woodland on the top of a hill overlooking Mexico City. Sinaia, it is fair to say, are not one of the league's better sides.

Bernal himself plays right midfield. Is he any good? 'No,' is the blunt assessment of a team-mate, 'but that's not important.' What is important is to get together for a bit of fun and then retire to the tacos stalls-cum-bars at the side of the field. Besides, as part of preparations for their role in *Rudo y Cursi*, Bernal and Diego Luna, a team-mate at Sinaia, had private coaching from Luis Zague, a naturalised Brazilian who played for Mexico in the 1994 World Cup, so perhaps their club's fortunes will be transformed.

'Football is one of the first things I learned as a boy, playing with my dad in the hallway of the apartment where we lived,' recalled Bernal in *El Universal*. 'My first match was a Pumas versus Chivas.' The Chivas (Goats) are Guadalajara's pride and joy, the second most popular team in Mexico, America of Mexico City being the first. And yet despite Bernal being a proud *tapatio*, his team is the Pumas, the affiliated team of UNAM, the Mexico City university (although its supporter base is not drawn exclusively from students but rather anyone from the southwest of the city).

Bernal takes in a Pumas game whenever he can, going along with any one of Diego Luna, Martín Altomaro (co-star of *De Tripas, Corazón*) or Osvaldo Benavides (co-star on *El Abuelo y Yo*), all fellow Pumas aficionados.

Bernal admits to having been reduced to tears twice while watching football and the Pumas were responsible for one of them. 'The first time was when Mexico lost to Germany in '86. I was on my own and very young but I cried. The second time was when Pumas lost the final to America, when Rios screwed up.' That was in 1987 when the Pumas goalkeeper gifted their deadly rivals the game; in 1986, Mexico hosted the World Cup and went out to West Germany in the quarter-finals on penalties.

While living in London, Bernal adopted Tottenham Hotspur, logical enough given that he lived in north-east London for most of his time in the capital. Although long having departed the capital, he keeps abreast of events at White Hart Lane and commented in British *GQ* in February 2007: 'This season has been pretty rubbish, no? If I was manager I'd find out why they hired this guy Berbatov.' Said Bulgarian striker, full name Dimitar Berbatov, went on to prove himself an astute acquisition, but was indeed struggling at the time of the interview.

Apart from football, Bernal's other favoured sporting pursuit is surfing, although he admits to being pretty hopeless. He is a much better dancer, and salsa music is another passion. Indeed, an outstanding dream is to set up a salsa group; he was once in a band, as he told *Hotdog* magazine: 'In *Science of Sleep*, when the character arrives at his mother's house, he brings out the carpet that says "Intestine Grosso", which means "Gross Intestines", and that was the name of my band. I used to dance and sing and play percussion instruments.' On *Rudo y Cursi* he has to sing as well as play football and Bernal has also recorded a duet with Devendra Banhart, the US folk singer.

These days, given all the travel, Bernal's chief leisure pursuit is reading, an activity he has enjoyed since his childhood. Bernal cites *The Stranger*, by Albert Camus, and *A Hero of Our Time*, by Mikhail Lermontov, as the two favourite books of his youth. The latter led to a lifelong passion for Russian literature. Another writer to have made a great impression on Bernal is Georg Büchner; a German playwright of the 1820s, best known for *Danton's Death*, *Lenz*, *Leonce und Lena* and the never-finished *Woyzeck*, all penned before he died of typhus aged 23. Büchner wrote of the unification of Germany and the French Revolution, yearning for such ideals to spread into the Rhineland. He was persecuted for his troubles and forced into exile. Of Büchner, Bernal has said: 'Ever since I read him, I understood on a practical level what one can achieve when telling a story.'

At the Guadalajara Book Fair of 2006, Bernal joined author José Saramago on stage at the Teatro Diana to read passages from the Nobel Prize winner's latest book, *Las Intermitencias de la Muerte* (*The Intermittancies of Death*). Proceeds from the performance went to charity. The encounter helped firm up an interest in the Portuguese writer's work, which proved significant when Bernal was then signed up for *Blindness*, the movie adaptation of Saramago's bestselling novel.

The King

Bernal's character in *The King* provides the perfect illustration of just how he approaches his craft differently from other actors. When the script was first bandied about, a number of up-and-coming young actors said that they liked it very much but that the lead role wasn't quite right for their profile. The part in question was that of 21-year-old Elvis Perez, the son of a deceased prostitute, who goes in search of the father he never knew after being discharged from the navy. Elvis is an ambiguous persona, gentle but menacing too, and as the film progresses he goes on to commit a series of terrifying and violent acts. It is easy to see why the latest batch of Hollywood starlets either balked at the chance to become a sociopathic killer or requested screenplay rewrites that would make Elvis more sympathetic to audiences. It is equally typical of Bernal that he jumped at the opportunity and loved Elvis just as he was, more interested in developing a reputation for playing complex characters than heart-throbs, dedicated to exploring his own depths as an actor.

The film was written by Milo Addica, a US native who shot to fame on the back of penning *Monster's Ball*, in which Halle Berry won an Oscar for her performance as a death-row widow who falls for Billy Bob Thornton's redneck prison warden. Despite the film's success, Addica was left unsatisfied by his peripheral role in its making. Believing in *The King* too much to let it go, he ended up producing the movie, thus ensuring maximum input. In fact the screenplay was co-written by Addica with James Marsh, the British documentary film-maker. Marsh also directed *The King*, so it was very much a hands-on approach for the two key figures involved.

Marsh and Attica had never met in person until they hooked up in Texas, where the film is set, to collaborate on the script. The idea of writing while scouting for locations came as a consequence of Marsh's background in documentary pictures, in which what the film-makers discover along the way often shapes the narrative.

One of Marsh's documentaries also inspired the name of the new feature and its chief protagonist: 1996's *The Burger and The King*, a film about the chefs who cooked for Elvis Presley. The concept for *The King*, meanwhile, was inspired by coming across an old photo of a young man called Joseph Sandow who was arrested for petty larceny in 1901. Elvis Perez's father, played by William Hurt, ends up with the name David Sandow.

Quite apart from impressing the film-makers with his enthusiasm for playing the part as dark as it was, Bernal also inspired a few changes to the script, adding an extra dimension to the tale. Milo Addica explained: 'When we met Gael, he certainly redefined the whole idea physically of what we were creating . . . so we rewrote the script when he committed, incorporating some of the Hispanic quality that he brought to the subject.' Such tinkering took time and contributed to the fact that, in the end, two years passed between Bernal's signing up to the project and it actually coming to fruition.

That he was prepared to be patient highlights Bernal's interest in the subject matter. Bernal has spoken about how easy the choice was to jump on board: 'Sometimes with the term "selective" it might seem like you choose things very carefully but in my case it's not that I've been careful; there have just been overwhelming reasons why I should do one thing and why I shouldn't consider another. It's been very definite.'

In the case of *The King*, the themes the movie addresses appealed. 'It contained all these complexities of issues, themes, situations and contexts that I'm really interested in, like the Mexican–United States border, the territory, faith, redemption, family, love – all these elements were contained in a small simple story and that is incredibly satisfying.'

The simple (as Bernal sees it) story revolves around Elvis, the ex-marine looking for his father. It turns out that Pop is a born-again Christian, the Reverend Sandow, a successful and prosperous pastor and a man none-too-keen to acquaint himself with his illegitimate son, the vestige of an unholy past he would rather forget. But Elvis is not so easily deterred and sets about infiltrating the family by any means necessary, starting with the seduction of the pastor's sixteen-year-old daughter, Malerie, his own half-sister. She soon falls pregnant and further misery is to come for the family once her brother, Paul, whom Sandow is raising in his own fundamentalist image, learns of the affair: he seeks to end the relationship by warning Elvis to stay away; Elvis murders his half-brother for his trouble.

So a meaty part for Bernal to say the least, although, as he himself has said, not one you can expect to fully get to the bottom of: 'A character like this, what happens, what he does, such an extraordinary situation, it is impossible for you to really get to understand how the character feels because you have never been even remotely close to this, to what he manages to do.' Bernal's approach is to relate to what you can: 'The only thing you do is empathise with his drama, with his [sense of] tragedy.'

In terms of preparing for the role: 'Yeah, there was research but for me I don't have a specific way of tackling a character – like I have to fill in A to Z on a list – it's always a case-by-case situation. And with this character it was about drawing him, because the character's journey and his emotional tragedy is pretty clear, it's pretty specific.'

Bernal also spent three months in Austin for rehearsals and while there he would frequently hop in his car, go for a drive and get lost in different neighbourhoods, especially those with a Mexican community of first and second generations.

He would stop and observe the people who lived there, as Bernal himself said, 'mixing with them, listening and getting into the context, soaking that up'.

The King was his first serious movie in the US, his only other being his supporting role in rom-com *I'm With Lucy*. Bernal found it an interesting part of the world in which to be: 'We were shooting in Corpus Christi, which is very small with only motels and refineries, and in Austin. That's an incredibly interesting town, one of the few in the US where segregation is not as marked as in other places, because of the university, I guess, and there are a lot of Mexicans there with a lot of money.' He had never even been to the region before but was pleased with how he was received: 'You start speaking Spanish and it's accepted. People don't go, like, "Whoa!" Texas is a country in itself and it's less hypocritical and more upfront than most of the United States. I was very well treated, actually.'

Filming began in late 2004 and was troubled from the outset, with funding cut just two days before Bernal was scheduled to arrive on set, the moneymen claiming it to be mean-spirited and unlikely to find an audience. Other potential backers were equally sceptical and scathing of its unpleasantness. Finally Ed Pressman, a producer committed to independent cinema, came to the rescue, albeit providing the barest minimum of budgets. In one sense this perhaps helped force the team to remain faithful to the script; as with the story itself, they had to say as much as possible with very limited resources.

It certainly made for a very tight shoot, just twenty-three days, meaning ten-plus scenes per day, a huge strain on the actors. The situation was ripe for disaster given that, with his documentary background, Marsh had no prior experience in handling actors, but he dealt with the situation admirably by placing his trust in them: 'Gael and William Hurt are both very experienced, so I just gave both of them a lot of responsibility and freedom to do what they wanted to do. I wasn't directing them in a very heavy-handed or particular way, I just saw what they wanted to do and helped them do that.'

A sensible approach, especially given Hurt's reputation for being a slightly prickly customer. As Marsh recalled: 'I think Gael liked working with William although that was often quite sparky.'

Slightly less 'sparky' for Bernal was filming the scenes with Addica, who performs a cameo. Addica was an actor before his writing career took off – the original idea behind writing *Monster's Ball* was to showcase his own thespian talent – and so it was natural he should take a role. As Addica joked, 'It was a great way for me to get to discipline Gael in the film and show him who's boss. It was very exciting.' On a more serious note, he added, 'We shot eleven scenes that day, if I recall, from nine to midnight, and it was a gruelling day. But it was great, obviously, as an actor on that level to work with Gael; it was very exciting. We were having a good time and we were working off of each other, and his concentration is such that he is in the room, he's present and that is what great acting is.'

Of course, Addica's more telling contribution was in writing a story as unflinching and rich in theme as his previous works. *Monster's Ball* explored the breakdown of a wife whose husband is on death row, while his second work, *Birth*, has Nicole Kidman believe that a ten-year-old boy is the reincarnation of her late husband. It is fair to say that Addica delves where other film-makers don't dare or care to go.

The King is certainly a journey into the deepest, darkest corners of small-town USA. It broaches subjects as charged as incest, fundamentalism and the fate of the outsider, and shocks with its violence. But that the violence is shocking says something in itself: there are but two violent scenes and it is their very spare nature that gives them their power; other, more commercial films are less careful, using violence as an almost cartoon constant.

Likewise the film's incest is not used merely to break taboos but to highlight just what a confused and disturbed character Elvis is: his quest to seduce his half-sister comes part through a desire for intimacy and to be loved, part through a need both to hurt and to get closer to his father. For Malerie, on the other hand, the process is that of a girl beginning to think for herself, to question her father's beliefs and then rebel against them. At first she merely submits herself to Elvis but soon she starts to take the initiative, her innocence long since lost.

Given the furore that surrounded the release of *The Crime of Father Amaro* in Mexico, Bernal is no stranger to upsetting conservative religious groups and *The King* certainly found critics from various church factions. The film is forthright in its display of double standards and cruelty within Christian fundamentalism. We are also in George Bush country and some fun is also poked at the Creationists: Paul leads the campaign to have Intelligent Design taught in his high school.

However, Christianity, in all its guises, is dealt with sensitively and the intention is rather to explore religious values than mock them. This is especially so with regard to themes of redemption and whether it is always possible, always even right to forgive. The born-again Christians are not ridiculed as such; they are given the chance to make fools of themselves, but the audience is asked to consider why these people are as they are, why they believe with such conviction what they believe.

Which is all well and good but, if not to lay the boot into the Bible-bashers, just what is the movie's point? Violent murder, incest, religious hypocrisy and broken homes are not fun topics, so for a film to inflict such misery on its audience without some sort of conclusion leaves an unsatisfactory and bitter taste. Elvis has clearly been dealt a bad hand in life but the context of his birth and the manner in which Sandow abandons him and his mother is not explained in any detail, making it difficult to judge the rights and wrongs. Perhaps the point is that no one is really to blame: the world is messed up and inconveniently there are no true culprits; thus we are denied absolution.

Indeed if there is any sense of an overlying message in the film it is that of judgement, or rather the importance of trying to understand before we judge. In *The King*, this requires viewers to sympathise with not especially likeable characters and it is to the immense credit of the actors that they just about manage to make them do so.

William Hurt is a brash and intimidating presence as Sandow and it is painful to witness the way in which his clumsy actions impinge on his family. Yet we understand that he is trying to do right. The scenes between Elvis and Malerie are delicately played and are some of the best in the movie thanks to beautifully restrained performances from Bernal and Pell James. Although we sense there to be a monster that lurks within Bernal's character, we also see his vulnerability when he uncertainly takes Malerie's hand for the first time and he almost doesn't dare look at her, nor she him, such is the couple's inexperience and apprehension.

This is one of many scenes in which actions speak louder than words, something of an Addica trademark. The writer himself has said, 'I like to create an environment where actors can behave as opposed to speak speak speak – dialogue is secondary to action.' This also makes for a script fairly sparse in dialogue, perhaps no bad thing considering that the movie was Bernal's first lead role in which his character is supposed to be a native English speaker (in *Dot the i*, he is a Brazilian with English parentage). Nevertheless, Bernal's US accent is near spotless, confident and never in doubt.

Bernal's is an impressive all-round performance. His charisma ensures that Elvis is a mixture of frightening self-assurance and sweet innocence. You are never sure how calculating Elvis is, what his real aims are. Is it to destroy or be accepted by the family, and does he even know himself? It is often noted that Bernal likes to leave his characters slightly open to interpretation, ensuring we are never quite certain what they are thinking. Never has this been more the case than in *The King*, where the unknown quantity of Elvis gives the film its unpredictability. Likewise, never have the trademark Bernal all-saying eyes been used so effectively, offering the occasional hint of the demon lurking behind the boyish smile.

Latin American New Wave Part VI: Lead Role

The King was Bernal's first leading role in a US feature film but it didn't herald a new direction. In these times of globalisation, it is only natural that a versatile actor should work all over the world and Bernal has made films in England, Spain, France and Canada too. If the script is good and the project right, he'll go wherever the work takes him.

Bernal was invited in June 2005 to join the Academy of Arts and Sciences, the body that votes at the Oscars, but he still keeps his distance from Hollywood. He is proud to say that Tijuana, to film *Babel*, is the nearest he has ever got to making a film in Tinseltown.

While he is politically and culturally committed to Mexico and Latin America, he is not fundamentally against Hollywood. The fact of the matter is that the Hollywood roles he is offered are stereotypical (Latin lover or sensitive but troubled boy from the barrio), the scripts too conventional; if the right sort of project and part came to him from Hollywood he might take it on. He cites Nicole Kidman as an actress he admires for making interesting films inside and outside the mainstream.

Bernal is fortunate in that he is an actor in demand (by the most interesting directors in the business to boot) and so he can pick and choose, although such fortune is based on talent and plenty of others do sell their talent to Hollywood to the highest bidder. Bernal is aware that he is at a stage in life – no children or real responsibilities – which allows him to take risks with his career choices but in *Fotogramas* also mused: 'Where is the risk in telling a story that needs to be told?'

Alfonso Cuarón admires Bernal's selectiveness, his dedication to projects he believes in, to challenging and bettering himself. 'He never fell into the easy seduction of trying to have a career, the easy thing of taking the roles that would expose him to mainstream audiences. He knows, whatever he does, it's like a marathon,' Cuarón said to the *LA Times*.

As for the roles which appeal to him, Bernal told *Fotogramas*: 'I am attracted by characters who make me someone I am not. Maybe it is no more than the classic cliché about actors who want to play a woman, Hitler or Jesus, but the characters that surprise me are the ones that I go for.'

Both *The Motorcycle Diaries* and *Bad Education* were eight-month projects, including pre-shoot preparation, and Bernal has said that he prefers this approach, allowing him to really develop a role. Yet one of his main merits as an actor is his instinctiveness. He has said he is at his best when the two combine. 'Instinct keeps you alert in the role. Intuition leads you to something inconclusive whereby you don't quite know yourself how it will end up, but it always makes for nice surprises. And then once that is in your hands, then comes the study, the research with the director, the setting it down, nurturing it until you reach a consensus.'

Bernal also thanks his instinct for avoiding the stereotypical Latino roles, citing as an example: 'Alfonso Arau [director of *Like Water for Chocolate*] offered me the role of Zapata but in English. A Mexican playing a Mexican in English! It clashed with my instinct.' His instinct favours Latin American films. Although not really a subscriber to the theory of the Latin American New Wave as a movement, Bernal is loyal to its cause. In fact, some people argue that he himself is it.

He was a leading figure in *Amores Perros, Y Tu Mamá También, The Crime of Father Amaro, The Motorcycle Diaries* and *Babel*, five of the region's most successful films. Could it be that quite apart from some continent-wide cinema trend, the whole boom has been based on the star appeal of one hot young actor?

Bernal's popularity, based on talent but no less his good looks, means he can single-handedly ensure a film gets an audience. His iconic status in Mexico is such that the three outright Mexican feature films he has made as an actor (ignoring his actor-director turn for *Déficit*) – namely *Amores Perros, Y Tu Mamá También* and *The Crime of Father Amaro* – feature among Mexico's top five all-time biggest box-office hits, the other two being *Sexo, Pudor y Lágrimas* and *Una Película de Huevos* (*A Film About Eggs*), the 2006 animation. When the NFT organised a festival to honour Mexican cinema in October 2006, it also paid homage to Mexico's most bankable star with a separate tribute to Bernal, including a talk and the screening of a selection of his films, both Mexican and non-Mexican.

Of course, many factors contributed to the Buena Onda phenomenon and Bernal was undoubtedly one of them, but singling him out as the overriding force is perhaps overdoing things.

Bernal himself told *Time* magazine that he saw it more as him having been in the right place at the right time. 'Destiny and luck have given me and many other actors the chance to be in a certain position where no one else has been.' In Mexico he has been described as an amulet for directors.

Also in *Time*, Salles observed: 'A film movement cannot develop solely on the efforts of directors. Italy had great directors like Visconti and Fellini but also actors like Marcello Mastroianni and Giulietta Masina. Now in Latin America you have Alejandro González Iñárritu and Alfonso Cuarón but also a generation of young, talented actors such as Gael.'

In terms of the movement's main directors, Bernal has worked with most of the hotshots: Iñárritu, Cuarón, Salles, Meirelles and Babenco. Extending the degrees of separation, Bernal's sometime girlfriend Dolores Fonzi made *El Aura* with *Nine Queens* director Fabián Bielinski. Pablo Stoll of *Whisky* fame was the production co-ordinator on the short *El Ojo en la Nuca* and another short, *The Last Post*, provides a slightly more tenuous link to Hugo Colace, director of photography on *La Ciénaga*, *Bombón: El Perro* and *Historias Mínimas*: Colace was the cinematographer on the Buenos Aires section of *The Last Post* shoot (which didn't in fact involve Bernal). As for the Buena Onda's two top directors of photography, Prieto and Lubezki, Bernal posed for their cameras on his first two films.

More than anyone else, Bernal has been at the epicentre of Latin American New Wave cinema. He would like increased intercontinental interaction in the region's cinema and believes that the key to establishing a Latin American industry is for them to work and market themselves as a group, in much the same way Asia does, as opposed to disparate individual countries. Certainly Bernal leads by example, making himself into the living proof that the continent can successfully work together.

The Science of Sleep

Coming on the back of heavy roles and intense projects in *The King* and *Bad Education*, it is easy to understand why Bernal jumped at the chance of joining in on Michel Gondry's absurdist *La Science des Rêves* (*The Science of Sleep*). Nevertheless, although it is a much more light-hearted piece than both preceding works, Bernal's character is no less complex and, once again, mentally unstable. He plays Stéphane, a Mexican adrift in Paris whose dominating creative side has no outlet in his dead-end job and so manifests itself in other aspects of his life: his wild imagination soon begins to take over, dreams and reality becoming confused.

The Science of Sleep was Frenchman Gondry's third feature film but the first he had written and directed himself. His two previous pictures (*Human Nature* and *The Eternal Sunshine of the Spotless Mind*) had been penned by Charlie Kaufman, although Gondry had significant input on the latter, indeed shared its Original Screenplay Academy Award. Kaufman had been the brains behind surreal pictures such as *Being John Malkovich* and *Adaptation*, both directed by Spike Jonze: like Kaufman, Gondry likes to push boundaries and challenge the viewer; like Jonze, Gondry started his career making highly original music videos.

Collaborations with the likes of Björk and the White Stripes began to win Gondry plaudits and industry attention: his stop-animation video using Lego in 'Fell in Love with a Girl' for the latter bagged him an MTV prize. Gondry's feature films transfer the experimental nature and boundary-pushing principles typical of video clips to the longer form of the medium. In fact, the idea for *The Science of Sleep* originated in Gondry's video for the Foo Fighters' hit, 'Everlong', in which two youngsters share dreams: there is even a clip in which one of the characters sports giant hands, just as Bernal would later do in the movie. Gondry was intrigued by developing the premise further, exploring the manner in which dreams might impact upon a relationship and how a relationship might affect dreams.

From there, he began to spin other ideas and obsessions into a story, adding many autobiographical elements. Before getting behind a camera, Gondry had worked in Paris at a calendar publishers, just as Bernal's character does in *The Science of Sleep*. Gondry himself, slipping back to his music-industry origins for allegory, at a *Guardian*/NFT talk he described the film as his first album: 'Let's say you sign the contract when you're twenty and you record the first album at twenty-one – you pour your whole existence between age nought and twenty-one, all jammed together, all the ideas that you accumulated, all come out in this first album. Then the second album is where you express all the thoughts between the first and second album, which may be about two years later. In my case, I kind of did it the other way around.' In typically eccentric fashion, he considers *The Eternal Sunshine of the Spotless Mind* as his second album: *Human Nature* he doesn't count, as on that he pretty much did as he was told.

The Science of Sleep tackles issues of insecurity with regard to the opposite sex and muses on the beauty and burden of having a vivid imagination and of being creative. The plot, in as much as there is one, revolves around Stéphane arriving back in Paris to be reunited with his French mother following the death of his Mexican father, with whom he had originally left the city when his parents split up. He moves back into the former family home. His *maman* has found him a supposedly creative job but it turns out to be merely functional, an office position at the calendar publishers, and although he makes suggestions for new designs he is ultimately forced to reserve his imaginative streak for his dreams. However, they soon begin to spill over into his daily life. When he meets his neighbour, Stéphanie, played by Charlotte Gainsbourg, she offers a new focus for his fantasies and he contrives elaborate ways to win her attention. At first she is attracted to him but his childish nature confuses her and his loose grip on reality ultimately pushes her away. Before long, their relationship exists more in Stéphane's head than anywhere else and the film's storyline becomes similarly fragmented between dream and reality.

Bernal's character, Stéphane, is clearly a version of Gondry himself, though, according to Gondry, this nearly cost the Mexican the part: 'The character of Stéphane is a sort of alter-ego ... at first I was worried because Gael is handsome and outgoing and I thought people might believe that that was how I saw myself. But he is a great actor and we got over the problem.'

The pair first met in Los Angeles when both were staying at the Château-Marmont hotel and Bernal was invited by Gondry's producer to the launch of a DVD compilation of music clips. Later in the night, actor and director bumped into each other outside the Shoe Stores bar, both of them the worse for wear. A typically showbiz night ensued, with an after-party at the hotel, ending with the likes of Winona Ryder being thrown in the swimming pool. The night resulted in hangovers all round as well as a friendship struck between Bernal and Gondry, who pledged to work together in the future.

At that point, Gondry was preparing to shoot *Eternal Sunshine of the Spotless Mind* but he had already begun work on the script for *The Science of Sleep*. Gondry rewrote it with Bernal in mind; the Mexican loved it and jumped on board. As reported in the *Independent*, all this was much to the irk of Welsh actor Rhys Ifans, who had worked under Gondry on *Human Nature* when the two had become close: Gondry had talked to Ifans about his ideas for *The Science of Sleep* and promised him the lead. Indeed, Ifans had even come up with the movie's title, as is acknowledged in the end credits (although whether Ifans' suggestion was 'The Science of Sleep' or 'The Science of Dreams', a more accurate translation of the French '*La Science des Rêves*', remains unclear). Ifans has since said that he felt let down and betrayed when he learned that Bernal had stepped into his shoes. Since their meeting in LA, it had become Bernal and Gondry exchanging ideas, recounting their dreams and developing Stéphane's character, rather than the director and Ifans.

Besides the chance to work with Gondry, Bernal told *El Universal* what most appealed was the chance for a bit of respite after some pretty heavy films. 'What caught my attention was the frivolity and the chance to experiment with the craft. I had just come from making *The King*, quite a dense film, and I had a tremendous desire to get lost in theatricality: at the end of the day, to be a bit more like I am, rather than these extraordinary characters who suffer great tragedy, who get knocked down again and again.' He was also seduced by the chance to cut loose after three quite structured pieces: 'I had just done *Bad Education*, *The King*, *The Motorcycle Diaries*, quite intense films, ones in which to a certain point I was restricted to a particular tone. And in this film [*The Science of Sleep*] the thing was to fly, to let yourself go.'

As well as suggestions for the script, Gondry encouraged improvisation on set and Bernal seems to have had tremendous input into the finished product. 'I should say that it is thanks to the spirit and contribution of Gael that I used so much fantasy,' Gondry has said.

Bernal himself has talked enthusiastically about improvisation: 'With Michel on this film, above all else that is what he wanted: he encourages these side remarks, encourages this complexity of momentum, he asks us if it [a scene] worked and, if not, without further ado, we change it right there and then.'

Gondry would always give Bernal and his co-star room to manoeuvre: 'When I worked with Charlotte and Gael, I would not give them a lot of direction – it's stupid because they have their own ideas and, if I give them my take before they try theirs, they will never get to know what they had in mind. In the scene where

Stéphane presents his calendar, in my mind he's very shy and awkward but Gael had worked on this presentation during the night and was very confident and very funny. So he asked if he could do it his way and I said yes. When he asked me later what my idea was, I said my idea doesn't matter. I get the credit anyway as the director.'

The shoot itself lasted seven weeks and took place in Paris, although the film's animated sequences had been produced elsewhere several months earlier. To help get the director in the mood, they filmed in the apartment block where Gondry had actually lived when he worked at his calendar job: indeed his son and former partner still resided in the block, two floors higher.

Gondry evidently enjoyed directing his two leads: 'It was stupendous. Gael always had ideas and suggestions and it was great fun. Charlotte acted in an incredible way, she did everything I asked of her. Part of the work was to adapt each personality and take the best from each one. The good thing was that there wasn't much time for rehearsals and so the filming was very intense and spontaneous, the chemistry developed very quickly.'

Bernal too has spoken of the unique filming atmosphere, that usually, as an actor, you have to arrive on set as if you own the place and know exactly what you are doing but, on this picture, there was less pretence and more of an appreciation of the team ethic and that the journey's final destination was as yet unknown. Certainly Gondry seems to have appreciated the collaborative side of things, saying that it is the first feature film of his which he enjoys watching: 'I think Charlotte and Gael did such a great job. Maybe it's because I wrote the screenplay and I feel as if they took my torment away from me and so, when I watch them on screen, I'm glad I'm not on my own. So I really like to watch *Science of Sleep* over and over, but maybe it's just because I'm a narcissist.'

Gondry has also spoken of how Bernal helped create a warm working environment: 'He's also just a machine of happiness. During the shoot, he would always make everybody happy and entertain them.'

Although it was clearly an open and inclusive set, Gondry did like to keep everyone on their toes. It is typical for a director to compliment his stars after each scene, to massage their egos, keep their confidence up, but Gondry likes to play it slightly differently. 'Actors are so used to being complimented, so sometimes I feel I need to put them a little off their balance, so they feel they don't know what they're doing and are refreshed. So when they ask: "Was I good?" I say: "Yes, but don't worry, if you were bad, I wouldn't tell you." I want them to feel comfortable but not too comfortable.'

Bernal was faced with discomfort of a whole different nature: in order to film a scene in which Stéphane is flying in one of his dreams, Gondry placed a big tank of water in front of a back-projection screen in which Bernal was to swim: the water was supposed to be warm, but it wasn't. Nevertheless, Bernal seems to have enjoyed these bizarre FX methods. 'The great thing about Michel is that all his effects are mechanical: you get to see them; they are not done in post-production. The shoot was like a puppet theatre. It demanded your concentration and energy – it was great fun.'

The film starts inside one of Stéphane's regular daydreams – or perhaps night-daydreams, the idea being that he is able to manipulate his sleeping dreams, as Gondry claims also to do: Stéphane is the presenter of a TV show, the set of which is constructed out of cardboard and other handicraft materials. The programme is something of a daytime-TV variety show and this is the cookery section, although Stéphane's recipes are for making dreams rather than dishes. The difference between his exciting fantasy night job as a TV personality and his actual mundane work at a calendar printers is clear enough but it is the way in which Bernal counterbalances the two that really sets the film's tone.

He presents with charisma and panache and it is Bernal's ability to exude confidence when playing the fantasy Stéphane and contrast it with the jittery nervousness of the Stéphane of reality that holds the film together. The audience is constantly being asked to decide whether a scene is taking place inside Stéphane's head or in the wider world, and the subtle changes in the way Bernal carries his character offer us our best clue.

Bernal's charm makes his character likeable in both spheres but particularly helps with the waking Stéphane: the unwavering enthusiasm that Bernal gives Stéphane keeps us on his side even when our sympathy for his vulnerability is tested by our exasperation at his utter ineptitude and inability to overcome his timidity. Whenever the going shows any signs of getting tough, Stéphane retreats inside the child within.

Undoubtedly, Stéphane finds himself in an unfortunate set of circumstances: adrift in an unfamiliar city, missing his father and stuck in a job that stifles the creative side to his character that so clearly needs an outlet. But his decisions are poor and he makes life harder for himself: he sleeps in the bedroom of his childhood, still furnished with toys and games; he proposes a wildly inappropriate calendar based on infamous disasters; when mistaken for the removal man, he doesn't speak up but rather goes along with the charade; he pretends to be attracted to Stéphanie's friend in order to speak to Stéphanie, to whom he actually is attracted.

At various junctures, Stéphane is seen playing in a band dressed in a furry animal suit and riding a life-sized stuffed horse: there is certainly a sense of pantomime about Bernal's performance. The *LA Times* praised the way Bernal brought to mind 'the comic grace and bemused innocence of the old silent film stars, with a Buster Keaton-ish body language that suits the movie's visually lyrical style'.

While Bernal brings to the table a hyperactivity that makes you fear for what Stéphane might do next, the sense of fun that Gainsbourg gives her character is more controlled, more self-assured, and the contrast works wonderfully.

Another benefit of Bernal and Gainsbourg's casting is the game of linguistic gymnastics. From the moment they first meet, conversation flits between French, English and Spanish; this both illustrates and symbolises their difficulties and erstwhile attempts at understanding one another.

On another level, these idiomatic games help emphasise Stéphane's sense of isolation; although originally from Paris, he has been away so long that he is uncomfortable speaking in French, as no doubt Bernal was. He makes a decent fist of it but *Le Monde* noted that 'the Mexican is not quite as adept at the Parisien accent as the Argentine' (a reference to his more successful mimicry in his portrayal of Che Guevara). That he had to attempt French at all was due to the casting process: French actress Miou-Miou had long been pencilled in to play the role of Stéphane's mother and she made it clear she did not wish to speak English, hence Bernal would have to brush up on his *français*. The Spanish angle similarly came as a consequence of Bernal's coming on board. So Gondry found his hand slightly forced, although, as he rightly contests, the mishmash of languages does fit the story.

Gondry said that he was also pleased to have the opportunity to highlight the fact that these days it is common – if still slightly surreal – for many non-native speakers to have full-on friendships or relationships in their second language, namely English. In this regard, the device works too.

The language barriers help coax particularly delicate and down-to-earth performances out of Bernal and Gainsbourg. The chemistry between the two leads is one of the film's major strengths. Unlike with his two stars in *Eternal Sunshine of the Spotless Mind* (Jim Carrey and Kate Winslet), Gondry was pleased to reveal that the pair gelled off screen as well as on it and that there being a connection was also a private boon. 'In the process of starting to work on the film, I met this person who was very creative and we had this bond and I decided to make Stéphanie a little bit like her, a person that I personally had feelings for. It was not easy. When I shot the film, I still had not a clear idea of whether this person liked me or not, and that was my direction to Charlotte, that I didn't know if she liked him or not. It was like I was trying to find out my own truth by asking her if she liked him. And she told me that she did, but she was wrong. But that's life.'

Be that as it may, critics have sniped that despite Stéphane's pursuit of Stéphanie there is no sense of sexual tension: he seems to desire her as a playmate more than as a lover. This leads to another major bugbear: that Gondry never seems to want to chastise Stéphane for his immaturity; rather he defends it as an integral component of creativity. Inevitably, in a film so evidently personal, such a charge has to be extended to the director and the film itself: that it is no more than childish play.

Advocates of the picture, such as those at the Sitges Film Festival in Spain who awarded it the People's Prize, would argue that one of its virtues is that it avoids the tired clichés of film romance and rises above typically lurid Hollywood sex appeal. Gondry, meanwhile, defends himself by saying that when you are in love you do behave like a child. But in a movie that relies on the audience sharing its sense of fun, this is a key issue. Certainly it is something that divides viewers: they either love its quirky inventiveness or grow weary of its lack of substance. To the latter, the novelty of the visual trickery soon wears off and the film becomes a sequence of near-random images that exist almost entirely in order for the director to experiment.

Gondry has said that he never puts an image in just because it looks pretty; that from pop videos, through adverts to feature films, narrative is always key. Yet there is no escaping the fact that fun and games with visuals is perhaps this film's real *raison d'être*. And there is nothing necessarily wrong in that: all forms of art have experimental proponents who counter escapism by periodically reminding the public that what they are viewing is art. Similarly, pushing boundaries and reinventing the craft – or at least what is expected of the craft – has a place in any artistic medium.

In this regard Gondry is not unlike his fellow countryman and contemporary, Jean-Luc Godard, and at its best *The Science of Sleep* does bring to mind the bold cinematic inventiveness of the great Nouvelle Vague director's earlier pieces; the problem is that at its worst it echoes Godard's later work in which, no matter the originality, many viewers ultimately drift away detached and distracted.

That said, Bernal himself is one of the film's most vocal advocates when it comes to its inventive nature, in the belief that its very uniqueness is justification enough. He has argued that the film 'makes you understand better what is cinema. This is how people like George Méliès and the Lumière brothers discovered it, who knew that you made cinema through such experiments, like the superimposing of images, dissolves, animations done square by square. This is how you understand the practical and abstract concepts of cinema.'

Warming to his theme, Bernal stated: 'Cinema is art, they are fictitious elements which converge and create a particular reality. Sometimes it is very difficult to trace a line over what happens in this reality. Personally, after a seeming bombardment of films which carry reality under the arm, I decided to throw it all out of the window and go tell a story about dreams, a love story which never happened nor will ever happen but to tell it with all the cinematic elements.'

In the same spirit of experiment and playfulness, when asked what he had learned from the role Bernal replied: 'To pay even more attention to your dreams. To respect them and live them, experiment, play with them. All human beings dream, it is a biological necessity. And I feel that subconsciously they help you, they are like a safety valve.'

Perhaps attentive to his dreams, on finishing *The Science of Sleep*, Bernal agreed to reunite the dream team and work again with Gondry on the director's planned adaptation of Rudy Rucker's *Master of Space and Time*.

The Science of Sleep has been criticised for being too long in duration, too short of plot. It is hard to dispute the gripe but that is not to say that Gondry should stick to shorter video clips, more that he perhaps does work better with a separate scriptwriter, someone who can apply a bit of discipline when required and tie all these ideas up with a convincing, controlling idea.

Bernal has described how the chance to give his imagination a chance to go out and play was what drew him to the project in the first place. Unlike Stéphane, both Bernal and Gondry have, in cinema, found an outlet for their creativity.

The Science of Sleep is a lot like Stéphane: at its most confident when dealing in fantasy but stuttering when forced to tackle the nitty-gritty. The film as a whole manages to be like its main protagonist, a misunderstood creative; a fine trick to pull off but ultimately perhaps not quite enough.

Blood Wedding

Bernal made some good friends on *The Science of Sleep* and his next project made it relatively easy for him to keep in contact. He took a role in the London stage show of the Federico García Lorca play *Blood Wedding*, and during rehearsals would make use of the Eurostar to head over to Paris for a weekend.

Blood Wedding was directed by Rufus Norris at the Almeida Theatre, located in Bernal's old north London stomping ground, Islington. Norris had staged a hugely successful production of *Festen* at the theatre the previous year.

Before the Almeida, Norris, as Associate Director at the Young Vic, had in 2003 put on a Lope de Vega play, *Peribáñez y el Comendador de Ocaña*, in which Bernal very nearly took a role. Norris and Bernal had met and hit it off ahead of casting but in the end the dates couldn't quite be worked into the actor's schedule.

Back then, Bernal had made both *Amores Perros* and *Y Tu Mamá También* but not yet *The Motorcycle Diaries* and *Bad Education*. By the time Norris next courted him, for *Blood Wedding* in 2005, Bernal's star shined considerably brighter. Given that Norris had been trying to cast Bernal in a play for a number of years, the director was justified in his claims to the press that he had chosen the Mexican for his acting abilities and not his box-office appeal.

'In a way that's the stock response that any director is going to give when asked why he cast a star. "Why did you cast somebody that ensured the show would sell out in four hours?" And you say it was because he was a good actor,' laughs Norris now. 'But I don't think anyone could argue that with Gael. I think he is fantastic and we were very lucky to get him.'

How they did get him was straightforward enough, although it did involve Norris and his wife, the writer Tanya Ronder, heading out to Mexico. Maggie Lunn was the casting director and executive producer at the Almeida. During the *Festen* run, she proposed a production of *Blood Wedding*, with Ronder adapting, Norris directing and Bernal starring.

'I just said, "Yeah, great, if we can get him then for sure",' recalls Norris. 'He very swiftly responded to say it would be great to talk about it, that it would be a great chance for him to come back to Britain, having trained here and made a lot of friends here, but also about wanting to do Lorca.'

Soon, Norris and Ronder found themselves in Mexico City. 'We texted each other and he said for us to go to this roundabout just outside this part of the city sometime the next day,' Norris says, taking up the story. 'So we went to this roundabout and on the button he and Pablo [Cruz] came haring round the corner in what I think was his mum's car and we headed up to the hills.'

A weekend of socialising ensued. 'We went up to his mum's house, which is in this tiny village a couple of hours away [from Mexico City] and chatted on the way. We got there, had something to eat, went for a swim, went for a walk, went to the village and then on the way back we passed a little bar – the only bar in this little village – and Gael said: "Do you fancy a quick drink?" And so it all begins.

'We went in and it was like something out of a spaghetti western, with swinging doors and these two guys leaning up against the bar in their hats and all the rest of it. On the walls there was some soft porn and then not far from it the statue of Mary and some sort of adorations. The two guys looked at us as we sat down and it was as if tumbleweed was going past outside and we thought: "Oh fuck, this all looks a bit . . ." But at the same time we knew we were there with Gael and everyone in Mexico knows who he is. The guys at the bar would be aware that he lives nearby or that he sometimes came down there.

'As it turned out they [the two men] were just gagging to get involved. Cut to ten minutes later and we are all round one table and they are saying: "Have some of this, have some of that." Three hours later, half the village is in there and we are legless.

'Tequila? Oh yeah – and some sort of obscure ice cream. Someone there ran an ice-cream stall so had gone and opened up the garage and dragged out their ice-cream cart. It all got out of hand but in a really fantastic way.'

They all awoke with sore heads the next day but the deal was sealed: Bernal would be treading the boards at the Almeida.

The play ran every day from 6 May to 18 June and rehearsals began five weeks before opening night. When there is a star turn in the camp, the rest of the cast and crew cannot help but be aware of their importance, that the show is sold out because of the big name. 'As a director, you can try and create a good environment but ultimately it is up to the star and how they behave with other people,' says Norris. 'From the word go, Gael was just another member of the company. There was absolutely none of that star stuff. I'm sure all his life he will loathe all that kind of thing.'

The cast was extremely mixed, incorporating nine different nationalities including Icelandic, Irish, Dutch, Portuguese, Madagascan – and a certain

Mexican. 'We did a lovely thing at the end of the first day of rehearsals. I had everyone gather round and I told them to sing a song in their native tongue. It was one of those gulp moments for actors who don't really know each other,' recalls the director, 'but I had some mates in the company, actors I'd worked with a lot, and Hano [Björn Hylnur Haraldsson], a lovely Icelandic actor, just stood up and sang some gorgeous Icelandic song and then one by one the others followed. Gael was one of the first in the queue, just got up and sang out this thing, I don't know what it was but some lovely Mexican number.'

Casting Bernal was nevertheless an artistic gamble – Norris had never seen him in the theatre before – but, as soon as they started, that Bernal had an electrifying stage presence was there for all to see. 'Yes, absolutely it was,' says Norris. 'He is full of celebration and life just kind of emanates from him – but in that light and dark way.'

Blood Wedding concerns a bride who steals away on her wedding night with a former lover, Leonardo. Her husband sets off to find them, resulting in tragedy for all concerned: Leonardo and the husband kill each other; the bride survives but will be ostracised by society as a whore, while Leonardo's own wife must live out her time in shame at her husband's actions. Bernal played Leonardo, the only character named.

Although performing a play provides little scope for improvisation, preparing the play does. 'Whenever he was let off the leash he was terrific and we had a lot of music in the show and he really got involved in all of that. He is a wonderful person to work with,' recalls Norris.

Still, *Blood Wedding* brings back mixed memories for the director. 'I don't think that either Gael or I would claim that *Blood Wedding* was the high point of our careers. We took a lot of risks with it and some of them paid off and some of them didn't. Somehow the process never quite took flight in the way that we had hoped it would.

'If I have an abiding feeling about it, it's that I wish I had delivered Bernal a better production. The show was a big hit and it did well and some parts of it worked very, very well but we didn't quite get the balance right with the chemistry, the various pheromone attachments, and in that play all that is really, really important. We had nine different nationalities in the cast from pretty much every continent and so the gamble increases massively in that sense – although I'm not at all sorry that we did that, I learned a great deal.'

It was the international cast who came in for most criticism among reviewers.

Some felt that in a play about Andalucian passions coming to the boil, North European actors and actresses just weren't appropriate.

There are evidently some very strong opinions in the theatre world about how one should put on a Lorca play. One of the reasons that Bernal, a big Lorca fan, had wanted to do the play was to avoid all that nonsense. 'He wanted to do a Lorca play but not in Spanish because there was a whole load of baggage that goes with it over there [Mexico or Spain]. As it happens there is here too, as we found out with the critics,' says Norris.

'We were quite bold with how we tried to do it and most of the responses were very good but some of the purists went for us. The reviews ranged from five stars in some of the nationals to – I think it was the *Evening Standard* whose opening line was something like: "A crime has been committed against theatre and the chief perpetrators are Rufus Norris and Tanya Ronda."

'It really divided them but that is a lot to do with Lorca. There is this romantic idea of how you do Lorca: that you have got to do it with Spanish accents and lots of people going ranga-tang-tang on a guitar; that you really can't fuck with it. And actually it is a really, really hard play to do – it is not even really a play, in fact, more of a poem and I don't think there has ever been a production in this country that has been lauded.'

Bernal's performance was generally praised if not completely celebrated. The *Guardian* said he was good but not incandescent enough, while others thought his performance suffered by the work of those around him (not managing to convince as sufficient causes for his emotional actions) and the part itself, 'a relatively two-dimensional character requiring a far stronger presence on stage' according to the *Stage*.

'From one or two critics there was some kind of pathetic bitching about the fact that Gael is not six feet tall,' recalls Norris with a shake of the head. 'And you think to yourself: "This is staggering. We are trying to encourage the likes of Gael, an international-class actor, to come [to the London stage] and you get this." I just thought that was pathetic, really.'

The production itself went well. 'It was pretty smooth and it warmed up and it got better as it went along and they were a very happy company, very committed. Hano and Gael shared a dressing room and they became big buddies and shortly afterwards a few of them from *Blood Wedding* all piled off to Iceland. As a director, you know things have gone well when these little trails open up from inside the company.'

That trail would lead Bernal back to Iceland in 2007 and back to the stage. While working on *Blood Wedding*, he was introduced to Gísli Örn Gardarsson, an Icelandic theatre director. A few years later, Bernal went to see Gardarsson's *Metamorphosis* in London. They met afterwards and the director told Bernal about his plans to stage *Tilsammans* (*Together*), the Swedish film by Lukas Moodyson (with whom Bernal would eventually make the movie *Mammoth*). Bernal said it was the best idea he had heard for a long time and asked to join in.

Blood Wedding sold out in a matter of hours, two months before it opened. During the production itself, queues started to form from around 3 p.m. every day in the hope of snaffling any tickets put back on resale. Crowds also gathered each night at the stage door. 'We had to find a back exit [for Bernal] so that he didn't have to emerge out of the dressing room into the hordes. Every day there were young girls and sometimes he would come out and do his obligatory signing and stuff. It was just a little insight into how boring all that side must be,' says Norris.

A different side of the fame game was seen by Norris in Mexico. 'You are out on the road somewhere and stop to buy something, whether it is from the solitary watermelon seller or whatever. So there is a guy there who stands on that road all day long, that's what he does for a job, and he gives you the stuff, you exchange money etc. . . . And just at the end he says to Gael: "Do you mind?" And Gael says: "No." And he heads off to his little shack and comes back with a piece of paper and gets him to sign it. There is no, "Oh, you're . . ." They just have a little chat about the football or whatever and that's it. I think there is a mutual love affair there which is great.'

Some of the director's most treasured moments linked to the *Blood Wedding* production hark back to being on the road in Mexico with Bernal. 'What was lovely was just driving with him through Mexico for what would have amounted altogether to about five hours with him just talking about the country. Like those long scenes in *Y Tu Mamá También* where you really got a sense of the politics of the director.' This time, Bernal was providing the voiceover. 'He is deeply politicised in a really intelligent way.'

Politico

In an early interview with Argentine newspaper *La Nación*, to promote *Y Tu Mamá También*, Bernal was asked what he wanted from his future: *'Quiero ser presidente güey!'* – 'I want to become president, dude,' was his reply. He was joking, but politics do play an important part in Bernal's life and are a fundamental element of his persona. Given that he grew up in a liberal left-wing household, with tales of the Cuban Revolution for bedtime stories, it could hardly have been otherwise. Yet Bernal himself might argue that it could hardly have been otherwise given the part of the world he grew up in. 'Whatever you do in Latin America involves taking a political standpoint,' he said.

Whereas he found London to be apathetic politically, it is hard not to take an interest in government in Mexico. Recent general elections are a case in point: in the UK, turnout gets ever lower as the electorate feels uninspired to choose between two parties converging on the centre ground. The 2006 election in Mexico, however, ended in massive turmoil and with thousands of protesters camping out on the capital's main streets for months on end.

Ahead of the vote, Manuel López Obrador, the popular former mayor of Mexico City, representing the centre-left Partido de la Revolución Democrática (Democratic Revolution Party – PRD), was ahead in the polls and clear favourite to become the new president. But following the July ballot, Felipe Calderón Hinojosa of the incumbent Partido Acción Nacional (National Action Party – PAN) emerged as the surprise winner. Yet Calderón had scored a mere 200,000 more votes than Obrador which, in a country with a population of 105 million, was minimal to say the least, especially given calls of foul play (and in a country of the size and range of Mexico, vigilance and monitoring is difficult).

Obrador and his supporters accused PAN of electoral fraud but independent adjudicators declared the vote, after a few re-counts here and there, acceptable. Other dissenters argued that the damage had been done before the poll, with negative and unfair campaigning (Obrador was made out to be the new Hugo Chávez, Venezuela's firebrand leader, scaring off many potential supporters). A new vote was called for by PRD and dismissed by PAN. The sorry affair dragged on, with Obrador's supporters only disbanding their downtown dissent encampments in the September.

Bernal spoke of the election at the NFT in October that same year.

> This has been one of the most difficult moments for democracy in
> Mexico. If they say fraud was committed here, then I believe that fraud
> was committed long before because there was a dirty war against one of
> the contestants. By the time of the election, if you were in Mexico and
> you were in parts from Morelia upwards, everyone voted for Calderón.
> This is something that people in Mexico City find hard to believe. And
> whoever won this election was going to win by this tiny margin, from
> one side or the other. Of course I sympathise with Andrés Manuel
> López Obrador to begin with, because it was the party that was much
> more in tune with my voting preference, but the margin was so tight and
> the whole thing went absolutely bonkers and it was impossible to follow.

Given such a scenario, it is easy to see why Bernal claims that it would be hard
to be a responsible citizen in Mexico and not have a political opinion. Nor were
the events of 2006 a one-off: Bernal remembers 1994 as an equally tumultuous
year which marked his youth. Back then the Partido Revolucionario Institucional
(Institutional Revolutionary Party – PRI), which would fall just weeks before the
release of *Amores Perros* after a seventy-year reign, were still firmly in power. There
would be two major political assassinations over the course of the year and a
massive currency devaluation, triggering widespread economic crisis.

On 1 January, the North American Free Trade Agreement (NAFTA) came
into being, having been drawn up in 1992. Besides hampering domestic cinema,
NAFTA was expected to (and did) benefit already wealthy businessmen and hit
the rural poor. On that same New Year's Day, there was an indigenous uprising
in the state of Chiapas, a region located in the extreme south of the country and
one of Mexico's poorest.

Revolutionaries labelling themselves the Zapatistas, masterminded by the
masked and pipe-smoking Subcomandante Marcos, led a peaceful takeover of
state institutions and demanded a fairer deal for their people. The government
reacted in predictably heavy-handed fashion, sending in troops to wage war.
Mexicans everywhere, and particularly those in the capital, who previously were
perhaps barely aware of this remote corner of their country, came out in support
of the Zapatistas.

'That movement polarised the country, but it also united a lot of people. We helped to stop the war. It felt that whatever we did would count. Something like a million and a half people demonstrated every day when the war started between the government and the guerrillas,' Bernal recalled in *Time Out*. 'I was very involved. I helped with sending food, writing and reading about the situation, and demonstrating about it on the marches.'

However, it wasn't solely Bernal's sense of justice that saw him getting involved. 'It was great. I was young, and it was fun. And I've got to say, I met my first girlfriend – my first real girlfriend – there as well. It was a great place to meet girls.'

Mexico, as with Latin America generally, is marked by extreme inequality. On a very visual level, the poverty of the poorest sectors of society contrasts sharply with the opulence of the rich elite: from pre-fabricated slums to penthouse villas in a hop, skip and a jump.

Every Mexican of Bernal's generation remembers exactly where they were when the great earthquake hit in 1985: the epicentre was near Acapulco on the Pacific coast but tremors could be felt as far away as Guadalajara. Officially the death toll in Mexico City was around the 10,000 mark, but locals believe that in reality it may have been up to ten times higher, the PRI then fiddling the figures. Furthermore, the damage need not have been so devastating had so many of the city's buildings not been erected on the cheap, ignoring the fact that Mexico lay on an earthquake fault line.

Most of Bernal's contemporaries will also recall at least two massive currency devaluations, when savings lost their value overnight.

Such events shape a child's conscience (indeed when asked by *El Universal* newspaper what event would mark the start of the movie of his life story, Bernal cited the 1985 earthquake) and bring sociopolitics to the fore.

'Ever since you're born in Mexico, you're faced and confronted with this situation, these impossibilities. You think why, why?' explained Bernal. 'You ask yourself these very elemental questions as a kid that are very valid, you know? Why should a person be poorer than the other, and why is five cents important for one person and not important for another?'

Fringe-theatre acting is hardly a get-rich profession but it is, nevertheless, an existence far removed from that of a rural Mexican peasant. Bernal's early upbringing would have been comfortable, all the more so once his parents moved to Mexico City and started to work in television. He himself began to earn a wage from stage acting aged ten.

But Bernal was encouraged to be inquisitive, to observe and seek to understand his surroundings and that in his country there were many people less fortunate than he. When he was fourteen, he partook in literacy programmes in the mountains in Mexico with indigenous people, the Huichol Indians in particular. 'That again inevitably awakens you and surprises you that actually we share the same place,' recounted Bernal. 'You find yourself in a more privileged situation just because you're born the way you are, you know, and they're underprivileged because of what they are, and yet we share the same territory, and it's ridiculous! This concept cannot be swallowed easily.'

Bernal has described the teaching programme as a journey of discovery and awareness for himself but also as a two-way process: 'It's a sense of giving back to the land where you come from. It's almost as if to recognise yourself in the place you live in you feel that you're giving something back to someone who is your brother, in a way, it feels so close. You're teaching people on a particular level to be free; they're teaching you on a spiritual level to be free. It's an exchange.'

Mexico has more than its fair share of problems but Bernal resolutely chooses to remain. 'In my case, the decision to live in Mexico is a personal one. It has nothing to do with a sense of duty or responsibility. But it is also, inevitably, a political decision.'

Given work commitments, Bernal is frequently on the road somewhere, either shooting a movie or promoting one, but when he is free to return home he heads back to Mexico, dividing his time between the capital and Cuernavaca, a city fifty kilometres south of Mexico City. The *LA Times* asked him why. 'Any explanation of why I like living there [Mexico] changes from day to day, and I still don't have it very well dissected. My family is there, my friends are there . . . I feel in touch with the territory.'

His popularity in Mexico is based on pride at his achievements but also in the pride he displays towards his native land. He has a very visual presence in Mexico and people do appreciate that he cares about the plight of his fellow countrymen and supports initiatives to boost equality, justice and culture. 'I feel I still have kind of an effervescent ideal of thinking that there is an initiative that you're born with, about trying to make the place where you are born better,' he says.

To such ends, Bernal went down to Chiapas, as the guest of ANEC (Asociación Nacional de Empresas Campesinas – National Association of Countryside Businesses) to visit farmers and learn about the difficulties faced by corn producers. Maize is the most important foodstuff for Mexicans but in recent years prices have soared. In essence, NAFTA allowed Mexico to be flooded with cheap corn from the US. Unable to compete with the subsidised giants across the frontier to their north, Mexican farmers are being forced to end a centuries-old tradition and stop growing corn, but a lack of domestic production makes Mexico an importer of its most basic staple, leaving it vulnerable to price hikes from abroad. It also makes for a less-nutritious (and tasty) diet, replacing the classic white tortillas derived from Mexican corn with the yellow ones made from US kernels. Bernal also noted the slight irony in the US market beating Mexico's into submission, then complaining when rural economic migrants are forced to seek their livelihood north of the border.

Following his field trip, Bernal accompanied Mary Robinson, the former President of Ireland and current UN High Commissioner for Human Rights, to the World Trade Organisation (WTO) summit in Hong Kong. He spent ten days there as a global ambassador for Oxfam, attending several meetings and forums and presenting his case study of Chiapas.

He was also entrusted with handing in the Make Trade Fair petition, a call for the removal of unjust trading conditions in global markets, which had been organised through Oxfam and signed by some 17.8 million people worldwide. In the company of Benin singer Angelique Kidjo and Chinese musician Anthony Wong, Bernal presented the petition to Pascal Lammy, the director general of the WTO. At the ceremony, Bernal said: 'Part of my family are farmers. I come to represent them as well as all the farmers in Mexico and across Latin America. The situation is explosive, it cannot go on like this.'

Bernal had previously been present in Edinburgh for the 'Make Poverty History' protests at the G8 summit, rather than at the Live8 concert in Hyde Park, and was one of several high-profile figures (Bono, Thom Yorke and Colin Firth among others) who posed for photos as part of Oxfam's 'Poverty Doesn't Fall from the Sky' campaign. In a symbolic gesture, the celebrities had various agricultural products tipped over their heads in order to highlight the rich world's practice of dumping undersold goods into poorer countries, who are then unable to compete on these unequal terms. Bernal was covered in cotton.

As well as working with Oxfam, Bernal is also heading a scheme in Mexico that aims to establish a custom whereby the proceeds from a film's premiere are donated to charity. He led the way by ensuring that the takings from *The Science of Sleep*'s debut were donated to the Casa de la Sal clinic, which helps treat HIV-positive children.

Long committed to promoting AIDS-prevention awareness in the developing world, Bernal's efforts were commended by the Aid for Aids Foundation, who gave him their 'My Hero' award. At the ceremony in New York in May 2007, Bernal said that he didn't feel himself an activist, rather he was merely conducting himself in a manner that befitted his upbringing.

'Latin Americans grow up politicised,' reiterated Bernal. 'Your politics are not divorced from who you are as a person, you're soaked in it. The military dictatorships were all in the recent past, within my memory, and that informs my life. Imagine how politicised all those Iraqi kids are going to be in ten years' time.'

He was a staunch and vocal critic of the Iraq war before the invasion and continued to be so once the bombs began to fall. In an anti-war concert in Madrid, Bernal told the audience that José María Aznar, the Spanish President who led Spain into the war alongside the US and UK, had opposed Latin America with his decision, given that Chile and Mexico had preserved the region's dignity by refusing to back the US at the UN security council, despite immense pressure.

Yet it was his words of protest at the 2003 Academy Awards that will live longest in the memory. The Oscar ceremony is watched live by more than thirty million people in the US alone and upsetting Hollywood's conservative establishment had accounted for more than one failed career before Bernal, someone who, as an actor, had yet to even taste Tinseltown. Speaking out against the invasion was risky to say the least.

Two weeks prior to the ceremony, he had been delighted to receive his invitation to make a presentation, especially as it was to introduce Caetano Veloso and Lila Downs and their performance of a song from *Frida*. He was less thrilled when the script arrived a week later, some hotchpotch about Latin American unity and being proud of his country's culture which introduced Veloso as the Brazilian Bob Dylan.

What's more, it became clear that the US would be at war come Oscar night; being for or against invading Iraq was the issue of the hour.

So Bernal composed his own speech, although he went along with the set script during rehearsals. On the night, friends were egging him on, most notably Pedro Almodóvar and Salma Hayek, the latter the producer and star of *Frida* who was with Bernal backstage as he necked a glass of champagne and walked on.

'The next song is from *Frida*. Frida Kahlo once said: "I don't paint my dreams, I paint my realities." The necessity for peace in the world is not a dream, it's a reality. We are not alone. If Frida Kahlo was alive, she would certainly be on our side against the war.'

Tim Robbins and Susan Sarandon had arrived on the red carpet flicking the peace sign in all directions and Chris Cooper, when collecting his Oscar for Best Supporting Actor, had wished everyone peace among all the problems that there were in the world. But Bernal was the first to mention the war by name, to speak of the elephant in the room.

He was heartily congratulated by Hollywood's right-on brigade afterwards, while its conservative wing were irate at the presumptuousness of the young upstart. Bernal said that he had been very nervous but that ultimately, 'There are so many people who really want to be part of Hollywood. But I don't care.' He added that if they had wanted someone to read from the script, they should have called one of their own.

'There was a need, an obligation to say something. The war had just started and I was representing Frida Kahlo, one of the reddest people there ever was on the planet,' he would tell *Fotogramas* once the dust had settled. 'What better platform. We are against the war, we are many, millions, we are everyone, we are all against the war. The consequences? No fucking idea. I knew I had a moral, social, political obligation, as far as I understood it. I had to be true to myself in such moments.'

So no regrets from Bernal, especially as he met his new girlfriend, a certain Natalie Portman, that night. 'For many reasons that night was perfect.'

Babel

Given that the treatment of Mexican immigrants by the United States is one of Bernal's primary political concerns, the role he took on in *Babel* proved particularly appropriate. Bernal filled the shoes of Santiago, a hot-headed young Mexican from Tijuana whose frustrations boil over at the border crossing into the US, with disastrous consequences for all concerned.

Babel was director Alejandro González Iñárritu's study of globalisation in which several interconnected stories from around the globe unravel at the same time. It was an ambitious project to say the very least, necessitating a long shoot split across three continents in order to depict narratives in Morocco, Japan and the area either side of the US-Mexican border.

Iñárritu's debut, *Amores Perros*, had been scripted by Guillermo Arriaga and the pair also joined forces on *21 Grams*, the director's second feature. *Babel* was to be their third collaboration and the conclusion of a loosely thematic trilogy based on tragic twists of fate. It was to be a hugely successful undertaking, with the finished product winning a whole host of prizes and securing a Best Picture Oscar nomination. It would also mark the end of their creative partnership: the duo would have a bitter fall-out during the course of the project's development.

All began harmoniously enough on *Babel*. Charged by Iñárritu to come up with a screenplay exploring the idea of symbolic borderlines, Arriaga produced his first draft in late 2004. Iñárritu then began to rework it, contemplating matters of setting and locations. As a nineteen-year-old, Iñárritu had travelled to Morocco, a trip that had made a deep impression on him, and he saw the new film as an ideal opportunity to return. Out of his own pocket, he funded a research trip to Morocco and Tunisia, inviting independent producers Steve Golin and John Kilik (ultimately then responsible for the likes of *The Eternal Sunshine of the Spotless Mind* and *Broken Flowers* respectively) along for the ride. This led to them co-producing *Babel* with Iñárritu and the film being backed by Paramount; it was actually the first project to get the green light from Paramount's new management team (Brad Grey had not long replaced Sherry Lansing) with a budget of US$25 million.

Given that Iñárritu had moved to Hollywood several years earlier and been forced to negotiate the Tijuana border crossing regularly himself, the region proved a natural inspiration for another segment of the film.

Japan, meanwhile, had fascinated Iñárritu when he visited the country to promote *21 Grams*.

Given the logistics, it would always be a complicated film to make, requiring permanent crew members, such as Iñárritu's regular cameraman Rodrigo Prieto, along for the whole ride and specialist teams in each of the three main locations. Iñárritu has since compared the process to making four different films.

For the Mexican section of the shoot (the California interiors were also shot in Tijuana), Iñárritu was able to call on some familiar faces with almost the whole *Amores Perros* crew answering the call. Iñárritu had invited most of them on board for *21 Grams* but, given that it had been a US production made north of the border, any non-English speakers from *Amores Perros* had to be left behind. A few members of the *Amores Perros* crew had inevitably moved on in the meantime (Carlos Hidalgo, for example, had given up assistant-director work to dedicate himself to cinematography) but the Mexican shoot of *Babel* was still very much a professional reunion.

One returnee was Tita Lombardo, production mananger on *Amores Perros* and line producer for the Mexican stage of *Babel*. 'It was a real pleasure to make the film because it was so unexpected for all concerned,' says Lombardo. 'The feeling was that we had lost Alejandro González Iñárritu, that his film-making would take place outside Mexico from now on, so it was a great and pleasant surprise to be working together again.' It is worth recalling that almost all the crew had been making their movie debuts with *Amores Perros*, having worked with Iñárritu for a number of years making commercials, so these were working relationships and emotional ties that went back a long way.

Given the spirit of nostalgia, it was only natural that Iñárritu would find a part for Bernal in the new venture. Furthermore, where Adriana Barraza had played Bernal's mother in *Amores Perros*, she would be his aunt in *Babel*.

Barraza, in a performance which would earn her a Best Supporting Actress Oscar nomination, played Amelia, a Mexican nanny to two small children in San Diego whose parents are on vacation in Morocco. A delay to their journey home means that Amelia is forced to take the little ones with her to her son's wedding, across the border in Tijuana. Her nephew Santiago (Bernal) drives them all down there. On their way back, Santiago, again at the wheel but now somewhat over-the-limit from the festivities, takes issue with a rude border official and makes a getaway into the desert, where he ends up abandoning Amelia and the children.

As it transpires, the holidaying parents of those children are Brad Pitt and Cate

Blanchett, or at least their alter egos Richard and Susan, who are on the trip of a lifetime in a desperate attempt to rescue their relationship from the deep misery into which it has sunk. What's more, the cause of their delay turns out to be that Susan is at death's door having been shot by a stray bullet.

That bullet was fired by one of a pair of Moroccan boys who had been fooling around with the rifle their shepherd father had recently acquired to protect his flock from jackals. As if they weren't in enough trouble, the boys' accidental gunshot is soon interpreted as a terrorist attack, making the accident an international incident for which culprits must be found.

Meanwhile, over in Japan, a deaf and mute teenage girl rebels against her distant widowed father by taking drugs and going out clubbing before, in her desperate need for affection, exposing herself in public and offering her body to the policeman who visits the apartment. The officer has come to trace the ownership of a gun, a rifle the girl's father had left behind on a hunting trip to Morocco as a present to the guide.

Thus *Babel* attempts to demonstrate how closely connected is everything in a globalised world.

The first scenes to be filmed were those set in Morocco. After unsuccessfully auditioning among Paris's Muslim community and then scouring Morocco's young professional performers, Iñárritu settled on non-actors for the roles of the two boys, advertising his search via the loudspeakers of village mosques.

Blanchett, meanwhile, was an actress Iñárritu had long admired, while Brad Pitt was selected for his all-American image and to play on his celebrity. 'I liked to punish him, make him look older, convert him into a human being and make it so that people [watching] forgot that this man was Brad Pitt,' Iñárritu would say. 'And Brad wasn't a star on the shoot because nobody knew who he was. We filmed in a village with no lights, in the middle of nowhere. The people were very humble and they didn't have television sets. I think this helped him because it was a difficult role for him to do.'

Difficult seems to sum up the whole Moroccan leg of the shoot. Although she didn't get involved until Mexico, that is how Lombardo understands it: 'Morocco seems to have been the hardest section to shoot due to logistics, language, general conditions and Hollywood stars to look after.' Japan appears to have been no cakewalk either: Iñárritu has described how there were no official permits or systems in which to rent locations so you just had to go and shoot; at one point they were threatened with jail having slowed down the morning traffic.

The known quantities of Mexico seem to have provided much-needed relief: 'Once in Mexico, "El Negro" [Iñárritu] was happy and relaxed. He was surrounded by familiarity, both of country, conditions and crew. He could even live at home,' notes Lombardo. 'It was a good job that the Mexican section came in the middle really because it would maybe have been too full-on to have headed straight to Japan from Morocco without the home respite.'

The Moroccan shoot began in early May and there was much deliberation about where to shoot next, Japan and Mexico changing place on the schedule a number of times as seasonal factors were considered. In the end, Mexico filled the sandwich and cast and crew just had to put up with the searing temperatures of the Sonoran Desert in September. 'There were five dehydration cases,' recalls Lombardo. 'I was co-ordinating ambulances back and forth from the hospital. Adriana even became very ill at one point.'

Filming took place in Puerto Peñasco, Sonora and Tijuana itself. 'Tijuana is pretty chaotic but if you can make a film in Mexico City, you can certainly handle Tijuana,' says Lombardo. 'It was a fairly straightforward shoot, although quite serious and characterised by time pressures. They had a date when they had to be filming in Japan and, as I understood it, there was no flexibility where Japan was concerned.'

Nevertheless there was a slight delay to the Mexican leg. 'It was supposed to be a four-week shoot but it took five, though this is nothing major or unusual,' recounts Lombardo, adding that, despite the time constraints, 'the shoot in Mexico was still fun, with meals and parties all together'.

There was a good atmosphere on set, fostered by familiarity but helped too by Iñárritu's growing stature. 'He was nervous at the start of making *Amores Perros* but on *Babel*, having by then established himself and achieved recognition, he had grown in confidence and was more sure of himself. This meant he was much more relaxed, which showed itself by him being much nicer to the crew,' laughs Lombardo.

That said, Iñárritu still liked to keep them on their toes. 'If a shot is already quite complicated, he likes to make it two, three, four, maybe five times more difficult,' says Lombardo. When out in the desert – which, Lombardo points out, is much of a muchness – Iñárritu and Prieto had quad bikes to whizz about on and decide exactly where they wanted to shoot. 'Once they were right in the distance, no smaller than ants, El Negro would radio in: "Here".'

As she co-ordinated the laying of tracks across the sand in order to transport all the equipment and set up camp where Iñárritu wanted to film, Lombardo couldn't help but think to herself: 'And why not right here?'

Filming in the desert brought a whole host of other problems, chief among them the issue of snakes. Given that they were filming with children, they had to be extra careful. They hired a snake-catcher. 'Everyday, El Negro would ask if any snakes had been caught and, as long as the snake-catcher produced at least a couple, he was happy,' remembers Lombardo with amusement. 'Maybe they were the same two every time, who knows?'

Joking aside, it was a serious concern: they filmed all night, through until five o'clock in the morning, and often Prieto was walking around shooting hand-held, following the kids and Adriana in the dark; anything could have jumped out.

That they were wandering about in the middle of the desert in the dead of night was all thanks to Santiago, Bernal's character. 'Santiago is a kid who ends up in the dramatic structure as being the catalyst of the tragedy that occurs in Tijuana,' explained the actor. 'He provides the vehicle and he is the vehicle of this tragedy. On a very immediate level you can just say that his reaction was a mistake fuelled by alcohol.'

That Santiago was still somewhat shiny by the time he was driving home is no surprise as at the wedding, he parties like the best of them. The wedding scene comes across as a gloriously festive celebration. It was filmed in the border village of Tecate using many locals and Iñárritu used party tunes instead of voices on the playback to get everyone in the mood. Certainly the tactic seems to have worked on Bernal, who cuts some moves: 'I didn't get to dance much in the film but I learned through my cousins who are from the north, they taught me,' he said.

He gives his dancefloor display with a gun tucked into his belt, which he then fires into the air, a juxtaposition of joy and menace that encapsulates his character. Santiago's natural charisma sees him take the children under his wing. In one memorable scene he surprises them with a demonstration of how to kill a chicken, flamboyantly wringing its neck (animal lovers will be pleased to learn that a mechanical chicken was used).

Bernal has spoken of watching the US and Mexican children mingling off camera as one of the pleasures of the shoot. Lombardo agrees: 'That was one of the nicest things about the shoot. The two US kids were lovely. They were discovering Mexico for the first time and everything was completely new to them so their reactions on screen are genuine.'

Iñárritu made sure: 'The kids would always be asking what was going to happen, what they were going to do, but El Negro is clever in that he doesn't really tell them, he just says, "Oh, you'll see", so that when things do happen, with the camera rolling, the reactions are natural.'

Instead of sending a team to film 'The Making of *Babel*' over five days, as Paramount had suggested, Iñárritu contracted two up-and-coming Mexican documentary film-makers (Carlos Armella and Pedro González-Rubio) to record the whole process. As part of this behind-the-scenes film, Bernal interviewed the two US youngsters. 'I just asked the kids what the differences are between Mexico and the United States that you see and they said: "Um, the food, um, oh and the people that sell in the streets." In the United States there's no people that sell in the streets. "Um, the language." That's it – those were the three basic differences.'

Of course, language was a major difference for everyone, throughout the shoot. *Babel* is the biblical tale in which God punishes mankind for its ambitions to build a tower to heaven by making people speak different languages. Given the scale of the undertaking, the parallels with making *Babel* the movie were all too obvious. Iñárritu says that at some points (in Morocco) the crew were speaking six different languages.

Language barriers made Iñárritu's task even more difficult. 'Directing actors and non-actors was one of the hardest things; directing people from very humble communities, or the deaf and dumb in Japan, all in a language that they didn't understand . . . to be able to orchestrate this madness and find a visual grammar, that was the difficult part.'

As befits its title, breakdown in communication is one of the movie's major themes. On the surface, there is Richard's and Susan's vulnerability due to their inability to speak Arabic and cope with their surrounds. On a larger scale, the random pot shot is misinterpreted as a terrorist attack. Communications may have improved in a technological sense but globalisation has not brought a corresponding advance in our understanding of the world or our respect for others.

Yet it is not always a language or cultural thing. Throughout the film, there are examples of people – and it is usually men – failing to communicate adequately with their children and partners, while governments are unable to agree on how to respond to crises or reach consensus on how best to manage their borders.

Immigration is one of the movie's hot topics, especially the concern of the Mexico section. Personal experience was a major factor for Iñárritu: 'As an immigrant, I have to cross the border every four months and I have had some very unpleasant experiences which helped me a lot on *Babel*, like when you end up faced with a xenophobic police official.'

Bernal said of his part: 'The character is also a means for showing this resentment and craziness that you encounter whenever you cross the border from Mexico to the USA. It's humiliating: you have to demonstrate your innocence before you can cross. The fact that you're greeted with suspicion and with a gun can be intimidating.'

Santiago decides to burst through border control rather than risk arrest and all its consequences (Amelia turns out to be an illegal immigrant; we can only presume Santiago is too). 'So maybe he sees a little opportunity to maybe escape and, in a whirlwind of alcohol, he sees it as something plausible but maybe it's not. Most of the time it doesn't work out,' said Bernal. 'But you can see it on a different level, in which he's reacting in a very primal way against the resentment or, as Alejandro calls it, "the rite of humiliation" that he has to go through every time he crosses the border.'

Babel was Bernal's first film made on Mexican soil since *The Crime of Father Amaro*, shot in late 2001, and, by a strange quirk of coincidence, they were filming in Puerto Peñasco, the small town where Bernal had shot parts of *El Abuelo y Yo* as a teenage soap star. As well as the chance to work again with old aquaintants, he particularly enjoyed getting to know Tijuana. 'There's something great about the spirit of these places, which is why I think Tijuana is one of the most humane places on earth,' he said. 'It's a town where you get the whole conflict of the world in one glass of water. Some people don't survive it but I have a lot of admiration for those who do, the ones who are reluctant to abandon it and become exiles.'

One day, while taking a break from filming, Bernal went for a walk in a park and came across the wall being built along the US-Mexico frontier. 'These people are victims of being born on the border, in a place where there's this stupid human imposition, this wall,' he observed.

For Iñárritu: 'The wall will be the biggest monument to stupidity ever made; it is shameful.' When *Babel* won the Golden Globe, Iñárritu was presented with the statue by Arnold Schwarzenegger: the director was not alone in appreciating the irony of the Governor of California giving a Mexican a prestigious award for a film (especially with the content of *Babel*) while building a wall to keep other Mexicans out just down the road.

Referring to *Babel* and the frontier restrictions generally, Bernal has said: 'If there was no border the story in Mexico would have been really happy. The kids would have gone back and they would have had a really good time, they would have discovered something new. But because of the border . . . that's the problem.'

Right from the project's inception, Iñárritu had been interested in symbolic borders as well as physical ones. 'Mental borders are more difficult to knock down. Stereotypes, prejudice created by religion, by governments and nationalists, all a bit stupid.'

Mental borders of quite another kind proved fundamental to *Babel*'s structure as a film. Iñárritu and Arriaga, following the blueprint they established for *Amores Perros* and used again in *21 Grams*, employ a non-linear narrative structure whereby the overall story must be pieced together in the viewer's head. Yet the movie is presented with skill, the jigsaw easy to assemble, and its very disjointed nature acts as a neat reflection of the dispersion of the stories; its jumps in chronology symbolic of the various time zones being navigated. Both are appropriate to the movie's central theme of the globalised world.

The butterfly effect, a chaos theory whereby an insect in the Amazon might, by fluttering its wings, trigger a chain of events that leads to a hurricane in Texas, is cleverly explored in *Babel*: a .270 Winchester hunting rifle is made in the US, bought in Tokyo and donated as a gift in North Africa; it ends up injuring an American in Morocco, which has terrible consequences on a family wedding in Mexico. In the modern world of mobile phones, cable television and the internet, it is easy for an audience to accept that the world is connected like never before.

Yet *Babel* doesn't merely want to remind us that we are all part of mankind, all really one and the same. There are no mobile phones, cable television sets or internet connections in the Moroccan village where Richard and Susan find themselves, and the treatment of people throughout the film, especially at the hands of police and authorities, varies greatly. As Iñárritu said, 'I tried to make a human palette in which nobody stands out, in which Brad Pitt is no more important than a Moroccan father, where everyone has the same importance. In an era when the life of a US citizen is deemed to be worth more than that of another human being, that is what I was trying to do.'

Something *Babel* is very keen to remind us of is that we all have in common a capacity for pain and suffering. Right from the off there is a sense that something soon is going to end in tears; what the viewer doesn't realise is that absolutely everything throughout the picture will. Neither *Amores Perros* nor *21 Grams* provided a laugh a minute, but few movies have ever so wallowed in misery as does *Babel*.

Iñárritu said that one of the main reasons he felt his movie would play well all over the world was that 'although you are watching people who belong to different religions, languages and continents, there is a universal thing which unites us: pain and joy, emotions basically and that is the power of cinema and the image'.

All of which is fine but begs the questions: why so much pain? why so little joy? The wedding scene in Mexico arrives like a breath of fresh air, though soon leads to more horror and despair.

That the world is an unfair and unjust place where terrible tragedies occur on a daily basis is not in dispute. However, this doesn't only have to be depicted through pain. Throughout the world, humans use laughter to counter their suffering and a splash of humour (dark humour for sure – but humour) can often be more effective in highlighting life's cruelties than can relentless images of misery.

This is a problem for *Babel* because there is a sense that Iñárritu and Arriaga believe that by infusing their movie with overblown gloominess they somehow automatically make it challenging and moving. Given the film's rather grand title and the fact that after tackling Mexico with *Amores Perros* and the US in *21 Grams*, *Babel* takes on no less than the world itself, there is a very real risk of it coming across as rather self-important.

Indeed, *Babel* does give the impression of being rather pleased with itself and, for many commentators, the sense of profundity that the movie wears so confidently on its sleeve is never justified. There is no guiding principle that unites the different narrative threads, no final conclusion or resolution.

This would not be so serious were it not for the fact that the Tokyo thread, the final one to be woven into the overall pattern, is by far the weakest link. That the rifle once belonged to the Japanese girl's father seems entirely irrelevant, especially considering the way the connections in the other stories bounced off one another so well. It also means that, as a dramatic finale to the film, it is all a bit anticlimactic.

Iñárritu said he 'was very aware of the danger of finishing this as four short pieces, four films that would not be related to one another and that all these diverse elements would create something that would not be congruent'. That was not in the end the case: the different stories do fit together to make a whole, it is just that the scale of the project deserved a better message to unify that whole.

That *Babel* is an accomplished piece of filming is not in doubt. The photography is beautiful and technically the movie is very well made. Iñárritu and Prieto used different film stocks to distinguish places (16mm for Morocco; 35mm for Mexico; anamorfica lenses for Japan), which adds another dimension to the story's dispersion.

The acting is strong too. Pitt's and Blanchett's portrait of a poisoned relationship is frightening, although most of their scenes take place after she has been shot, when there is nothing much more for her to do than lie prostrate while he runs around in frantic anguish. The natural performances of both the Moroccan and US children are superb, while Rinko Kikuchi ably conveys the Japanese girl's slippery sensitivity.

Elsewhere, Barraza earns her Oscar nod with an assured performance and she and Bernal complement one another well. 'It wouldn't have been the same if we hadn't had that back story,' Bernal has said in reference to them being reunited after *Amores Perros*. Barraza's Amelia displays a maturity and level-headedness that Bernal's Santiago so clearly lacks.

Santiago is something of a reckless maverick and, in spite of his warmth, sparkle and affability, the viewer somehow knows not to place too much trust in him. In many ways he personifies Tijuana, a place at once charming and deadly, and this suits Bernal down to the ground: not for the first time he refuses to launch a fully formed character into his scenes but infuses his persona with an unpredictability that maintains the film's suspense.

Iñárritu clearly appreciates this quality. 'I felt the same as I felt doing *Amores Perros*, which is that Gael has a way to approach things that is very fresh, to not over-rationalise or over-intellectualise, and I believe in the power of innocence more than experience.'

Lombardo noted the same sort of commitment from Bernal as she had on *Amores Perros*. 'Gael is the sort of person who is very quiet and full of concentration on set, then completely different away from the set. He is very dedicated to his work.'

Bernal's reflections on them all working together again was that they had all advanced while retaining their enthusiasm. 'Now what I can see is that we're a bit more aware of the craft, of the artistic rigour, and the things that are not important that we shouldn't bother about. But at the same time we have the same instinctive energy, maybe the same stamina but with an added bonus in that maybe now we are more curious, because the more you do the more you think you don't know anything.'

But not everyone was patting each other on the back and celebrating another job well done. An almighty spat had erupted between Iñárritu and Arriaga relating to intellectual ownership of the work, with the writer demanding more recognition.

The original script was Arriaga's and there were those who said he was unhappy with amendments made by Iñárritu. For example, originally the deaf and mute

Japanese teenager had been a Spanish girl who had lost her sight. Increasing murmurings from Arriaga is thought to have led to his being contractually forbidden from visiting the set by Iñárritu. Arriaga then declared their working relationship dead and buried.

The plot thickened when Iñárritu took the curious decision to send a letter for publication to *Chilango*, Mexico City's weekly listings magazine. The letter lamented Arriaga's 'unjustified obsession with claiming the sole authority of a film', adding that the scriptwriter seemed 'not to recognise that making cinema is an art of deep collaboration'.

It went on to say: 'You were not – and you've never let yourself feel like – part of this team and your declarations are an unfortunate low conclusion to this marvellous and collective process that we have all lived through and now celebrate.' Although written by Iñárritu, the letter was signed by the whole production team, including Bernal.

Somewhat taken aback, Arriaga attempted to put the record straight, telling the press that he didn't want to be known as the film's author because he understood well the collective process involved. In fact, that was exactly what he had been objecting to in the first place: in line with a congress of scriptwriters in Europe, he merely wished to reassert the recognition of the writer; to protest against movies which declared themselves to be 'A film by . . .' rather than which used the breakdown 'Directed by . . . Photographed by . . . Written by . . .'

What appeared to have irked Arriaga in the first place was hearing Iñárritu refer to 'his trilogy' one too many times. The writer asserted that he had thought up the storylines for *Babel* long before he had ever met Iñárritu. Thus the crux of the argument seemed to be that, though Arriaga may have devised the original stories, Iñárritu had conceived of the globalisation concept. In short, they came up with the plot for *Babel* together.

When asked to comment, Bernal and the other signatories to Iñárritu's letter (Rodrigo Prieto, Adriana Barraza, Gustavo Santaolalla, Briggitte Brocht, Martín Hernández and Stephen Mirrione) said that they had merely been affirming their belief that film-making was a collective process.

So the whole public slanging match seems to have been something of a misunderstanding. Director and writer appeared slightly ashamed that the disagreement had got so out of hand and each publicly wished the other good luck with their future films, sentiments taken to be genuine.

Arriaga and Iñárritu both still attended the 2007 Oscar ceremony, where *Babel* was beaten to Best Picture by Martin Scorsese's *The Departed*, but there was much regret that in Mexico's finest cinematic hour (a record eight Mexicans were nominated) two of its film industry's key figures were engaged in such a squabble. Perhaps the bigger shame will prove to be the end of such an invigorating artistic partnership.

Latin American New Wave
Part VII: Exile

The Oscars in 2007 saw a Latin American invasion and, of the eighteen Hispanics among the candidates, nine of them were from Mexico: directors Alejandro González Iñárritu, Guillermo del Toro and Alfonso Cuarón; actress Adriana Barraza; scriptwriter Guillermo Arriaga; photographers Guillermo Navarro and Emmanuel Lubezki; sound engineer Fernando Cámara; art director Eugenio Caballero. Bernal, meanwhile, presented the award for Best Documentary Short.

Indeed, following in the wake of the Latin American New Wave, Hollywood had gradually been infusing itself with a growing Latino presence. Given that over half of California's population is Hispanic, this was perhaps not before time. Hollywood producers also seemed to be waking up to the notion that, as a demographic, Hispanics like going to the movies.

Films such as *The Legend of Zorro*, starring Antonio Banderas, and *Bandidas*, featuring Salma Hayek and Penélope Cruz, may have been typical lowbrow Hollywood fare but they did slightly break the mould by placing Hispanics in the heroic lead roles (Spaniards in the case of Banderas and Cruz). But such films were not too far removed from Hollywood's usual stereotypical take on goings-on south of the border.

The first images that come to mind when most people think of Mexico are usually moustachioed, sombrero-wearing cowboys slugging tequila and carrying on with corrupt cops and drug smugglers. Such a narrow vision of a country of more than 100 million people is a reflection of Hollywood's ignorant depiction of its neighbours.

Celluloid adventures on the other side of the Rio Bravo traditionally saw US mores being put to the test as stranded gringos get overwhelmed by a lawless land inhabited by locals out to trick and cheat them. Mexico is painted as an exotic, mythical place where anything goes. Pictures such as John Huston's 1948 *The Treasure of the Sierra Madre*, starring Humphrey Bogart, and *The Wild Bunch* in 1969, by Samuel Peckinpah, trade on such clichés.

More recent features, such as *The Mexican* with Brad Pitt, do make fun of the

US's unenlightened vision of the country at its southern border but still pander to the lowest common denominator. Even the much praised *Traffic*, which won Puerto Rican Benicio del Toro a Best Supporting Actor Oscar, relied on playing to audience prejudices and, despite its realism credentials, Mexican audiences couldn't overlook the fact that Del Toro's Tijuana policeman seemed to speak with a Colombian accent.

In terms of Hispanic talent breaking into the US mainstream, Latin Americans have long had a significant presence in Hollywood, albeit traditionally a presence based on exotic typecasting. Mexican Ricardo Montalbán and Argentine Fernando Lamas were two of the first-ever Latin lovers while the likes of Brazil's Carmen Miranda provided the tropical kitsch. These days stars such as Banderas, Hayek, Cruz and Jennifer Lopez have been content to conform to type.

Nevertheless, a number of Latino character actors have emerged. Rosie Perez, Jessica Alba and Rosario Dawson are all US born and bred, while the likes of Andy García, John Leguizamo and Benicio del Toro all moved over when very young. Behind the lens, US native Roberto Rodríguez first shot to prominence making the low-budget *El Mariachi*, which he filmed in the Mexican town of his parents. He has gone on to make the likes of *From Dusk Till Dawn* and *Sin City*.

Maximising this talent with films that address Latin audiences is not something that has come naturally to Hollywood. *Maria Full of Grace*, about a young Colombian girl tempted into becoming a drug mule, was written and directed by US native Joshua Marston but made entirely in Spanish and bagged a Best Actress Oscar nomination for its Colombian lead, Catalina Sandino Moreno. But a more typical offering might be *Spanglish*, concerning a live-in Mexican maid (played by Spaniard Paz Vega), which is formulaic in its Hollywood sentimentality and depiction of Latin Americans.

Part of the problem for the US film industry has been deciding upon just what the Buena Onda success equates to in market terms. Latinos make up the largest and fastest-growing minority in the US so it would seem logical to assume they have been flocking to see these movies. However, a closer look at the numbers reveals that these films have really been embraced by the art-house crowd.

After the likes of *Amores Perros*, *Y Tu Mamá También*, *The Crime of Father Amaro* and *The Motorcycle Diaries*, everyone was waiting for the next Latin American smash hit. Many expected it to be *Secuestro Express*, a flashy kidnap thriller from Venezuela written and directed by Caracas native Jonathan

221

Jakubowicz. Although it was edgy and offered enough gritty realism to get up the noses of the Venezuelan administration, it lacked depth and proved to be only a minor success.

If nothing else, *Secuestro Express* proved that you couldn't just feed the Hispanic market any old fare from back home and expect a hit. The original Latin American New Wave films were so successful fundamentally because they were very good movies. That nothing out of Latin America has quite matched them since is primarily because the talent involved in making those films has moved elsewhere. The first Buena Onda films were made by savvy film-makers with ambition and skill. It is little wonder that the leading players were courted by Hollywood and Europe and that they in turn allowed themselves to be so indulged.

The 2005 Bafta awards featured Alfonso Cuarón's *Harry Potter and the Prisoner of Azkaban*, made and financed in Britain, among its nominations for Best British Picture. A year later, *The Constant Gardener*, another British-financed flick but directed by *City of God* helmer Fernando Meirelles, did likewise and got Best Director and Best Overall Film nods to boot. Baftas were then dished out to *Children of Men* in 2007, for cinematography and production design, this another Cuarón-directed British project.

The 2006 Cannes Film Festival had two Mexicans going for the top prize Palme d'Or, Iñárritu's *Babel* (Hollywood-financed, if not controlled) and Guillermo del Toro's *El Labarinto del Fauno* (*Pan's Labyrinth*), a Spanish-made (although also Mexican financed) gothic fantasy feature set in the aftermath of that country's civil war. *The Devil's Backbone*, del Toro's 2001 picture, had been made under similar conditions.

Guillermo Arriaga and Iñárritu had turned their attention to the US for *Amores Perros* follow-up *21 Grams*. Arriaga next penned *The Three Burials of Melquiades Estrada* for the directorial debut of US actor Tommy Lee Jones, although he also scripted the Mexican film *Búfalo de la Noche* (*Buffalo of the Night*). Cinematographers Rodrigo Prieto and Emmanuel Lubezki could be found plying their trade on all sorts of films, all over the world. As well as teaming up with Iñárritu on *Babel*, Prieto was Oscar-nominated for his work with Ang Lee on *Brokeback Mountain*. Lubezki picked up a Bafta for photographing *Children of Men* but also shot the likes of *Ali*, *The Assasination of Richard Nixon* and *Cat in a Hat*. Actor Emilio Echevarría, El Chivo in *Amores Perros*, bagged the role of Raoul, a Cuban agent, in the James Bond film *Die Another Day*.

Since 2004, Juan José Campanella has dedicated his time to US television rather than Argentine cinema. Walter Salles is developing a project to adapt Jack Kerouac's *On the Road* for the big screen. As for Bernal, after making a series of films in far-flung places, *Babel* marked his first shoot in Mexico since *The Crime of Father Amaro* in 2002.

As well as the more high-profile figures, many Mexican technicians have been working steadily north of the border. Director of photography Carlos Hidalgo, who has worked on Hollywood films such as *Clear and Present Danger* and Mexican ones such as *Amores Perros*, speaks of pioneers such as Luis Mandoki, a Mexican director who moved to Hollywood in the 1980s, and the general conundrum. 'The generation of Mandoki opened the door and bit by bit more and more people followed. Because in Mexico there is no industry. In Mexico the truth is we make cinema for love not money. Because we want to tell stories. But if you want to make cinema with all the toys, all the possibilities, or as a business, you have to go elsewhere. I think Mexico will need many years before it becomes a business.'

In so many ways, moving to Hollywood echoes the wider issue of immigration brought up in *Babel*: it is a question of moving towards better opportunities. Alberto Aziz Nassif, in an article entitled '*Estado débil, cine pobre*' ('Weak state, poor cinema') published in Mexico's *El Universal* in April 2007, wrote:

> In almost all walks of public life you come across the same problems: lack of adequate state regulation, areas of monopoly, government incompetence, absolute exposure to the US market and poor overall results for the country. Of course, the specifics vary but it is becoming evermore pressing that the state improves its regulatory capacity, offers better instruments of support and financing and a policy at state-level that defines a project for the country. In this case, these matters concern Mexican cinema, an industry with serious deficiencies and one which has never been able to recover since its golden era.

State support for cinema in Mexico has tended to come in six-year cycles, creating relative booms and busts at the whim of the latest government's interest in or scorn for film. Vicente Fox proved himself to be of the latter camp when, in 2003, he announced a plan to withdraw all state support for the CCC, close IMCINE and sell the government-owned Churrubusco Film Studios to real-estate speculators.

As Alfonso Cuarón commented at the time: 'The irony is that, at a moment when Mexican cinema is getting so much attention, the government is planning to close down the institutions which sustain it.' He was not alone in his thoughts and widespread condemnation forced the proposal to be scrapped.

Still, state support for film production is not what it once was, which was not much anyway. A Mexican film-maker submitting a project to IMCINE today will receive a grant up to a maximum of US$700,000. Given that most movies cost about US$2 million to make, private backing is required for the shortfall.

This is not in itself a bad thing. As Nassif points out, cinema is just one of many sectors in need of better support and the top priorities for Mexico arguably lie elsewhere. What the government needs to do is encourage private investment and first steps were made in December 2006 with new initiatives which followed the Brazilian model of offering tax breaks to businesses in return for aid for film production.

The scheme is not universally supported. Detractors argue that in terms of promoting culture it is biased towards film while more generally it allows big companies not to pay their proper taxes. 'It's true,' says producer Federico González Compeán. 'The only argument in favour of this law is that it helps cinema grow, which is its objective, but it is not a policy of true development. Instead of handing in what they should to the treasury, people say, "One for you, two for me – I'm going to make a film, pass it on to that." There are a lot of things missing.'

Director Antonio Urrutia has a different gripe: 'The new law allows crap films to get made by people who don't know what they are doing. Maybe they have links to a company boss and say I want to make a film and get the money.'

Hidalgo reserves judgement: 'The new law is not working properly but is an advance of sorts.' As far as Filmoteca director Iván Trujillo is concerned: 'It has been approved but hardly applied. It wasn't even mentioned in the last fiscal report so it is hard for companies to implement it.'

Most people agree that regulation of the film distribution market would be a better initiative. Private backers need to see good prospects of making a return on their investment and conditions as they stand are highly unfavourable to producers.

Two major companies dominate the cinema exhibition landscape: Cinemex controls half the very significant Mexico City market; Cinépolis controls half the country as a whole. Their power is such that they can dictate their own unfavourable terms to Mexican distributors. These terms are that the exhibitor retains 60 per cent of the return with the other 40 per cent split between the producer and distributor. In most countries, it is a fifty-fifty arrangement.

Of the 40 per cent left to the producer and distributor, the split usually favours the latter. The producer can end up trying to cover production costs from as little as 10 per cent of the box-office return.

'The rotten part of the story is the distribution and exhibitors,' agrees Hidalgo. 'The producer gets eight to twelve cents of each peso so the one who made the film and got the financing together is not the one who earns the money from it. The one earning the money is the one selling popcorn or distributing it. Until this changes, it is going to remain difficult.'

The sheer might of the exhibitors has also blighted initiatives to impose screen quotas for Mexican films or have a percentage of ticket prices reinvested into cinema, as in Argentina.

Given the thin slice of the wedge exhibitors leave for them, distributors are reluctant to take risks on Mexican films, which often need more promoting: Hollywood's star system ensures its films come fully packaged and ready to go. Furthermore, the practice of forcing distributors into buying a US hit as part of a bundle is still rife.

'Because the North American market is so big and we are so close to it, we are really just another state,' despairs Compeán. 'If you give them [the distributor] a Mexican film and it doesn't work they don't care, they just bring in a North American one the next day. If there is no scarcity you can't negotiate with a Mexican product.'

Distribution problems for local fare mean that, although film production is on the up in Mexico, a corresponding increase in exposure has not been achieved. Around fifty films were made in Mexico in both 2005 and 2006 but only half of them made it into cinemas, let alone were given an adequate chance to shine.

Meagre box-office percentages matter more for Mexican producers than in other parts of the world. 'From your investment you should get 30 per cent back from box-office; 25/30 from television; 25/30 from DVD sales. Then come sales abroad,' explains Trujillo. 'But in Mexico the producer depends almost entirely, about 90 per cent, on box office. The other two don't exist: the DVD market is represented by piracy and TV is a monopoly which pays whatever suits it.'

Compeán adds, 'Television has always paid small amounts for films. It started to change and began to increase but is going back down again: the TV companies always resist. It is a monopoly. Either you go with one or the other and, when one isn't really very interested in national cinema, you have to go with the other and they say: "This is the offer, take it or leave it." This is a very important factor for our cinema. Also, in countries like Spain, television companies must divert a share of their profits back into film but here in Mexico there is no such scheme.'

In both the cinema and television sectors, film-makers suffer the consequences of a weak state which allows powerful monopolies to set the rules. If exhibition, both on the large and small screen, was regulated to better favour home product, more investors would be persuaded to sink funds into Mexican films and perhaps the country's top talent would return.

With just a little helpful legislation, a self-sufficient national film industry could be born. Leaving everything to the will of the free market is not the solution for sectors such as film, nor is it appropriate. There are very strong arguments as to why governments should protect domestic culture.

With its visual and sonic scope, as a cultural outlet film is a powerful medium, particularly so in regions with high levels of illiteracy. This makes it one of the best cultural platforms for nurturing a sense of national identity. A country as huge and diverse as Mexico requires a wide range of films in order to reflect its many realities. Cinema is perhaps the most effective way to help the general public learn about themselves as a people and appreciate the country as a whole. What's more, it can inform others about Mexico, helping to develop better international understanding.

Bernal has said he believes culture to be 'the only link between social and economic development'. Disgruntled Mexicans point out that the government's cultural budget for 2007 was, at 0.6 per cent of GDP, significantly less than the 1 per cent recommended by the United Nations Educational, Scientific and Cultural Organisation.

Trujillo makes unfavourable comparisons with other countries. 'In Argentina they protect cinema as an important part of culture, in Brazil, Chile, France and Spain too. In France they have it very clear: "Our cinema is not just about money but the defence of our culture against attacks from North America." For them it is a matter of identity.'

Hidalgo tends to agree but is sceptical about FOPROCINE, the Mexican state organ in charge of funding cultural film projects. 'It is a lost fund for auteur cinema. I'm sorry but all films have to be a business. It is not right that people's taxes become money to be thrown away: "Oh, it doesn't matter," and off they go to make whatever film they want. That's not the way to do it.'

That said, there is certainly more room for government spending on culture and this could be channelled into producing films that might make a loss but prove their social value. At the same time, improving the trading conditions for producers would ensure that private finance funded more commercially minded projects. There is also the little matter of film – and culture in general – being able to contribute positively to the economy in import/export terms. The talent is certainly there in Mexico, so why not make the most of it?

'There is a theory that one can talk about a national film industry when you are making one film per year for every one million people: that it is perhaps not healthy to make more,' says Trujillo. 'Spain is making about one hundred and there isn't enough time for them to fill screens and in Argentina they make more films than they can show too. But countries with a successful cinema industry are doing it. Chile makes about fifteen, which corresponds to their number of millions [sixteen] and is the number of films they can consume domestically. If you can do that you can have a healthy domestic industry and not have to rely on foreign sales. But Mexico is only making around forty and still few films can recover their money internally.'

Given Mexico's population of 105 million, there ought to be enough of an audience to justify making more domestic cinema. 'There is an enormous market and huge demand,' says Bernal in frustration. 'There should be a certain perseverance so that the industry can be more creative. In recent summers, the most successful films have been Mexican.'

So if there is domestic demand for domestic productions, what is stopping the exhibitors from supplying it? Many people suspect that it is because the big cinema chains are in cahoots with the US film industry, making them not only disinclined but opposed to supporting Mexican films. There are even plans afoot to further boost US imports by dubbing them into Spanish: at present they come subtitled. Hope comes with signs of the US studios looking to make serious investment in production south of the border. If the majors did get involved in this manner, the climate would certainly change.

For now, according to figures in Brazil's distinguished weekly magazine *Carta Capital*, national films corresponded to just 6 per cent of tickets sold in Mexico in 2006. In Brazil the figure was 14 per cent, and in Argentina 10 per cent. These numbers demonstrate that Mexico lags behind the two other principal film-making countries in Latin America, even though Brazil and Argentina are plagued by most of the same structural problems as Mexico.

'The Brazilian market doesn't sustain a film made through private finance: not even pulling in five million viewers does the film pay for itself. *Carandiru*, *City of God*, *Central Station* and *Dois Filhos de Francisco* (*Two Sons of Francisco* –

a 2005 domestic hit concerning and featuring two Brazilian country music stars) only broke even,' Hector Babenco has said of the situation in his adopted country. 'The rules of the market are very severe and the market is competing with other simpler pastimes. The people who ought to be watching Brazilian films don't have the twenty *reais* [US$11] to do so. If the cinema cost six *reais* [US$3], everyone would go.'

Still, Brazil's fiscal incentive for the business sector to finance film is more efficient and more established than Mexico's (which is in something of a probation period and could be dropped at any moment) while Argentina still makes use of its box-office levies. As with Mexico, there is a growing appreciation of the benefits of the big screen acting as a giant national mirror, that this helps countries better define who they are and what they want to be, but, throughout the continent, distribution conditions favour Hollywood, which is why so few of the continent's films play in neighbouring countries, why Mexicans don't get the chance to see Argentinian films and vice versa. DVD piracy is a common problem, as is monopolistic television.

These issues must be addressed across Latin America if a sustainable cinema industry is to be established in the region and the recent good work is to leave a permanent legacy. Otherwise, the continent's talent will be lost abroad for good.

Déficit

Nothing demonstrates what Bernal is all about more than Canana, the production company he set up with Diego Luna and Pablo Cruz. Its aim is to aid and promote Mexican film-making and encourage cinema which tackles subjects typically ignored by commercially driven production houses. Thus, it is not so much a business as a social project committed to developing national cinema. If they were looking to make a fast buck, they themselves have agreed, they would surely be investing in something else.

Bernal and Luna found themselves at the centre of a buzz of creative energy within Mexican film that was going to waste due to lack of opportunity. Ever keen to pay their dues to the medium that had launched their own careers, they sought to find a way of assisting these people to get their films made. Thus Bernal and Luna, who had previously toyed with the idea of forming a theatre troupe, began exploring the possibility of setting up a production company. The problem was that they had no idea how to run a business. On the other hand, Pablo Cruz, a longtime friend who Bernal had first met in London as a student, certainly did. He had established his own television advertising company in Spain, Lift, which had proved a successful venture. So much so that he was able to sell up, cash in and join Bernal and Luna on Canana. The company was finally formed in May 2005.

Canana is the Spanish word for the bullet belts that Mexican revolutionaries would wear. The name works well, suggesting as it does a certain type of guerilla film-making, a shoot-from-the-hip philosophy. Bernal, Luna and Cruz had all been involved in projects that had thrived on a get-up-and-go attitude. The Mexican cinema industry was not what it should and could be but waiting for the powers-that-be to put things right was undoubtedly a waste of time: the domestic film industry would probably never get the support it deserved. If you wanted to make a movie, you had to take the initiative. Bernal summed up their concept in saying, 'Doing films in Mexico is pretty difficult; it's not yet a self-sustaining industry. But one thing you can do is manage to make films without very much money.'

Cruz has expressed similar sentiments: 'There is no more time for complaining about a lack of resources.' He says that getting films made is a tough business anywhere and although it is inevitably tougher still in any country where extreme poverty is a fact of life, this not only makes practical sense but morally justifies a low-budget approach. 'You have to be aware of what is happening in the country and it is crazy to spend three million dollars on a film,' he says. 'The Canana objective is to produce at reasonable prices. A production house usually has a three, four, five million budget but we don't. We have maybe a quarter of that money and we aim to make three films with it.'

While Bernal and Luna are the more visible representatives of Canana, lending their combined star status to projects in order to secure funding and promote distribution, Cruz is the brains behind the operation. Having started out as a cameraman, his passion for Ken Loach films led him to Britain. As well as crossing paths with Bernal, Cruz studied Film Theory at the London College of Printing. Afterwards, he produced films in Africa before starting his Spanish advertising adventure.

In September 2007, *Variety* magazine listed Cruz among its Ten Producers to Watch. He told the magazine that he was flattered and said of Canana, 'We're not making films just for entertainment's sake. We are doing films about the reality we are living. We are trying to change things, or at least contribute, with the stories we share.'

Be that as it may, the success with Lift shows that he is also a smooth operator. He believes there is a market for films that show Mexico as it really is, both at home and abroad. One of Canana's first moves was to fund domestic distribution for *El Violín*, a black-and-white picture by Francisco Vargas which depicted peasant revolutionaries. Despite huge critical acclaim on the festival circuit, not least when playing in the *Un Certain Regard* section at Cannes, no Mexican distributor would back it in its home country. Canana believed in the film and that it would find its audience. It duly did, proving a smash hit and outperforming several more illustrious releases.

The fate of *El Violín* in Mexico perfectly demonstrated Canana's credentials. Cruz describes another film, *Cochochi*, as a prime example of why the production house exists. It is a film about the Rarámuri Indians, a native people of the Tarahumara Sierra mountains in northwest Mexico. The film tells the tale of two young brothers and the search for a missing horse, exploring as it goes the lives and culture of the Rarámuri people and all in their native tongue. Canana's sponsorship of the film helped attract other funding partners, not least Donald K Ranvaud's London-based Buena Onda Ltd as co-producers, boosting *Cochochi*'s budget to US$400,000.

Cochochi will be distributed by Focus Features as part of a partnership agreement with Canana. Focus were involved with *Y Tu Mamá También* (in the guise of Good Machine International) and then *The Motorcycle Diaries* and *Bad Education*, so have long had a working relationship with Bernal and Luna.

Bernal's relationship with the Cannes Film Festival no doubt helped another Canana-backed movie, *Drama/Mex* by Gerardo Naranjo, premiere at Critic's Week. The film, which also played the 2007 London Film Festival, concerns three intertwined stories set in Acapulco.

Of course, running your own production company allows for certain perks, directing your own film being the obvious one. Luna decided to turn his hand to documentary film-making, choosing legendary boxer Julio César Chávez as his subject. Chávez was one of Mexico's most prominent sportsmen when Luna and Bernal were growing up and his story is one of great glory and tremendous tragedy. The champ was manipulated throughout his life by promoters and even used by the president. Luna's film premiered at the Tribeca Film Festival in New York and Bernal was there to support his buddy.

Bernal himself was involved with the making of another documentary, *Santa Muerte* (*Dead Saint*) by Eva Aridjis, for which he provides the narration. In fact, documentaries are a key component of Canana's operations and played a major role in getting the company founded in the first place.

Having marvelled at *Trópico de Cáncer* (*Tropic of Cancer*), a film made by their good friend Eugenio Polgovsky as part of his film studies course at CCC, Bernal was dismayed that such a fine film would never really be seen. He scratched his head about how best to get the film out there, as he told the *Guardian*/NFT audience:

> So how do you distribute a film when you have no money? You tell everybody that it's good and they should see it. So that's basically what we did. And we had a brilliant proposal from a very close friend – he suggested that we make a rock tour, but for documentaries. I was very drunk at the time so it sounded amazing. But it was hard to pick it up and put it into a structure. So we got together twenty documentaries and we were going to take them around the country. How? With what money? That's when we had to start thinking about things that we had no clue how to do.

This led to Cruz providing his expertise and Canana coming into being. Canana's first project then became Ambulante, a touring documentary film festival. The project found a partner in the Morelia Film Festival and was supported by Cinépolis, one of Mexico's largest cinema chains, which provided facilities in fifteen cities, some of which had never before had a documentary screened at a cinema. In order to stimulate interest in what was, therefore, quite a revolutionary concept, Bernal and Luna got to work on the publicity front, generating press coverage, and an entrance fee of half the usual cinema admission price was negotiated.

In the end, nineteen films were shown over the course of a week, of which twelve were Mexican productions. Naturally among them was *Trópico de Cáncer*, a film which showed the families who dedicate their lives to selling animals, dead or alive, to travellers on the San Luis Potosí motorway in order to make ends meet. Another notable national production was *Toro Negro* by Pedro González Rubio and Carlos Armella, which concerned the life of an indigenous bullfighter and led to the directing duo being invited to shoot the 'Making of *Babel*'.

Ambulante proved successful, attracting respectable if modest crowds and leading to some of the Mexican films being shown as part of the NFT's Mexican Cinema Now season and Manchester's Festival Viva.

It spawned a second version the following year, the tour growing in size and scope: thirty films were shown at nineteen cinemas in fifteen cities and drew some twenty thousand spectators. The section of films was this time split into four categories: The Official Selection; Injerto, for experimental films; Witness, for films which denounce human-rights violations; Dictator's Cut, for films which had been the victims of censorship and about which Bernal said it was almost a social obligation to go and see. This time, a selection of the films toured Norway and plans were put in place to take Ambulante to Spain. A partnership with fashion label Gucci was also established whereby the Italian designer would provide a grant to help finance the completion of up to eight already up-and-running documentaries, which would then show at the festival in 2008 (a major problem for documentary film-makers is getting stuck in post-production).

Of course, it wasn't just *Trópico de Cáncer* that inspired the boys to enter the documentary world. The Canana gang explained that documentaries helped the country to understand who it was and what it wanted to be; that the youth of Mexico should become more politically engaged and that this was a good way to provoke debate; that in an election year (as 2006 was) it was especially important to consider the state of things.

Beyond the general cultural and educational benefits to the public and the promotion of documentary films in the marketplace, the Canana team also wanted to inspire new film-makers. Shooting a documentary movie required few resources beyond a good idea and a well of enthusiasm.

Many people commented upon how Canana had put government institutions to shame, demonstrating quickly and efficiently how to go about promoting culture in Mexico.

Securing increased screen time for documentaries on the nation's television sets is the next goal. As with the rest of Latin America, Mexican television is dominated by the fantastical soap operas which present a romanticised version of the country, so documentaries could indeed provide a strong counterbalance.

An interest in improving quality and variety on the small screen had been one of Bernal's main goals with Canana. Indeed, it led to his directorial debut, as it turned out on the big screen, as he told the NFT.

> The film that I did came out of a workshop for a TV series called *Ruta 32*. We were going to do a series of stories set in all thirty-two states in Mexico. I wanted to do this because I'm from Guadalajara and I've never seen a film or anything on TV that portrays my city, and it's a city of about five million people. So it was one of those obvious things – why not? But it was very hard to sell that format on TV. 'We want to do this series of stories in each state.' 'What are the stories about?' 'Well, one is about how the military is colluding with the drug traffickers. One is about people getting kidnapped at the beach. One is about the kidnapping of a woman at the border in Ciudad Juarez.' We didn't get any response from any of the TV stations or private financiers we pitched this to. We are still hoping to do this one day, if only to document Mexico at this time. But I had this story that I had written, set in the state of Morelos, south of Mexico City, and that became a film because that was the easiest way to get finance.

That the story set in Morelos eventually became a film is all the more interesting given the unlikely setting for its original conception. While in London as part of his *Blood Wedding* run in summer 2005, Bernal and two friends were ambling through Whitechapel one morning after the night before. 'We were really hung over. And all of a sudden one of us started to dance. It was very cold. One of us said, "Imagine we were going to Tepoztlán. Imagine if we were going to a swimming pool," Bernal remembered. Tepoztlán is a village in Mexico City's surrounds where the well-to-do of the capital have weekend retreats. 'We imagined this yuppie guy who goes to his parents' place, and tries to stop his girlfriend getting there.'

Kyzza Terrazas had been one of Bernal's fellow sore-head sufferers that morning and ended up taking the initial idea and transforming it into a working script. 'Gael had this anecdote about this rich kid that had a party at his country house with some of his friends. His girlfriend was supposed to come, but he meets another girl that he likes. He starts giving his girlfriend wrong directions as to how to get to the house,' explained Terrazas. 'That was the skeleton that Gael had in mind, and he invited me to collaborate on the screenplay. What I tried to do was bring that world to life.'

The title, *Déficit*, was thought to be apt on many levels: the characters may be wealthy but they are all found lacking in some way. Besides, *Déficit* was a word that Bernal's generation had, along with devaluation and crisis, become familiar with from a young age, without fully comprehending its meaning or influence on their lives.

With the script complete and being pitched, confusion regarding the television project and funding abounded until there arrived a moment when they decided to just go ahead and make it. Canana was supposed to be promoting a pro-active approach so it was time to lead by example.

Assembling the actors proved harder than imagined: Bernal found it awkward to be on the opposite side of the casting couch. That said, in the end, the key decisions looked after themselves, as Bernal told *El Universal*: 'I didn't know Camila but I knew she was the character right away when I saw her and the same thing happened with Tenoch and then there are my mates Malcolm and Alvaro, for whom I especially wrote two characters.' Camila Sodi is a rising star in Mexico, appearing opposite Diego Luna in Guillermo Arriaga's *Buffalo of the Night* and now also said to be Luna's real-life squeeze. Malcolm Llanas and Álvaro Verduzco, meanwhile, have been friends with Bernal since childhood. Keeping it familiar, Eugenio Polgovsky, director of *Trópico de Cáncer*, the film that had inspired the founding of Canana, took on photography duties.

The main acting role went to the director himself. Bernal plays Cristobal, the boy who seemingly has it all: he enjoys a wealthy lifestyle, is an economics student headed for Harvard and has a wide circle of friends, for whom he and his sister

Elisa (Sodi) throw a party at the family summer house. As the reunion gets under way, Cristobal takes a fancy to Dolores, an Argentine beauty brought along by another friend. Via his mobile, Cristobal begins to give his own girlfriend misleading directions to the house, hoping that she will get sufficiently lost to give him time to make a move on Dolores.

The story is simple enough but the viewer soon begins to appreciate that Cristobal's world is not all it is cracked up to be. The plush house, as Cristobal well knows, is the consequence of being the son of a corrupt politician. He has an uncomfortable relationship with the gardener who was a boyhood friend until class boundaries reared their ugly head. In fact, social barriers are everywhere to be seen and begin to reveal themselves to Cristobal and the others as the fiesta gets out of hand and their lives begin to unravel.

Filming took place in March 2006 in Tepoztlán itself. Almost all the footage was shot at a house, a short distance from the village itself. Some scenes where filmed away from the villa, including some by a riverbed and the foothills of the Tepozteco Hills, which were interrupted by a herd of cows and an irate pastor, disgusted that he was being asked to take the animals for water elsewhere because of something so trivial as a film.

The shoot is said to have been a serious one, in keeping with the director's focused approach to his craft, although relaxing in many ways too – there was barely any mobile-phone reception due to the surrounding hills, for example – and with a good spirit in the camp.

An urge to call the shots had been something Bernal had carried around with him since drama school, when he had become interested in directing in the theatre. Then he started making films and that desire had naturally carried over to movies. On the likes of *Y Tu Mamá También*, which he made while still a drama student, he was constantly asking technical questions of the crew, fascinated by the film-making process. As Bernal told *indieWIRE*, it was inevitable that he would direct eventually and this opportunity simply presented itself.

'You need to find a unified reason why the film needs to exist,' he added. The political undercurrent of the tale was Bernal's reason and, although he says that if you point and shoot a camera anywhere in Mexico it cannot help but be a critique, in focusing on the well-to-do, *Déficit* does attempt to tackle a section of society rarely held under the microscope.

He says he is proud of what he made, that it was a beautiful experience and that he will likely try again, although acting remains his passion because you have more time to take everything in, whereas directing 'was quite stressful and overwhelming, you never stop, a hundred miles an hour'. When asked how he found directing himself, Bernal quipped: 'A terrible actor, unbearable actor. Doesn't listen to me; just does what he wants!'

Given that he has worked with directors of the pedigree of Pedro Almodóvar, Walter Salles, Alejandro González Iñárritu and Alfonso Cuarón, he had plenty of great role models to draw upon and, in the latter three, good friends to turn to. 'There were certain situations where I thought about the mentors, Alfonso Cuarón specifically. But you have to murder your mentors in a way,' said Bernal, although he did seek their help in post-production. 'They were really good at mentioning a couple of things and I'd go, "Oh shit, yes, I know I have to re-edit this".'

Salles, Iñárritu and Cuarón were all present at the film's premiere in Cannes, along with Carlos Reygadas, Diego Luna and Javier Bardem, another good friend of Bernal's. Coincidentally, the film screened at Miramar where, seven years earlier, Bernal had burst onto the world stage in *Amores Perros*. *Déficit* was warmly received and Iñárritu said that he, Salles and Cuarón were pleased to declare it a good first step on the directorial learning curve. 'You can say that it has its faults but making a film, carrying it under the arm, is a heroic act for anybody, actor, famous or not.'

Other observers paid similar homage, giving the picture the benefit of the doubt due to the integrity with which it had been made, but finding the faults harder to ignore. *Screen International* stated that if sincere commitment and high spirits were enough, the film would be a masterpiece, but lamented the poor sound quality, rendering the banter between the partying youngsters incomprehensible, and that 'Bernal and his cinematographer seem to have no idea where to put the camera'.

Harsh words, perhaps, although Bernal himself has acknowledged that there were things he did when filming and editing that he would not repeat, preferring not to go into the specifics.

Another dissenter was a member of the audience at the Morelia Film Festival where it made its Mexican debut. In an open forum after the screening, the young buck chipped in saying, 'I didn't like the film. I don't know . . . I just didn't understand what you were trying to say.' Bernal took it all in his stride: 'I'm not going to explain the film. If I did that would be cheating. And if the film didn't grab you, that's your prerogative, I thank you for your comments.' Besides, another member of the Morelia audience was director Stephen Frears and he gave it his seal of approval.

Most commentators agreed that it was a first work of promise and merit, a fair overall achievement on a low budget. Bernal's own acting performance was seen to lack its usual spark and subtlety, doubtless a consequence of his energies being more thinly spread across disciplines.

Most praise was directed at the themes the movie explored and the precise and succinct way it was done. Few films in Mexico – or indeed books, television shows and plays – examine the complacent rich. The privileged classes are shown up in all their decadence here and neatly rubbed up against the marginalised in the form of the gardener, thus introducing issues such as racist prejudice and the legacy of colonialism. For some, such meaty topics were merely introduced with no follow-through, but others found delicacy in the film's portrayal of everyday Mexicans incapable of living harmoniously together.

Déficit was a modest production, filmed in digital (then transposed to 35mm for the big screen) and, clocking in at 75 minutes, economical for a feature. Thus, its technical and thematic scope had to be kept in perspective too. Given that part of its purpose was to blaze a trail for young film-makers and show that producing a movie need not be an all-singing, all-dancing, special-effects affair, *Déficit* can be deemed a qualified success.

'Directing is really about putting yourself out there, to be slapped in a way. You know that in the kitchen, you're gonna get burned. It's very scary but very exciting as well,' said Bernal, adding that most important of all, 'if you have something to say, you have nothing to lose and you probably learn from the experience.'

The Past

In *El Pasado* (*The Past*), Bernal plays Rímini, a man with love troubles: his current partner suffers terrible jealousies, his ex has become delusional about the nature of their relationship and he has a stalker. The Argentinian media played with the notion of life imitating art, given that Bernal was filming *The Past* when Natalie Portman arrived in Buenos Aires unannounced.

The Past is an adaptation of Alan Pauls' 2003 novel, directed by Hector Babenco of *Carandiru* fame. This made for the second time Bernal was appearing in a Pauls film: *Vidas Privadas* was co-scripted by Pauls and Fito Páez.

Pauls himself was surprised when Babenco approached him about adapting the book to the screen. He saw his 530-page novel as a very literary work. Babenco collaborated with co-writer Marta Góes for eighteen months developing the screenplay and had to cut vast subplots and peripheral figures to make it work. The film version of *The Past* thus focuses primarily on two people whereas the book had at least one other very prominent couple. Pauls says that it is always hard to see your novel carved up but, given his experience as a scriptwriter, was aware that a six-hour movie documenting every passage of the novel would be inappropriate. That said, it still took Babenco and Góes nine treatments before they were satisfied with their script.

The film begins with the amicable separation of Rímini and Sofía (played by Anália Couceyro) after twelve years as husband and wife. They go about the task of splitting up their shared life and all its belongings maturely and look destined to remain firm friends. However, once Rímini starts dating Vera (Moro Anghileri), Sofía loses her poise and begins to act evermore irrationally.

The premise of the book was that once a relationship ends, the two lovers become ghosts to one another. Sofia certainly haunts Rímini and Babenco says he is attracted to films with characters slightly removed from reality, people who hide their crazy side behind a front of normality.

When Babenco told Pauls that he had lined up Bernal to play Rímini, the author couldn't picture the Mexican as his main character, although he wasn't against the idea. 'I like Gael a lot because he is a very good actor and is very intelligent. But at the same time, I had to allow myself to discover him, in order to start to see him as Rímini. Rímini is a bit faceless. He could be invisible. He is practically just a gaze, a point of view.' There can be nobody more suited to playing a pair of eyes than Bernal. Babenco says he chose Bernal because he wanted someone who could work with silence and play a taciturn figure, one evidently pained but resigned to the destructive forces surrounding him.

'I spoke to them [the producers] in Argentina and they claimed Gael would be impossible to get. By chance, I read that Gael was showing in *Blood Wedding* in London so I asked Walter Salles for his email and sent a message to say that I was coming to London to see the play and that I'd like to have a coffee with him,' Babenco told *Carta Capital*. 'I still didn't even have a script. I told Bernal that I was writing a project called *The Past* and he said he would like me to send the script when it was ready.'

But when it was ready, Babenco had another idea. 'I remembered that Stanley Kubrick didn't even let the financiers see the script. He used to call people to his house to read the script together. So I asked Gael where he was. If he was in Mexico I would go to Mexico. If he was in Thailand I'd go there. Two or three days later he said he was in Buenos Aires. I picked a hotel in the city and asked him to invite a few actress friends over and we read for two nights in a row.'

Bernal got back to Babenco a fortnight later to commit. 'He said: "Pay me whatever but don't be mean." We arrived at a sum which was about a third of what he earned with Almodóvar.'

On Bernal's behalf, the attraction was not so much the film itself but the chance to work with the Argentine-born Brazilian director. Aged fourteen, Bernal's father had taken him to see *Pixote* at the cinema and Babenco's movie had made a strong impression.

Bernal's involvement upped the stakes in the film's profile and especially in terms of expectation: Babenco and Bernal working together on a new film had a good ring to it. It also impacted upon the casting process. Every young female actor wanted the chance to star opposite Bernal and casting took five months.

Cast and crew convened in Buenos Aires from late June 2006. The shoot was tough at times (the director has described it as a bullfight) with Babenco meeting resistance to his approach from the locals. Argentine by birth he may be, but his methods seemed alien to them. For Bernal, it was also an occasionally unpleasant ride thanks to the constant paparazzi attention.

Reaction to the film was mixed. Babenco has said that he showed it informally a few times in Argentina when it was finished, to unfavourable response: he surmises that Argentines perhaps don't like being shown home truths.

More generally, women found it hard to relate to certain characters. Babenco pointed out that the film is told from Rímini's perspective; it is subjective. He also added, 'In all relationships, the woman is in command, whether passively or actively. The man is a plaything until at some moment he gets tired and explodes. He goes in search of another reality but the woman continues to think about him.' It should perhaps be noted that Babenco has been married four times.

'The man in the film is a victim of all these events because he provokes none of them,' added Babenco, 'they are created by life.' Rímini may be the victim but nor does he help himself, just going around in circles. 'Gael is passive, he has this tinge, not like typical leads these days. He is more like an Antonioini hero, the sort who finds himself in the depth of a crisis and, having no counterargument, keeps quiet. Silence is his statement.'

As well as giving another outing to his Argentine accent, Bernal tried to bring his usual depth and range to the role. Given that Rímini is not masking a mysterious side but rather riding his own existential storm, the multi-layered performance, of a character with less substance, is not quite as successful as in other outings.

The movie did, however, mark a personal milestone for Bernal. As he matures as a person and performer, so his status as an actor becomes ever more distinguished. *The Past* was the first time Bernal had ever played a father in a film.

Mexican (not Mexican't)

Latin America's meteoric rise in world cinema is particularly impressive for its timing, with the world fully embracing globalisation: competition is much greater and tougher in a globalised world, making Mexico's 2007 Oscar-night presence, for example, all the more impressive.

That said, more efficient global networks do make it easier for work to be shown around the world. Cinema has always been a far-reaching product but distribution has broadened in scope in recent years. This is a consequence of commercial practicalities but also of increased awareness of and interest in other corners of the globe among the public in general, including cinema audiences.

For evidence one need look no further than Bernal's filmography. Between *The Past* and *The Motorcycle Diaries* he shot films in the US, Spain, France and most of Latin America; he worked with directors from Mexico, Brazil, Argentina, France, Spain and England. His latest projects will make him even more well travelled.

The internet has been a major factor behind the march of globalisation: in *Mammoth* Bernal takes the role of an internet visionary. What's more, it is an English-language film directed by Swedish director Lukas Moodysson (of *Fucking Åmål* [*Show Me Love*] and *Together*) and tells the tale of a young and successful New Yorker (played by the Mexican) whose life reaches something of an epiphany while he's holidaying with his young family in Thailand, which the film shoot substitutes with the Philippines. It is a Swedish/Danish/German co-production.

Blindness, meanwhile, is an adaptation of Portuguese author José Saramago's 1995 bestselling novel and is directed by Brazilian Fernando Meirelles. The film is deliberately international: given that the book is a study of how easily modern civilisation can unravel, Meirelles wanted to create a microcosm of the world in his movie and so set about assembling a mixed cast to be representative of all of humanity. Hence US stars Julianne Moore, Mark Ruffallo and Danny Glover are joined by Bernal, the Brazilian Alice Braga and the Japanese Iskye Isseya.

The story tells of an epidemic of blindness which hits an unnamed modern city. The outbreak of sudden whiteness seemingly spares no one and panic and disorder prove just as contagious. But a doctor's wife (Moore) proves lucky: she retains her vision and guides her husband (Ruffalo) and five strangers to safety.

At the start of the epidemic, those afflicted are thrown into quarantine by the authorities, inside an abandoned lunatic asylum. Inside the hospital, the society that develops is ugly and anarchic in its blindness, with the criminally minded and the physically powerful preying on the weak. Rising to the top is Bernal as King of Ward 3. He quickly seizes food supplies, which he then distributes in exchange for money and sexual favours.

To prepare his cast, Meirelles co-ordinated a series of workshops, having his actors wander about in blindfolds to better understand the challenges of being blind. On one occasion he even left the blindfolded cast at the gate and told them to go find their wards. The exercise proved useful for all: some people tried to work together, others went it alone; some got lost and some got pretty cross; all were able to appreciate the importance of trust. At one point they were given food to share out but, unbeknown to them, Meirelles crept in and stole half of it. Accusations of treachery burst forth.

Filming began in July 2007 inside the Ontario Reformatory in Guelph, a former prison located about 100 kilometres outside Toronto, Canada: Bernal arrived three weeks into the shoot. Meirelles says that he had thought of casting Bernal because he liked the idea of having a good-looking villain with the face of an innocent boy, especially given that the blind are unaware of such things. Their paths then crossed by chance and Bernal agreed to join up.

Meirelles had also heard that Bernal likes to get involved in the development of his character, which suited the Brazilian as he encourages his actors to improvise. In his blog of the shoot, Meirelles explains how Bernal reshaped his character, bringing an extra dimension to the whole film. On his first day of rehearsals, Bernal was blindfolded and told to walk down a corridor full of hospital junk everywhere. He stepped on a small glass bottle and paused to pick it up, took off the cap and smelled the substance. It was nail varnish. He considered sticking his fingers in but decided against it.

'Gael thought that the same thing might occur to his character,' writes Meirelles, 'and that the King of Ward 3 could easily have painted nails for the scene when he organises an orgy with the women from the other wards. I thought the idea was a bit unnecessary but I cut him some slack because I didn't want to discourage him on his first day.' When it came around to filming the scene, Meirelles indulged the actor and told him to casually and incidentally pick up the bottle.

'Only he went much further and did the whole scene focused on the nail varnish rather than on his lines,' writes Meirelles. 'He found the little flask, picked it up, opened it, smelled it, painted each finger, blew on them and tapped them on the side of the bottle which then fell to the floor. He leaves the scene still searching for it. He then goes about speaking to the other characters completely distracted, still thinking of the polish. In each take, he added another element to this parallel story. The result was very amusing. The cruel villain ends up seeming like some mixed-up type who has smoked three joints, unaware of the suffering that he is causing all around him. Someone who is more irresponsible than wicked and perhaps therefore even more shocking. We liked the way it turned out.'

From there on, they developed other scenes along the same lines, giving the villain an almost comical side so that, although the viewer hates him for how he behaves, a sense of sympathy also emerges via these glimpses of the lost, confused and vulnerable boy underneath.

Blindness is a subject both telling and challenging for cinema, such a visual art. As Meirelles explained: 'When you have two characters in a dialogue, emotion is expressed by the way people look at each other, through the eyes. Especially in the cut, the edit, you usually cut when someone looks over. Film is all about point-of-view and in this film there is none.' Given that much of Bernal's screen magic comes generally from his eyes, this is perhaps especially resonant to scenes involving the King of Ward 3.

Bernal remains true to his roots and has a couple of Mexican pictures in the pipeline too. *Pedro Páramo* is one of Mexico's best-loved novels and Bernal is to take on the title role. Juan Rulfo's 1955 classic sees Páramo head to his mother's middle-of-nowhere village only to discover it to be a ghost town – literally. The film adaptation has been handled by Spaniard Mateo Gil, who will direct, while Mexican Eugenio Caballero will provide art direction and, along with Bernal, make sure plenty of *mexicanidad* is maintained. The shoot will take in Mexico (Bernal's native Jalisco is favoured), Spain and Portugal and the movie will be a co-production between the same three countries, Canana picking up the Mexican tab.

The Crime of Father Amaro made a successful transition from page to screen with Vicente Leñero in charge of the screenplay. Leñero is now working on a new script with a working title of *Mexico 68*, based around the massacre at the Plaza de las Tres Culturas. Alfonso Cuarón is keen to direct and Bernal has been linked with the project. It is hard to imagine how he could resist the dual temptation of teaming up with his old mentor and getting to play an activist at one of Mexico's defining political moments.

That Cuarón and Bernal are still keen to work in Mexico suggests that the situation in Mexican cinema is far from doom and gloom. Iñárritu is not abandoning the ship just yet either: 'Mexico is an incredible country. As an artist it offers incredible material to work with. You have to stay home, stay in touch and feel the pulse of life.'

For all its faults, Mexico is undoubtedly an inspirational place. As Bernal told *El Mundo*:

> We are a country of many eggs and much impotence. We are the children of whores and machos. It is a continent full of contradictions. There are many tales to tell and many people to tell them. That is why cinema is very important in exorcising our demons. *Amores Perros* marked a milestone in a world cinema that was on the wane. It is an upturn towards youth, towards blood, to the entrails and the visceral and I believe that we have to make tacos out of these ingredients and eat them whole to inspire us.'

Along with the inspiration, there is no shortage of talent. Paradoxically, one of the traditional problems in establishing a film industry in Latin America has been the abundance of talent: in their eagerness for work, or at least to be making movies, *cineastas* have been too quick to undercut one another, to squabble over funding or to compete aggressively for parts.

'By offering crumbs to a passionate and enthusiastic group you create divisions as they end up fighting amongst themselves,' says Diana Bracho, president of the Mexican Film Academy (2002–06). She believes that provoking disharmony in the cinema sector was long a tactic of the authorities in their aim to quash dissent. While in the academy chair she concentrated efforts on fostering greater unity between film-makers, to have them appreciate that they were all striving for common goals.

Speaking at the Morelia Film Festival, Cuarón agreed: 'We have to understand that together we are stronger. For me, feeling protected by the [film-making] community is very significant because I emerged from a generation that was small-minded.'

These days there is a loyalty and camaraderie among Mexican film-makers that has not been seen before. Alejandro González Iñárritu, Alfonso Cuarón and Guillermo del Toro, the so-called three amigos, may make vastly different types of movies to Carlos Reygadas, but Reygadas has spoken of the mutual respect between all of them. This respect is based on artistic integrity but also on an appreciation of what each one has gone through to get their films made in Mexico.

In his NFT talk, Bernal spoke of Reygadas and the state of play generally:

> In Mexico, all that we need is just a push. People are already interested in investing in films, in making them and telling stories. And people are starting to realise that you don't need a lot to make a film. Sure, for a big film, you still need a Hollywood budget, but for a small little film it is quite immediate the way you can get the money. Carlos Reygadas is a great example. Nobody had heard of him before, he was a lawyer and then he did one brilliant film, and then another brilliant film, and nobody knew how he got it together but he's done it in a very independent way and I hope that this continues.

These sentiments were shared by Iñárritu in *Little White Lies* magazine:

> Facts show that there is not much the government is doing to really help and promote young film-makers. Some things have happened, like some tax reductions, but not as much as you would have thought six years ago. I think the most important thing – more than the government – is that Gael, Alfonso, Guillermo or Carlos Reygadas, or Rodrigo García or me, have been inspiring young film-makers, in order that they say: 'You know, there is a way to make films in this way.' I think that, for me, is the most valuable thing. And Gael has been opening the doors for many actors to say: 'Fuck it. I'm not trapped in this TV soap-opera life. I can be an actor, and I can expect more in my life.' Or directors are not going to feel trapped – they can think a little bit.

The new mantra seems to be: stop complaining and get on with things. Cuarón's son, Jonás, got hold of a camera and shot *Año Uña* (*Year of the Nail*) with US$7,000, then took it on the festival circuit. His daddy's name and contacts list obviously helped but Cuarón senior says he was struck and inspired by his son's approach – exploring new mediums for getting films shown, such as the internet, and editing on a personal computer.

Iñárritu was equally inspired by Carlos Armella and Pedro González, the two young film-makers he contracted to shoot the 'Making of *Babel*' but whose previous work had been the documentary *Toro Negro*, made with zero support.

Don't sit about complaining about lack of government help, said Iñárritu: 'To be always justifying yourself saying that "I'm not doing anything because the government hand-out isn't reaching me" is bullshit. The best statement an artist can make is through his work, his film, his picture, with whatever resources he has.'

Both Cuarón and Iñárritu cited Bernal and *Déficit* as a fine example of being pro-active. As for themselves, at Cannes 2007, they announced the foundation of a new production company called Cha Cha Cha, which they had founded with Guillermo del Toro, Alfonso's brother Carlos and Rodrigo García, the Colombian director of *Nueve Vidas* (*Nine Lives*).

Using their combined might, they persuaded Universal Pictures to pour US$100 million into the Cha Cha Cha pot and commit Focus Features to handle distribution and international sales. The cash will fund five projects, one helmed by each of the Cha Cha Cha founders, who will have complete artistic control. The spin-off of a Hollywood major entering the Mexican production arena could provide the impetus for resolving the box-office bias towards US exhibitors.

The first project out of the Cha Cha Cha stable is something of a love-in for the Mexican wing of the Buena Onda movement. With Iñárritu, Alfonso Cuarón and del Toro producing, Carlos Cuarón, writer of *Y Tu Mamá También*, makes his debut in the director's chair and the road-trippers themselves have the lead roles: the film is called *Rudo y Cursi*; Luna is Rudo and Bernal plays Cursi.

Comparisons with *Y Tu Mamá También* are inevitable and, as it happens, *Rudo y Cursi* (literally *Rough and Tacky*) also features an excursion to a beach. Carlos Cuarón was even inspired to write the story while on many of the production road trips for *Y Tu Mamá También*. Yet to call it a follow-up or even a sequel would be wide of the mark. For starters, while *Y Tu Mamá También* was about friendship, Rudo and Cursi are brothers, so questions of fraternity are on the agenda.

Described as a family drama with a comic tone, it is the tale of two brothers from a small village who work on a banana plantation. Rudo is married, Cursi a musician of sorts, but neither are satisfied with their lot and together they head to Mexico City in search of their dreams. Once in the capital, they put their football skills to work and make a bid for the big time.

Carlos Cuarón says he pitched the idea to Bernal and Luna over dinner two years earlier with nothing so much as a script to show them but they snapped his hand off in their enthusiasm. Given Bernal's and Luna's love of football, not to mention the chance to work together again and reunite with a whole production team of friends, it is no wonder the pair jumped on board.

Under a massive weight of expectation, the cameras finally rolled in mid-2007. 'The pressure was on for Carlos because of everyone around him – the holy trinity [Iñárritu, Alfonso Cuarón and del Toro] and then Gael and Diego and the high-profile nature of it being the first Cha Cha Cha film, the big budget etc. – sometimes you could see the pressure of it all on his face,' says Tita Lombardo, who acted as line producer. 'The flip side was the talent involved in the project and the confidence that this couldn't help but shine through in the end.'

Alongside Cha Cha Cha, Bernal's and Luna's own company, Canana, is co-producing *Rudo y Cursi* and so another domestic and international hit seems assured.

In the decade since *Amores Perros* was first pitched, the film-making rules and landscape have changed immeasurably but getting a movie made in Mexico remains a tricky business. The film industry is still neglected despite the unprecedented box-office success and critical acclaim of recent years but the Buena Onda brigade are now applying the same rigour and determination they used in getting films off the ground to lifting the industry itself. Given the ambition and talent involved, one would be a fool not to back them.

The prospects look equally bright for Gael García Bernal. His boyish good looks defy the approach of his thirtieth birthday and his popularity continues to mount. As an actor, he has a growing reputation as someone who brings supreme dedication to his craft and complexity to his roles. He has made his directorial debut and Canana is establishing itself as a significant production player, at the same time providing an outlet for Bernal himself to contribute towards progress and change in Mexico, to do justice to his strong political convictions. There seems to be no stopping him. Perhaps he should run for president after all.

Bernal's Career

Significant Theatre Performances

El Rapto de las Estrellas (*The Kidnapping of the Stars*)
Directed by Teresa Suárez, the Poliforum, Mexico City, 1988–89

El Abuelo y Yo (*The Grandfather and I*)
Directed by Pedro Damián, toured Mexico 1992

The Three Sisters directed by Alan Dunnet; *The Comedy of Errors* directed by Alan Hooper; *Mother Courage and her Children*, directed by Peta Lily; *The Rivals*, directed by Paul Tomlinson; *The Lights*, directed by Kristine Landon-Smith. All while a student at Central School of Speech and Drama, London, 1997–2000

Blood Wedding
Directed by Rufus Norris, the Almeida, London, May–June 2005

Television (major roles only)

El Abuelo y Yo (*The Grandfather and I*)
Director: Pedro Damián/ Juan Carlos Muñoz
Bernal's role: Daniel
Premiered: Mexico March 1991

Fidel
Director: David Attwood
Bernal's role: Che Guevara
Premiered: US 27 January 2002

Short Films

De Tripas, Corazón (Guts and Heart)
Director: Antonio Urrutia
Bernal's role: Martin
Nominated for Best Short Film, Live Action Oscar, 1997

Cerebro (Brain)
Director: Andrés León Becker
Bernal's role: the nameless Young Boy
Premiered: 2001 Guadalajara Film Festival

El Ojo en la Nuca (The Eye of the Nape)
Director: Rodrigo Plá
Bernal's role: Pablo
Premiered: 2000 Guadalajara Film Festival

The Last Post
Director: Dominic Santana
Bernal's role: Jose Francisco
Nominated for Best Short Film BAFTA, 2001

Feature Films

Amores Perros
Director: Alejandro González Inárritu
Bernal's role: Octavio
Premiered: 14 May 2000, Cannes Film Festival
UK Distributor: Optimum Releasing (released 18 May 2001)
Nominated for Best Foreign Language Film Oscar, 2001
Winner Best Film not in the English Language BAFTA, 2002

Y Tu Mamá También (And Your Mother Too)
Director: Alfonso Cuarón
Bernal's role: Julio Zapata

Premiered: 8 June 2001, Mexico
UK Distributor: Icon (released 12 April 2002)
Nominated for Best Writing, Original Screenplay Oscar, 2003
Nominated for Best Film not in the English Language and Best Original Screenplay BAFTAs, 2003

Vidas Privadas (*Private Lives*)
Director: Fito Páez
Bernal's role: Gustavo 'Gana' Bertolini
Premiered: 2 November 2001, Spain
UK Distributor: None

Sin Noticias De Dios (*Don't Tempt Me*)
Director: Agustín Díaz Yanes
Bernal's role: Davenport
Premiered: 30 November 2001, Spain
UK Distributor: None

El Crimen De Padre Amaro (*The Crime of Father Amaro*)
Director: Carlos Carrera
Bernal's role: Father Amaro
Premiered: 16 August 2002, Mexico
UK Distributor: Columbia Pictures (released 20 June 2003)
Nominated Best Foreign Language Film Oscar, 2003

I'm with Lucy
Director: Jon Sherman
Bernal's role: Gabriel
Premiered: 30 August 2002, Deauville Festival of American Cinema, France
UK Distributor: None

Dot the i
Director: Matthew Parkhill
Bernal's role: Kit Winter
Premiered: 18 January 2003, Sundance Film Festival, USA
UK Distributor: Momentum Pictures (released on DVD only)

Diarios De Motocicleta (*The Motorcycle Diaries*)
Director: Walter Salles
Bernal's role: Ernesto Guevara de la Serna
Premiered: 15 January 2004, Sundance Film Festival, USA
UK Distributor: Pathé Distribution (released 27 August 2004)
Winner Best Achievement in Music Written for Motion Pictures, Original Song
Oscar and Nominated for Best Writing, Adapted Screenplay Oscar, 2005
Winner Anthony Asquith Award for Film Music and Best Film not in the
English Language BAFTAs, Nominated for Best Cinematography, Best Film,
Best Performance by an Actor in a Leading Role (Bernal), Best Performance by
an Actor in a Supporting Role and Best Adapted Screenplay BAFTAs, 2005

La Mala Educación (*Bad Education*)
Director: Pedro Almodóvar
Bernal's role: Ángel/Juan/Zahara
Premiered: 19 March 2004, Spain
UK Distributor: Focus Features (released 21 May 2004)
Nominated Best Foreign Film not in the English Language BAFTA, 2005

The King
Director: James Marsh
Bernal's role: Elvis Valderez
Premiered: 15 May 2005, Cannes Film Festival, France
UK Distributor: ContentFilm International (released 19 May 2006)

La Science des Rêves (*The Science of Sleep*)
Director: Michel Gondry
Bernal's role: Stéphane Miroux
Premiered: 11 February 2006, Berlin International Film Festival, Germany
UK Distributor: Gaumont International (released 16 February 2007)

Babel
Director: Alejandro González Inárritu
Bernal's role: Santiago
Premiered: 23 May 2006, Cannes Film Festival, France
UK Distributor: Paramount (released 19 January 2007)

Winner Best Achievement in Music Written for Motion Pictures, Original Score Oscar, Nominated for Best Achievement in Directing, Best Achievement in Editing, Best Motion Picture, two times Best Performance by an Actress in a Supporting Role (Adriana Barraza and Rinko Kikuchi) and Best Writing, Original Screenplay Oscars, 2007. Winner Anthony Asquith Award for Film Music BAFTA, Nominated for Best Cinematography, Best Editing, Best Film, Best Screenplay – Original, Best Sound, David Lean Award for Direction BAFTAs, 2007

Déficit
Director: Gael García Bernal
Bernal's role: Cristobal
Premiered: 21 May 2007, Cannes Film Festival, France
UK Distributor: Revolver Entertainment (release date to be confirmed (TBC))

El Pasado (*The Past*)
Director: Hector Babenco
Bernal's role: Rímini
Premiered: 10 September 2007, Toronto Film Festival, Canada
UK Distributor: TBC

Rudo y Cursi
Director: Carlos Cuarón
Bernal's role: Toto
Premiered: 31 August 2008, Venice Film Festival, Italy
UK Distributor: TBC

Blindness
Director: Fernando Meirelles
Bernal's role: King of Ward 3
Premiered: 31 August 2008, Venice Film Festival, Italy
UK Distributor: Pathé Distribution (released 14 November 2008)

Bernal's Personal Honours and Awards

2000 Winner of Premio ACE (Hispanic Achievement Awards) as Best Actor – Cinema, for *Amores Perros*

2000 Joint Winner of the Silver Hugo for Best Actor at the Chicago International Film Festival, shared with Emilio Echevarría, both for *Amores Perros*

2001 Winner of the Silver Ariel (Mexico) as Best Actor for *Amores Perros*

2001 Joint Winner of the Marcello Mastroianni Award at the Venice Film Festival for *Y Tu Mamá También*, shared with Diego Luna

2001 Joint Winner of Best Actor at the Valdivia International Film Festival for *Y Tu Mamá También*, shared with Diego Luna

2003 Chopard Trophy as Male Revelation at the Cannes Film Festival

2003 Winner of the Silver Goddess for Best Actor, awarded by the Mexican Cinema Journalists for *The Crime of Father Amaro*

2004 Winner of Best Actor at the Valdivia International Film Festival for *Bad Education*

2004 Joint Winner of the Jury Award for Best Actor at the Fort Lauderdale International Film Festival, shared with Fele Martínez, both for *Bad Education*

2005 Winner of Chlotrudis (Independent Film Society) Award, Best Actor for *Bad Education*

2005 Winner of Glitter (International Gay Film Awards) Award as Best Actor for *Bad Education*

2005 Winner of Premio ACE as Best Actor – Cinema, for *The Motorcycle Diaries*

2006 Joint Winner of Best Ensemble Cast at Gotham Awards, shared with Brad Pitt, Cate Blanchett, Kôji Yakusho, Adriana Barraza, Rinko Kikuchi, Said Tarchani, Boubker Ait El Caid, for *Babel*

2007 Joint Winner of Best Ensemble Cast at Palm Springs International Film Festival, shared with Brad Pitt, Cate Blanchett, Kôji Yakusho, Adriana Barraza, Rinko Kikuchi, Said Tarchani, Boubker Ait El Caid, for *Babel*

Bibliography

Books

Jorge Alaya Blanco, *La Fugacidad del Cine Mexicano*, Oceano, 2001

Stephanie Dennison and Song Hwee Lim (editors*), Remapping World Cinema – identity, culture and politics in film* (Chapter Three: Latin American Cinema: From underdevelopment to post modernism by Michael Chanan), Wallflower Press, 2006

Alberto Elena and Marina Díaz López (editors), *24 Frames – The Cinema of Latin America*, Wallflower Press, 2003

Stephen M Hart, *A Companion to Latin American Film*, TAMESIS, 2004

John Hill and Pamela Church Gibson (editors), *World Cinema – Critical Approaches* (chapter entitled: South American Cinema by Julianne Burton-Carvajal), Oxford University Press, 2000

Jorge Alberto Lozoya, *Cine Mexico*, Lunwerg Editores and IMCINE, 1992–2006

César Maranghello, *Breve Historia del Cine Argentino*, LAERTES, 2005

Lúcia Nagib (editor), *The New Brazilian Cinema*, I.B. TAURIS, 2003

Deborah Shaw, *Contemporary Cinema of Latin America – 10 Key Films*, Continuum, 2003

Teresa Toledo and Walter Carvalho (editors), *Made in Spanish 2002 – Construyendo el Cine (Latinoamericano)*, Festival Internacional de Cine de San Sebastián, 2002

Paul Julian Smith, *BFI Modern Classics – Amores Perros*, BFI Publishing, 2003

James Wood, *The Faber Book of Mexican Cinema*, Faber and Faber, 2006

Specific press/online articles in chronological order

Orgullosa por el éxito de Gael, Salvador Franco Reyes, *El Universal*, 23 April 2001

Aztec Cameras, John Patterson, *Guardian*, 18 May 2001

Pup Fiction, Edward Lawrenson (and Bernardo Pérez Soler for interview with Alejandro González Iñárritu), *Sight & Sound*, May 2001

Gael García Bernal – Amores Chavos, Alberto Armendáriz, *La Nacion*, 28 October 2001

Actor Intuitivo, Julieta Marhialay, *Fotogramas*, December 2001

Bust and Boom, Geoffrey Macnab, *Guardian*, 30 January 2002

Heaven's Mouth, Paul Julian Smith, *Sight & Sound*, April 2002

Stamp of Approval, Joe Queenan, *Guardian*, 13 July 2002

First Steps in Latin, Xan Brooks, *Guardian*, 19 July 2002

Mexican Rave, David Gritten, *Telegraph*, 19 September 2002

Putting the Gang to Rights, Alex Bellos, *Guardian*, 8 December 2002

Padre, Padre: Mexico's native son Gael García Bernal stars in the controversial 'The Crime of Father Amaro', Erin Torneo, indieWIRE, 11 December 2002

On a Wing and a Prayer, Walter Salles, *Guardian*, 21 December 2002

Angels with Dirty Faces, Ismail Xavier, *Sight & Sound*, January 2003

El nuevo 'chico Almodódovar,' Juan Villoro, *El País*, 22 February 2004

'Mi hijo Gael fue un niño normal' dice la madre del protagonista, Emilio Godoy, *El Mundo*, 7 March 2004

El ciclón que llegó de México, Paula Ponga, *Fotogramas*, March 2004

Protects and Survive, Ali Jaafar, *Sight & Sound*, May 2004

A Mexican Rave, Ryan Gilbey, *Sunday Times*, 16 May 2004

All I Desire, Paul Julian Smith, *Sight & Sound*, June 2004

Mexican Rave, Gaby Wood, *Observer*, 1 August 2004

Guardian/NFT Interview – Walter Salles, with Geoff Andrew, *Guardian*, 26 August 2004

Against the Current, Nick James, *Sight & Sound*, September 2004

Guardian/NFT Interview – Gael García Bernal, with Geoff Andrew, *Guardian*, 16 October 2004

Gael García Bernal: He plays everybody's favourite revolutionary on screen, but he's not just play acting, Juliette Binoche, *Interview*, November 2004

Talk of the Town, Chris McLean, *Telegraph*, 25 April 2005

The Language of Love, Kate Kellaway, *Observer*, 1 May 2005

Times Talk – Gael García Bernal, with Alex O'Connell, *The Times*, 30 October 2005

Alza la voz por los agricultores, Gael García Bernal, *El Universal*, 20 December 2005

Conversa entre Hector Babenco e Alan Pauls, Silvana Arantes, *Folha de São Paulo*, 28 March 2006

Gael García Bernal Interview, Dave Calhoun, *Time Out*, 25 April 2006

Gael García Bernal: Journeys of the soul, Chris Sullivan, *Independent*, 8 May 2006

Border Crossing, Ali Jaafar (and *On Set – Babel*, Fernando Sólorzano), *Sight & Sound*, July 2006

Come into my World, Sam Davies, *Sight & Sound*, August 2006

The New Aztec Camera, Chris Sullivan, *Independent*, 8 September 2006

Buena Onda – The Bigger Picture, Angel Gurria-Quintana, *Financial Times*, 6 October 2006

Gael García: La realidad es que el país es un desmadre tremendo, Juan Jose Olivares, *La Jornada*, 17 November 2006

Mexican Actor on Road to Discovery, Reed Johnson, *LA Times*, 31 December 2006

Bernal Has the Magic Movie Touch, Gary Flockhart, *Scotsman*, 19 January 2007

Cine Mexicano: una industria desaprovechada, Editorial, *La Jornada*, 27 January 2007

El cine mexicano entra en su edad de oro, Antonio O Ávila, *El País*, 28 January 2007

Guardian/NFT Interview – Michel Gondry, with Sandra Hebron, *Guardian*, 7 February 2007

Jurado, un diario Berlinés, Gael García Bernal, *Letras Libres*, April 2007

Estado débil, cine pobre, Alberto Aziz Nassif, *El Universal*, 10 April 2007

Viva la revolucion!, Geoffrey Macnab, *Independent*, 8 June 2007

Com a palavra, Babenco, Ana Paula Sosa, *Carta Capital*, 19 October 2007

Newspapers (by country)

All newspapers listed below were consulted with varying degrees of regularity. A special mention must go to *El Universal*: this Mexican newspaper's archive was a constant source of information.

Mexico: *El Informador; La Jornada; El Siglo de Torreón; El Siglo de Durango; El Universal*

Argentina: *Clarín; La Nación*

Brazil: *Estado de São Paulo; Folha de São Paulo*

Spain: *El Mundo; El País*

UK: *Guardian; Independent; Observer; Scotsman; Sunday Herald; Telegraph; The Times*

US: *Chicago Tribune; LA Times; Milwaukee Journal Sentinel; NY Daily News; Washington Post*

Plus cited tabloid gossip in Sex Mex care of: *Daily Mail*, *Hot Stuff*, *Sunday Mirror*

Magazines
Mexico: *Chilango*
Brazil: *Carta Capital*
France: *Revista Jalouse*
Spain: *Fotogramas*
UK: *Another Magazine / Another Man Magazine*, *Hot Dog*, *Little White Lies*, *GQ*, *Sight & Sound*
US: *Entertainment Weekly*, *Time*, *Variety*
International: *Screen International*

Websites
www.bbc.co.uk (BBC online)
http://blogdeblindness.blogspot.com
www.Close-Up.com
www.ClubCultura.com
Cyber Forum
http://gaelonline.com/
www.hollywood.com
http://icelandreview.com/
www.IMDB.com (Internet Movie Database)
www.indieWIRE.com
www.mexicanwave.com
www.MRQE.com (Movie Review Query Engine)
www.reel.com
www.thenitmustbetrue.com
www.univision.com
www.wenn.com (World Entertainment News Network)

Index